Two Weeks
of Life

Two Weeks of Life

A memoir
of
love, death,
&
politics

ELEANOR CLIFT

BASIC
BOOKS

A Member of the Perseus Books Group
New York

Published by Basic Books
A Member of the Perseus Books Group

Books published by Basic Books are available at special discounts for
bulk purchases in the United States by corporations, institutions, and other
organizations. For more information, please contact the Special Markets
Department at the Perseus Books Group, 2300 Chestnut Street, Suite 200,
Philadelphia, PA 19103, or call (800) 255-1514, or e-mail
special.markets@perseusbooks.com.

DESIGN BY JANE RAESE
Text set in 11/15 Janson

Cataloging-in-Publication Data is available from the Library of Congress.
ISBN 978-0-465-00251-1

2 4 6 8 10 9 7 5 3 1

TO THE A-TEAM

Contents

CONTENTS

Preface

WHEN MY HUSBAND PASSED AWAY after a long and courageous battle with cancer, I wrote a tribute to him that *Newsweek* published on its Web site. It was titled "Dying with Courage," and it reflected on his struggle and mine.

At the same time that hospice workers were helping me care for Tom as he lay dying in a hospital bed in our living room, I was called upon as a journalist to comment on the controversy over the fate of a brain-damaged woman in a Florida hospice. *Two Weeks of Life* is the book that emerged out of these parallel experiences. It is written in diary form and recounts the events of the final weeks of two lives, one ending in a quiet death at home, the other drawing the U.S. Congress and President Bush into an unprecedented display of government intervention. Terri Schiavo had been in a vegetative state for fifteen years, and her husband wanted to remove her feeding tube and let her die. Her parents objected. When the Florida courts upheld Michael Schiavo's request, the ensuing uproar gripped the nation in a cable-news orgy of media excess. Politicians rushed in to exploit the divisions in American society over end-of-life decisions, and Americans were forced, many for the first time, to confront the kind of death they might want for themselves or their loved ones. The questions are profound as medical decisions intersect with moral and ethical considerations.

Who decides when to pull the plug? Is receiving food and water an inalienable right, or a medical treatment? When a life is judged not worth living, what are the implications for people with disabilities? My husband died peaceably at home. I didn't have to wrestle with these questions. I knew what Tom wanted, and this book is a love story as much as it is a journey to life's end.

We were supposed to grow old together. I was ambivalent at first about pairing these two very different deaths, but once my journalistic juices kicked in, I got comfortable with the idea. It was a way to order my thoughts and come to terms with how my life had been radically altered. I also knew Tom would approve. He was very public about his disease. As a journalist in the Washington Bureau of the *Cleveland Plain Dealer*, he had written a dozen columns over five years, beginning with his initial diagnosis of kidney cancer and continuing throughout the onset of metastatic disease, which he compared to being on the ninetieth floor of the World Trade Center. He didn't know if he would get out alive, but he was sure going to try. And try he did, until there were no more draconian treatments and it was time for hospice care. Not much changed in Tom's condition during these last two weeks, and I tell the story of our life together through flashbacks, with the goal of showing how Tom's intellect and will shaped his approach to death. They say write what you know, and I know this because I lived it.

This is not a political book, or at least it shouldn't have been. It is a story about dying in America and the choices we make. Like it or not, it's something we all have to deal with for ourselves, and for our loved ones. This is a memoir of that time in my life and the discoveries I made. To the extent I did things right, it was because I cared about Tom and listened to him, and he was able to maintain his dignity and control to the extent his illness let him right up to the end. Terri Schiavo didn't have the luxury of knowing what awaited her, and her wishes had to be deciphered through exhaustive court proceedings in which one side accused the other of murdering an innocent human being, while the other proclaimed that the rights of an individual were being trampled. Part of this memoir is my reporting about the high-decibel, often hysterical debate that reached its crescendo during these two weeks along with the players responsible for propelling Terri Schiavo onto the national agenda. I'm a journalist by training and instinct. That reporting is the vehicle for my journey to make sense of the physical, ethical and moral issues legitimately raised by both sides in the debate.

The overwhelming majority of Americans do not think government should get involved in personal end-of-life decisions. Former Republican senator John Danforth, an ordained Episcopal priest, is one of a growing number of Republicans who worries that his party is blurring the separation of church and state on which the country was founded. He calls his party's interference in the Schiavo case "unprincipled, just a cave in to these religious groups." The controversy is about more than end-of-life issues, he says; it's also about what he calls "edges of life" issues like stem cell research, which the Republican-led legislature in his home state of Missouri is trying to ban. In the Senate, Danforth cosponsored the Patient Self-Determination Act, which requires hospitals and health-care institutions to advise people of their right to refuse medical treatment, and to ask them if they have an advance directive that spells out their wishes in the event of a medical crisis. It was totally uncontroversial when it passed in the early 1990s, which Danforth suspects would not be the case today. Yet despite all the publicity around Schiavo, according to the *Washington Post*, only about a quarter of adults have put their wishes in writing, and fewer than half of adults over the age of fifty have a durable power of attorney, meaning they have authorized someone else to make decisions for them should they become unable. Iowa senator Tom Harkin, who joined with Republicans in the legislative effort to prolong Schiavo's life, now calls it "a terrible blot on the Senate." Brought into the fight by disability groups, Harkin was bothered enough by the outcome that he assigned two of his legal aides to see if they could find a legislative vehicle that would address a situation like Terri's, where a person is profoundly disabled and their wishes are not clear. After a year, he gave up, concluding government should stay out and settling for language in an appropriations bill for the Health and Human Services Department to promote awareness of advance directives.

Government can't do this for us, and when it tries, the politicians pay a price. Democratic strategist James Carville, forecasting the political turnover on Capitol Hill that would occur in November '06, called the stampede into the Schiavo case "the first chapter in the undoing of the Republican majority."

Hospice played a central role in the last four months of Tom's life, making possible the closest thing to what I imagine is a good death when death is inevitable and imminent.

By telling his story and mine, I hope to get people thinking in a more open and thoughtful way about dying. This
book is not a downer; far from it. Tom's sense of humor and
perspective about his illness carry the narrative, and one of
the people I spent time with while writing the book was
legendary humorist Art Buchwald, who had checked into a
hospice expecting to die. When he didn't, he turned his stay
into an extended Paris-style salon where he joked about
death along with everything else. It was liberating for him,
and for his visitors. Lifting the curtain on death lessens the
mystery and the fear. Death is part of life, and worthy of the
same honesty and humor we accord all milestones.

I.

THURSDAY, MARCH 17, 2005

Who Decides?

The uncertainty we all live with is not that we will die — that is a given — but when and how.
— Tom Brazaitis in a January 2001 column

My husband and life partner of more than twenty years is lying in a hospital bed in our living room. He is in the final weeks of his life after a long and courageous battle against cancer. Sunlight streams through the picture windows, and the television is tuned to Turner Classic Movies. Tom especially likes the musicals. The room does not beckon death, but I know it is coming. We've been enrolled in hospice since shortly after Thanksgiving when the oncologist suggested Tom "take a break" from chemotherapy and regain his strength with home care. The doctor presented the choice before us in such glowing terms that Tom at first thought it was good news. It was only when he saw me crying that he realized the recommendation to enter into the healing community of a home hospice was not another stop on the road to recovery.

I didn't know much about hospice, but I knew enough to understand admission was equivalent to a death sentence that Tom had six months or less to live. Going into hospice meant giving up on further treatment and accepting what is known as palliative care, a fancy term for comfort care, which is principally pain relief for a patient like Tom with Stage 4 cancer that had spread to his bones and brain. After living with cancer and keeping its worst effects at bay for more than four years, I knew that what Tom called the "End Game" was finally upon us. Hospice is the last stop, where you go to die, and I hated the thought of it. But I came to learn that for the terminally ill, and those who love and care for them, it can also mean a more peaceful ushering in of the inevitable. The fight is over, and there's an acceptance that is liberating.

As Tom lies dying quietly at home, another kind of death is playing out on the national stage, one that will have implications far beyond anyone's imaginings, when a young woman named Terri Schiavo collapsed at home early on the morning of February 25, 1990. Her husband, finding her on the floor in the hallway unconscious and gasping for air, called 911. He also roused Terri's father, Bob Schindler, who called his son, Bobby, Terri's younger brother. "Get over to your sister's—something's wrong," he said. Bobby lived maybe a quarter mile away, and he threw on his clothes and jumped in his car, arriving at the apartment before the paramedics.

At first he wasn't overly concerned. Terri was lying on her hands facedown, her head tilted to one side. She was breathing, although it was labored breathing, almost like she was snoring. "C'mon, Terri, get up," Bobby said, shaking her shoulder. She didn't respond. The paramedics showed up within seconds, and Bobby then knew almost immediately that something was terribly wrong.

Terri Schiavo was in full cardiac arrest when the rescue team arrived, and it took seven electrical shocks to her heart to restore a normal rhythm. A medical chain of events triggered by a low potassium level, probably caused by her erratic eating habits, led to the cardiac arrest and the severe loss of oxygen that left Terri, at age twenty-six, a husk of her former self. She was in a coma for about a month and then lapsed into what neurologists call a permanent vegetative state (PVS).

Nearly fifteen years later, she is able to breathe on her own and has normal wake and sleep cycles but has lost higher brain function and the ability to think. When she is awake, her eyes are open and she smiles and sometimes seems aware of her surroundings. Whether she is truly responsive or acting out of some basic primal reflex is now the subject of a national debate. One thing is certain: Terri is not terminally ill in the sense that term is generally used. There is no disease process ravaging her body. With excellent care, she could live fifty years. What's at issue is the quality of her life, and who decides whether she would want to live in such a compromised state. Terri is in a Florida hospice, where she has been for the past five years, a record stay in a facility thought of as death's door, while her husband and parents fight over who decides her fate.

An NBC News–*Washington Post* poll asked the question: Would you want to be kept alive in Terri Schiavo's condition? Eight percent said yes. Eighty-seven percent said no. Given those lopsided numbers, what possessed the U.S. Congress and the president of the United States to intervene to keep her alive?

Florida's courts repeatedly side with her husband, who says he is acting on what he believes are his wife's wishes, and that she would not want to be kept alive in a vegetative state. Her parents dispute both his assessment of her condition and his right to decide, arguing that he lives with another woman and has therefore forfeited his marital rights. The courts don't back down, and in twenty-four hours Terri is scheduled to have her feeding tube removed by order of the court, triggering a political and media frenzy over when and how to end life.

Terri's father, Bob Schindler, is an open, friendly bear of a man with a walrus mustache and thinning white hair. He grew up in Philadelphia and retains a city accent shaped by the streets, despite having lived in Florida for the past decade. Asked a year later how his daughter's case reached the highest levels of the government in Washington, Schindler shrugs and tells me he doesn't know. He is eager to talk about the years of contention with Terri's husband, Michael Schiavo, and the violent argument they had on Valentine's Day 1993 about Terri's care in light of the $1.6 million malpractice judgment Michael had been awarded.

At the time of her collapse, Terri had been seeing a fertility doctor, who should have detected her life-threatening low potassium. The Schindlers wanted that money spent on aggressive rehabilitation for their daughter. Schiavo had concluded Terri's situation was hopeless and would pay only for basic nursing home care. He put DNR (Do Not Resuscitate) on her records, and the following year, in 1994, when she had a urinary tract infection, he didn't want her treated with antibiotics. That's when the Schindlers first went to court to try to remove Schiavo as Terri's legal guardian, the first salvo in what would become the longest right-to-die case in American law.

"I told one reporter, I admit she had brain damage, but I believe she had less brain damage than a majority of reporters who were writing about her. She had nothing but a feeding tube," Bob Schindler says, pointing to the media types who blithely asserted she couldn't breathe on her own. "She was mobile—we could bring her home to celebrate holidays, take her to the mall. He stopped all that rehabilitation and warehoused her."

Michael Schiavo isn't the most sympathetic figure. He seems a little too eager to end his wife's life. Why doesn't he just let her parents care for her? On the other side, the Schindlers are so relentless it's fair to wonder if they aren't in denial and simply unable to accept the judgment of so many doctors and judges that Terri cannot be rehabilitated and deserves a dignified death.

As if he wants to let me know that he's not a fanatic, Bob Schindler volunteers in our conversation that he took his mother off a ventilator. "Her kidneys totally failed. She was all yellow. She didn't have a written directive, but I said, 'Get her off that thing.' I put her on it because she had difficulty breathing. But I saw the condition she was in and I asked, 'Can she survive this?' I'm pragmatic enough to realize it was hopeless. I cursed God at the time for putting me in that position—for forcing me to make that decision," he said, adding, "I shouldn't put it like that."

As her husband relates the story of his mother's passing, Mary Schindler shakes her head and says, "That was different, that was different."

The Schiavo affair has ballooned beyond a family custody dispute into a crusade for fundamentalist Christians. Their political power is substantial. They claim credit, deservedly so, for electing President Bush to a second term, and they have a pipeline to the leaders of the House and Senate. On Capitol Hill, where legislation usually proceeds at a glacial pace, the House moves quickly to pass a bill that could block the removal of Terri's feeding tube, and the Senate follows suit. Senate majority leader Bill Frist, a heart surgeon by training, takes to the Senate floor to declare doctors wrong when they say Terri is in a persistent vegetative state. Asked how he arrived at that conclusion, he says he spent an hour or so in his office watching a video of Terri, and "speaking more as a physician" than as a U.S. senator he concluded Terri "certainly seems to respond to visual stimuli." Frist's diagnosis boosted the credibility of the "Save Terri" forces. He'd been a prominent transplant surgeon before entering politics, and was often called upon, he said in his Senate speech, to decide whether someone was brain dead. Short of brain death, he explained, there are other mental incapacitations, from coma to persistent vegetative state to the relatively new minimally conscious state, which the Schindlers believed was a more accurate term for Terri.

There was no reason for television viewers watching Frist expound on the Senate floor to question his medical expertise. He'd been a physician for much of his adult life; he hadn't even voted until he was in his forties. But to much of the medical profession and especially among those familiar with PVS, Frist's words were shockingly irresponsible. "If he really believed that, he should be kept away from sharp objects within his grasp," said Dr. Carlos Gomez with Capital Hospice, who explains to me that Frist couldn't possibly diagnose PVS without being in the room with Terri and observing her over a period of time. "You've got to see, touch, listen—that's why medicine is called an art, not a hard science. I could have gone either way on the Schiavo case. I could have argued for a middle position, but there wasn't a middle position. It was either stay on [the feeding tube] ad infinitum, or she gets off."

Actually, there is a middle position, and that is to transfer custody of Terri from her husband to her parents. "Which I would have argued for except Mr. Schiavo by law is the one that's allowed to make these decisions for all sorts of logical and psychological reasons," says Gomez, who, like many observers of this family feud from hell, wonders, "Why after seven years of caring for her did he change his mind? That is a question I can't answer. The people I would be angry at are the medical people who gave the Schindlers the advice that she could be rehabilitated."

By late today, Thursday, the House and Senate haven't yet agreed on how to word legislation to save Terri. The House bill is broadly written and could open the floodgates for other disgruntled family members unhappy with court rulings. Senate negotiators want a more narrowly focused bill that would apply only to Terri. In the meantime, to satisfy the growing political frenzy, Republicans announce they will issue subpoenas for Schiavo, her husband, and her caregivers to appear before the House Committee on

Government Reform to testify about the quality of long-term care for incapacitated patients. It's a ploy to trigger federal laws that make it a crime for anyone, including a judge, to interfere with the ability of an individual to comply with a subpoena to appear before Congress, a backdoor way to prevent further court rulings. Norman Ornstein, a congressional scholar with the American Enterprise Institute, says he has not seen anything like this, ever. "The idea of a congressional committee issuing a subpoena—not to get a witness, but to block an action in a state court—is almost bizarre." Republicans say Schiavo's caregivers tell them she could be brought to Washington in a wheelchair.

For fifteen days in March, you couldn't turn on a television in America without seeing a video of the dark-haired Terri, looking vulnerable, her head gently swaying, and her expression sweet but vacant. Who would want to kill this woman? The video transformed what would otherwise have been a family feud into a social phenomenon. Dr. Ronald Cranford, a neurologist, recalls the July day in 2002 when he took his camera into Terri's room at the Woodside Hospice to videotape his examination of her, selected pieces of which would later make their way into America's living rooms. Cranford was brought into the case by the side representing Michael Schiavo, Terri's husband, who was petitioning the court to withdraw her feeding tube, an act that would allow her to die. Her parents, Bob and Mary Schindler, were fighting the removal of the feeding tube, and they were at Terri's bedside when Cranford showed up with his camera. Michael Schiavo was also present, along with his lawyer, George Felos, an outspoken right-to-die advocate.

It was Cranford's idea that the half-dozen medical doctors consulting on the case videotape their examinations so they could be used at trial. Four of them did so, submitting their video to Judge George Greer, the Florida judge overseeing the case. Cranford's examination lasted just forty-two minutes, which would later become an issue. Bob Schindler says Cranford flattered Terri, telling her, "Good, Terri. Good, Terri," because she appeared to follow his commands. "You heard me, Terri," he said, cheering her on, according to the Schindlers. "Then he turned around and said it was all reflex," says Schindler in obvious disgust. Dismissing Cranford as a hired gun, Schindler insists his daughter responded. "He calls himself 'Dr. Death,'" Schindler says of Cranford, who by his own count has provided expert testimony in at least nine major right-to-die cases. "More than any other neurologist or physician," says Cranford, which is why he refers to himself as "Dr. Death," not to disrespect his line of work but to acknowledge the reality of the most avoided topic in America.

What Cranford was looking for was evidence of "visual pursuit" or visual tracking that would suggest a higher level of consciousness than PVS. He passed a brightly colored balloon back and forth, and it appeared for about fifteen seconds that Terri was following the balloon with her eyes. It was the one clinical feature that gave him pause in an otherwise unambiguous case of PVS. But he couldn't get her to repeat it, and he concluded based on her flat EEG and CT scans over twelve years showing severe, irreversible brain damage that her eye movements during that brief period were random.

But those few seconds would prove a powerful piece of propaganda for right-to-life activists determined to sustain

Terri's life. People who'd never seen a person in a vegetative state looked at that video and said, "My God, it looks like she's interacting," says Cranford.

The Schindlers were represented by William Hammesfahr, a Florida neurologist who videotaped Terri for more than three hours and concluded she was responsive. "Raise your leg," he instructed as the Schindlers watched. He had his hand on the top of her leg, anticipating movement, and the Schindlers swear they could see her leg going up. "Just a little bit," Bob Schindler concedes. But when they looked on the video, they couldn't see it. Neither could Judge Greer, who said the lengthy videotape submitted by Hammesfahr did not support his assertions. Hammesfahr was the only one of eight neurologists who examined Terri over a period of a dozen years who said she was aware of her environment and responsive to commands and could respond to medical treatment. He testified that he and Mary Schindler gave Terri more than a hundred commands and asked her dozens of questions during the examination, and that Terri squeezed his finger on command, but the video did not bear that out in a convincing way for anybody who wasn't a true believer. Some of Hammesfahr's unorthodox medical treatments have since gained him attention on quackwatch.com.

Taken together, the videos, whatever their intent, helped persuade Judge Greer that Terri was in a vegetative state. He ordered the tapes not to be released to the press, but an edited version found its way to the media and helped elevate the case nearly three years later to national prominence. The six selected segments edited for public consumption added up to four minutes and twenty-eight seconds, including the section with the balloon passing back and forth that Cranford taped. Christian conservatives took up Terri's cause, pointing to the videos showing her following the balloon and smiling in response to her mother as evidence that Terri is a person who can be rehabilitated. Based on the video and the emotional response they generated, conservative groups backing the Schindlers gathered thirty-three affidavits signed by physicians around the country disputing the court's findings that Terri was in a permanent vegetative state with no hope of recovery.

Though Cranford disagrees with the Schindlers, he thinks they are the ones who suffer the most in this tug of war over their daughter. Prompted by the publicity, outside doctors and medical professionals who never examined Terri had "cruelly deceived" them into believing she could get better or at least had a chance for improvement with various treatments they advocated. Letting Terri die would take away any opportunity she had to recover. A facility in Alberta, Canada, offered to care for Terri free of charge and provide accommodations for the Schindlers as well. There were doctors in China calling who felt they were more advanced than medical professionals here, and were eager for a chance to outshine the West. Cranford faults the legion of doctors who in his view distorted the facts and offered unprofessional advice. But he doesn't blame the Schindlers. They feel like they are the last chance Terri will ever have, and they are acting according to their beliefs.

I TELL TOM that I am really getting into the caregiver role. "Better watch out," he says. "I hear they're recruiting from the ranks."

Tom's wry sense of humor remains even as his speech becomes diminished. He is resigned. He doesn't fight his situation. His ability to fully comprehend is compromised, which is a blessing. I remember how frightened we both were when he first went off to the Cleveland Clinic for a grueling course of experimental treatment. He e-mailed a reader who had become a pen pal that he hadn't felt this anxious since the night before he flew to Germany to begin active duty in the army. It was 1962, and his odds of coming home safe and sound then were better than they are today, he wrote. "I keep waiting for flashes of insight that are reputed to those who know they are on the stretch run of life. Hell, we're all dying, and we'll be dead for a long time. But I had plans ... Don't we all."

Tom was diagnosed with renal cell carcinoma, or kidney cancer, in the summer of 1999. It is a stealthy cancer and signaled its presence only once it was well along with blood in the urine. Our primary doctor wasn't even alarmed. Tom was a runner, and he said that sometimes happens. "No big deal," he said. Coincidentally, Tom had an appointment with his urologist because like any male in his fifties, he was monitoring his prostate. When Tom mentioned having had blood in his urine, the urologist ordered an immediate CAT scan that showed a large mass on his left kidney. Tom was disbelieving. "I ran five miles this morning," he told the doctor. He was in the hospital and operated on to remove his kidney within a week. The surgery went well. "I got it all," the doctor said. And in fairness, he did get it all, that is, all that he could see. But a year and a month later, in August 2000, a follow-up CAT scan showed metastases to the lung.

You always think these things happen to somebody else, and there was no history of cancer in Tom's family. Neither of us thought he was vulnerable. In retrospect, he had complained about fatigue, but doctors don't take that seriously. They blame it on stress or a midlife crisis, and they prescribe Prozac if they prescribe anything. I've come to understand that fatigue is a side effect of cancer, and if we had pressed the case and somebody had gotten an ultrasound of Tom's abdomen, they would have seen this tumor because the physician told us it had been growing for years. It's a very slow-growing cancer in its early stages.

"What do you mean by fatigue? I mean, all of us get tired," Diane Rehm asked Tom when we appeared on her show on public radio the day before Thanksgiving, November 2003. We were there because Diane is a friend, and we believed that sharing Tom's story was a public service to other people. Tom agreed that feeling tired at the end of the day is normal, but what he felt was different, a pervasive fatigue that clung to him almost from the moment he woke up.

Still, that was ancient history. We were in a new place now, a scary place, one that required us to summon additional reserves of whatever it was that had gotten us this far. Is it strength ... hope ... love ... resignation? Maybe it's all of what makes us human. When you're diagnosed with a terminal illness, or with a life-threatening illness, two things happen, says Dr. Roy Elam, a palliative care physician in Nashville, Tennessee. One is the search for the cure, and two, the search for meaning, which Tom found in counseling others through his column and on the Internet, and which we found in our love for each other.

"How has the cancer—the developing illness, the treatments—affected your relationship with Eleanor?" Diane asked.

"Well, I would start by saying that a diagnosis of cancer really makes you examine your life because you realize suddenly that it's not forever. We all are in this boat. I just happen to be having to make some decisions earlier than most people. But as far as my relationship with Eleanor is concerned, it's brought us closer together. I'm positive of that. During those times when she was administering the shots and I was going through the side effects, when I'd get really delirious is when I'd really express my love for her like I haven't, you know, when I'm just in my normal state. I just felt so close to her. And when we were in Cleveland recently for a benefit for kidney cancer, we went to an ice show together, and we held hands, and there was a playing of the song 'If Ever I Should Leave You' from *Camelot*, and the two of us were in tears. At the same time, when the song was over and the tears were over, we're facing this together."

Tom had experienced headaches, and an MRI in September 2003 revealed that his kidney cancer had spread to the brain. There were two tumors visible, although they didn't call them tumors. They used the word *lesions*, or *nodules*, which somehow seemed more manageable. And when you're going through something as deadly as brain cancer, language is important.

At the Cleveland Clinic, where Tom was being treated, he underwent gamma ray surgery, which is outpatient radiation. They screwed a frame to his head and then targeted the lesions with high blasts of radiation. An MRI six weeks later showed one of them had almost disappeared, but the other had actually grown. Plus three other tumors—okay, that's what they were—showed up. So Tom did another gamma ray treatment, and he also had open-brain surgery to remove the largest tumor. They drilled a hole in his skull. He compared it to ice fishing. The surgeon antici-pated that the procedure would take five hours, but it took only three, and he called me immediately after to say Tom was awake and talking. He put Tom on the phone. The de-cision to go ahead with the surgery happened suddenly, so I was in Washington. Tom didn't sound at all compromised by what he had just been through. He wanted to talk about where, if he did further radiation, he might get a toupee that was better looking than the one television correspon-dent Sam Donaldson wore. Sam would understand Tom's attempt to lighten the mood. A cancer survivor himself, when Sam was diagnosed with melanoma he answered calls from well-wishers by bellowing into the phone, "Melanoma Central."

Tom had resisted whole-brain radiation in part because he didn't want to lose his hair. It was thinning but it was dark and it was all over his head, and he didn't want to give it up to the cancer. But he'd gotten past that. The lesions, nodules, tiny tumors, whatever we called them, were pop-ping up with enough regularity that radiating the whole brain was really his only option. One doctor said he could expect an IQ loss of ten points, and like most people, he didn't think he could afford that. The alternative was to do nothing, and that would allow the cancer to progress un-impeded.

Tom did what he always does. He went to the Internet and did all the research he could, and he contacted various people who'd been through it and could offer advice. There were a lot of horror stories about whole-brain radiation, and I was getting wobbly about it. But when we met with the physician at Sibley Hospital in Washington, and he explained the treatment only takes fifteen minutes a day, and Tom could park right outside, and the Muzak is playing, it doesn't seem nearly so threatening as it does when you read about it in scientific papers.

"Tom, what are the odds?" Diane asked during the 2003 interview.

"Nobody is willing to state the odds because it's so variable from person to person," Tom replied.

As it turns out, that's not quite true. We've traveled a long road together with this illness, and now Tom is in the hospital bed in our living room and his neurologist is on the phone from Cleveland. He tells me that people with brain metastases usually last less than a year. When there's "meningeal spread," meaning the cancer is in the spinal fluid, three months is the average. I ask whether these are new tumors in the brain that are robbing Tom of his ability to think clearly and leaving him bedridden, or whether healthy brain tissue was destroyed during the radiation. There's no way to know unless you do an autopsy, the doctor says. He does know that Tom will sleep for much longer periods of time and eventually not wake up.

FRIDAY, MARCH 18, 2005

Pulling the Plug

Right now, murder is being committed against a defenseless American citizen in Florida. ... Mrs. Schiavo's life is not slipping away—it is being violently wrenched from her body in an act of medical terrorism. Mr. Schiavo's attorney's characterization of the premeditated starvation and dehydration of a helpless woman as her "dying process" is as disturbing as it is unacceptable. What is happening to her is not compassion, it is homicide. She doesn't need to die, and as long as Terri Schiavo can breathe and her supporters can pray, we will not rest.

—House majority leader Tom DeLay

TERRI SCHIAVO'S FEEDING TUBE is removed about 1:45 P.M., and the nation begins a death watch. Cable television cameras stake out the Woodside Hospice in Pinellas Park, Florida, as protesters stand outside shouting and bomb threats are called in.

This is not the first time Terri has been denied the sustenance necessary to sustain her life in the past fifteen years. In 2001, she went without food and water for two days before an appellate court judge ordered the tube reinserted, and in 2003, it was six days before Governor Jeb Bush was able to push through a special session of the Florida legislature "Terri's Law," which reinstalled the feeding tube on the grounds that protecting the frail and vulnerable shouldn't be the exclusive province of the courts. "I hope that what we have done is in keeping with what Terri wanted, and if it is not, God have mercy on all of us," senate president Jim King said after the bill passed. Filled with self-recrimination, King told reporters Terri's Law was probably the worst vote he'd ever cast. He vowed that if the issue ever came back to the state senate that he wouldn't vote for it again.

Death normally occurs within three to fourteen days after artificial nutrition and hydration are stopped, so the element of time hangs heavy over those wanting to "save" Terri. This is like the third act of a tragic drama with all the key players filling their assigned roles. There's the husband, a cloddish figure who seems incapable of at least pretending to understand the anguish of his in-laws, and, from the media's point of view, a little too eager even after fifteen years to hasten his wife's death. The aggrieved parents are sympathetic up to a point, but impervious to the true state of Terri's condition, despite the weight of medical facts. Terri's fiercely protective brother, Bobby, tells all who will listen that it doesn't matter that Terri is brain-damaged. He loves her and would want her alive if she were ten times worse off. Bobby's fervor makes him a popular speaker at Christian pro-life rallies. At a press conference when a reporter asks if it is appropriate for the federal government to intrude and override a family decision, Bobby heatedly replies, "Who's the family?" Shouldn't the family who lived with Terri for twenty-five years have some say?

The young woman at the center of the controversy is un-remarkable, which is why so many Americans look into her sweet but empty expression and think there, but for the grace of God, could be my daughter, or sister. Like any young girl, Terri had her dreams. She loved romance. She read Danielle Steele novels and saw *An Officer and a Gentleman* with Richard Gere and Debra Winger four times in one day. In details gleaned by Joan Didion for her piece in the *New York Review of Books*, we learn that Terri bought her little brother, Bobby, his first Bruce Springsteen album and that she hung out at the mall but didn't date. In high school, her weight ballooned to 250 pounds, and she was self-conscious about her appearance. The product of a devoutly Catholic home and schools, she did okay academically but lacked ambition. She didn't have big plans for anything beyond wanting to get married and have children. While her peers pumped up their résumés to impress college recruiters, the lone entry for Terri in her senior yearbook was "Library Aide," which she and a friend settled on just to have something next to their names.

After graduation, according to her parents, she tried several different diets to lose weight, eventually settling on the NutriSystem diet, a regimen that had prepackaged, calorie-controlled meals arriving daily on her doorstep. The discipline allowed her to drop more than 100 pounds in a relatively short time, a period of months.

She was a petite 110 when she first met Michael Schiavo in a psychology class during her second semester at Bucks County Community College. He paid attention to her, which was a new experience for a woman just discovering she was attractive after years of hiding behind extra pounds.

He is said to be the first boy she ever kissed. They married in 1984 when she was not quite twenty-one, and he was eight months older.

Thanks to the crash NutriSystem plan, she'd lost the weight, but not the habits of dieting, which for Terri meant eating copious amounts of salad, treating herself to an over-sized omelet on weekends, and drinking large quantities of ice tea. The likely cause of the low potassium level that apparently prompted her collapse is an eating disorder characterized by the gorging and purging that is known as bulimia, which wreaks havoc on the body's chemical and hormonal balances. She never confessed to family or friends that she had an eating disorder, and no one testified in the many court filings over the years to observing her engage in this type of behavior. Still, it is not unreasonable to conclude that her history of dieting and weight loss compromised her system and played some role in her untimely collapse.

The marriage, by some accounts, was troubled. Terri had no clear focus in terms of a job or career, and her tendency to put on weight was a recurring theme, with Michael reportedly threatening to leave her if she got heavy again. Michael would later say on national television it was her father's demeaning of her that caused Terri's eating disorder. In any event, the economics of modern life combined with the unfocused career plans of the young couple led them to live with Terri's parents, an arrangement that continued even after Bob Schindler retired and the family moved to Florida.

Michael took restaurant jobs while Terri clerked at an insurance company. She was 9 to 5, while he worked mostly nights, an imbalance that left Terri with a lot of time on her hands. She dyed her hair blonde and lay around the pool hour after hour drinking ice tea, consuming several quarts a day, according to Didion's account. The couple was trying to get pregnant, and it wasn't happening. Even though her marriage wasn't great, Terri knew one thing: she wanted a family. "If you're Catholic, you could be married to Genghis Khan and you still want to have children—there's something redemptive about it," says the Reverend Pat Mahoney, a Presbyterian minister with the Christian Defense Fund who became a Schindler family confidant.

Terri was in fertility treatments when the event occurred that would rob her of her future. It was early morning, well before dawn, when Michael awoke to a loud thump, the sound of Terri falling to the floor in the hallway outside their bedroom. Michael placed a call to 911 at 5:40 A.M. When the emergency responders arrived and began treating Terri twelve minutes later, Bobby Schindler, Terri's brother, was also on the scene. Both he and Michael described Terri as lying prone and breathing, or at least doing what they interpreted as breathing, "making gurgling noises." The rescue crew managed after several attempts with a defibrillator to get her heart beating normally again. Terri's heart survived, but Terri's brain, deprived of oxygen, had been damaged beyond repair.

Michael Schiavo filed a medical negligence suit against Terri's primary care physician and the gynecologist overseeing her fertility treatments, charging that the low potassium level that triggered Terri's cardiac arrest should have been discovered. During the course of the jury trial, the Schindlers testified that Michael was a loving and caring husband who could be entrusted with Terri's care. They put aside their qualms about Michael because a lot of money was at stake, enough to care for Terri the rest of her natural life. Michael testified in the November 1992 malpractice trial that he was taking a nursing course to help him care for Terri, and he promised the Schindlers that whatever money he received from the suit would go to Terri's rehabilitation. Asked during the court proceeding about his intentions, he said he wanted to bring Terri home, and if he had the resources to care for her at home, he would "in a heartbeat." He said he believed in his marriage vows, and when asked to be more explicit, he said, "I married my wife because I love her and I want to spend the rest of my life with her. I'm going to do that."

The jury decided in favor of Terri, and after court costs and attorney's fees, the remaining sum of about $700,000 was put in a guardianship fund controlled by a bank. Michael was not the guardian of her property and had no control over the money. His expenses for Terri's care were paid out of the fund, with all expenditures subject to scrutiny by the bank. In a separate court judgment, Michael was awarded $300,000 for the loss of companionship that he suffered as Terri's spouse.

The money was deposited in January 1993, and just weeks later, on Valentine's Day, the fragile détente between the Schindlers and Michael Schiavo that had existed throughout the trial broke apart with an angry encounter at Terri's bedside in the nursing home where she was being maintained. "If it weren't for Mary, it would have been pretty ugly," says Bob Schindler, recalling how his wife had to pull him away to keep him from physically striking his son-in-law.

Michael stormed out of the room and said he was going to get an attorney, which he did, and he tried to ban the Schindlers from seeing Terri. He couldn't legally keep the Schindlers away, but he erected a blockade of sorts by keeping them in the dark about any medical information about Terri. "We would go to her caretakers and ask, 'How is Terri?' and they couldn't tell us anything. That was the case from 1993 until the day she died," Bob Schindler says, recalling how in August 2004, when they arrived at the hospice for a visit and discovered Terri wasn't there, he had to make a "major commotion" before one of the nurses offered a clue. "When someone is sick, where do they go?" she said. With that, the Schindlers raced to the nearest hospital, where they had to threaten to walk on every floor and into every room before they learned Terri was on the sixth floor. She had aspirated food into her lungs, a common occurrence with PVS patients, which Schindler blames on the hospice feeding her in a horizontal position when she should have been at a 45-degree angle.

The Schindlers expected Michael to use the money from the medical malpractice award to aggressively treat and rehabilitate Terri, a goal that Michael had concluded was futile. "When the money came in and he had her in a nursing home, then I got on his case," says Schindler. When Terri's parents discovered that Michael had put DNR on her chart, and that he had contacted a local mortuary to make funeral arrangements, they viewed Michael as the enemy, the sole person who stood in the way of their daughter's well-being.

Their fury mounted when, in 1994, Terri had a urinary tract infection that Michael didn't want the doctors to treat. The Schindlers filed an action to have him removed as Terri's guardian. In the deposition, when Michael was asked why he sought to refuse medical treatment, principally antibiotics, knowing she would develop sepsis (blood poisoning) and die, he responded, "I don't think she'd want to live like that." When Schindler tells the story, he emphasizes the pronoun *I*, and notes with contempt that Michael at the time was "shacking up with the girl he eventually married."

What would Terri have wanted? Michael successfully argued in a string of legal battles that he was carrying out Terri's wishes, that he and others heard her say on different occasions that she would not want to "live on tubes," once after watching an episode of *ER* and another time after observing Michael's grandmother on life support. Michael's brother and sister-in-law backed up his account, while the Schindlers, devout pro-life Catholics, could not imagine their daughter in the bloom of youth entertaining such dark thoughts, much less expressing them in a serious way. They thought Michael was a gold digger wanting to hasten Terri to her death and collect the balance in the trust account. Bob Schindler contacted an actuary to give him an idea of what the principal should be, but he had no access to the records. Whatever Michael's motives might have been at various points, his actions were based on a body of medical and moral reasoning that had undergone repeated court scrutiny. By the time Terri died, all that remained was $60,000 to $70,000 in her guardianship account. The bulk of that money ($40,000) went to Michael's lawyer.

Workers at the Woodside Hospice caring for Terri refer to the media onslaught and round-the-clock protesters as "The Siege." Being accused of murder and starving someone to death is a complete corruption of what hospice is all about, yet the National Hospice and Palliative Care Organization does little to correct the misimpressions. After a long internal discussion that includes the CEO of the hospice where Schiavo is receiving care, they decide not to get in the middle of what is essentially a custody dispute between Schiavo's husband and her parents. Their message is that hospice is there to provide care for whatever decision a family makes. It is a high-minded position but one that allows a lot of religiously infused misinformation to go unchallenged.

Ken Connor is a private lawyer, originally from Florida, who's been involved in what he calls "sanctity-of-life issues" for many years. When Florida governor Jeb Bush saw the Schiavo case once again spinning out of control, he asked Connor to represent him in leveraging the state's power to keep Terri alive.

They had gotten to know each other in 1994 when they both ran for governor in the Republican primary, and Bush turned to his onetime rival for help when the constitutionality of the hastily passed Terri's Law was challenged in October 2003. "How do you measure success in this case?" Connor had asked the governor's staff. "Their initial response was if we can keep Terri alive until the next legislative session, we can get this law fixed." In other words, the governor's legal team knew Terri's Law was flawed and had anticipated it would be struck down. The Florida judge who on May 6, 2004, ruled Terri's Law unconstitutional quoted U.S. Supreme Court Justice Antonin Scalia, an icon among conservatives: "The legislature cannot intervene in final judicial acts." The Florida Supreme Court upheld the lower court ruling, seven to zero. Three of those judges were appointed by Jeb Bush. Governor Bush and his allies were able to keep Terri alive through two legislative sessions, but they couldn't muster enough votes in the Florida legislature to get a fix that would satisfy the court. The U.S. Supreme Court refused to hear the case, which meant the Florida ruling that Terri's Law was unconstitutional would stand.

Now Connor is in Washington where he and the pro-life forces he represents are counting on Congress to take up Terri's cause. The House has just adjourned for Easter recess, and the Senate is still at work on a stopgap bill to save Terri. Pro-life activists feel they are winning. But Connor sees all the frenzy in Washington for what it is—a lot of noise signifying nothing. He calls Florida representative Dave Weldon, a physician who had helped bring Terri's case to the attention of House leader Tom DeLay. "This is crazy—this is the worst of all possible worlds," he tells Weldon. "Everybody can act like they tried to do something for this poor woman, wring their hands and stare and say we tried and fell short, and create the pretense they did something when in fact they did nothing because unless the House comes back in session, this woman is going to die."

Connor tells Weldon that DeLay is vulnerable, that he's at the center of a burgeoning corruption scandal and needs all the friends he can get, "and we're going to call it like it is, which is the Republican leaders diddled while Terri Schiavo died. Plain and simple—and you need to understand

that we're not going to let the House off the hook here because it's chosen to take a powder while the Senate is still in
session."

In a speech to the Family Research Council, a conservative pro-life group for which he recently served as president, Connor blisters DeLay for creating the impression of
having done something when in fact it is all symbolic and
guaranteed to fail. He urges the audience of conservative
activists to call DeLay and let him know how they feel,
which they do, and the message apparently gets through
because DeLay calls the House back into session—an extraordinary move on a holiday—and scrambles to assemble
enough members for a quorum that could resolve the differences between the House and Senate bills and produce
legislation for President Bush to sign over the weekend.

While commentators marveled at the speed with which
Congress was acting, the story was different behind the
scenes. Connor believes his side has lost the legal momentum, and he blames DeLay. "It makes a huge difference
who's defending the status quo," he explains. During the
time the House is on break, Terri's feeding tube is removed,
which means that Terri's lawyers have to push for its rein-
sertion—a change in the status quo—a different burden
than they would have if the feeding tube had been in place.

In Florida, Judge Greer is in the crosshairs of the politicians. It is Friday afternoon, and he is on the interstate
heading out of town when he gets a call on his cell phone
from Washington. It is the lead counsel of the House Select
Subcommittee on Government Reform wanting permission
from Greer to hold a hearing in Terri Schiavo's hospice
room. Greer has repeatedly ruled in favor of removing the

feeding tube, the first time in 2000, then in 2003, and again in 2005. He requires round-the-clock police protection and is spirited away at the end of each day to a hideaway for his safety. The staff attorney calling on behalf of the Republican majority tells Greer that Congress is prepared to pass all this great legislation governing health care reform and they need to schedule field trips to observe firsthand the kind of medical treatment in place. "How many other field hearings are on the schedule?" Greer asks. After a pregnant pause, the staffer replies, "None."

Even if there were a dozen hearings, Greer wouldn't grant the request. It is an obvious bid for grandstanding by politicians and serves no legitimate purpose. Greer is a polite and careful man, and he seems most offended by Congress's casual disregard for the processes of law and government. He had presided over two major trials in the Schiavo case "and lots of minor ones outside the courtroom," he adds with a wry laugh as he recounts the experience a year later at a bioethics conference at the University of Pennsylvania. The first trial lasted five days; the second, several years later, took seven days. By his count, including himself, thirty judges and supreme court justices in both the state of Florida and the federal system reviewed the evidence submitted by the opposing sides. There was a score or more of witnesses whose testimony was subject to the rules of evidence and cross-examination. Greer wrote nine pages of rulings to explain his thinking each step of the way, and there are some forty to fifty volumes documenting the case stored at the circuit court in Clearwater, Florida. The legal backup is "gigantic," he says. "I don't know of any state decision that's been subject to that kind of scrutiny."

And here comes Congress rushing in with no testimony, no expertise, as if all that hard work by all those legal minds never happened.

Greer is old-school. He doesn't think judges should call attention to themselves. This case landed in his court and brought him a lot of unwanted publicity when he didn't rule the way his profile might have suggested he would. He's a Republican and a conservative Christian, and except for sharing a house at Florida State University for one semester with future rock star Jim Morrison, he's never done anything the slightest bit risqué. Judges in Florida run for election nonpartisan, and all Greer did was faithfully follow the law, or so he believed, in ruling the way he did in the Schiavo case. So it was quite a shock to Greer when the pastor at his church, Calvary Baptist Church in Clearwater, wrote him a letter saying "it might be easier for all of us" if he didn't attend worship services. A proud and principled Southern Baptist, Greer left the church.

TOM'S PRIMARY-CARE NURSE, a young woman named Daphne, rolls her eyes at the right-wing commentators deploring the barbarism of letting Schiavo starve. She is appalled by reports that people are attempting to sneak in food to save Terri. Did they think they could stuff a roast beef sandwich down her throat? Didn't they understand that feeding her would kill her, which is what they were trying to avoid? Daphne explains in her straightforward way that a person nearing the end of life does not suffer hunger pains; your stomach doesn't growl, and you don't gnaw on the sheets. Withholding food eases the strain on a body when there are dwindling reserves. Tom is still eating pretty heartily, but she warns there will come a day when he will refuse food, and that I shouldn't force it. Starving to death is actually a fairly painless way to go.

In the dying process, there is a slowing down of all systems, which includes the digestive process. It can't handle what it once did—everything is slower; the need is less. Daphne explains you can go a long time without eating depending on how many fat reserves you have on board. But you can go without drinking only one to two weeks. The effects of dehydration are much more life-threatening. But there's not any pain associated with it. In fact, there's a sense of well-being, a happy delirium, she calls it.

Daphne Aberle is a third-generation nurse. Her mother and grandmother worked in public health, and she was raised with ayurveda medicine, a holistic system of medicine from India. *Ayurveda* means "knowledge of life." Her mother was a religion major before she was a nurse, and Daphne has a strong sense of spirituality that she describes as a mix of Hindu and Roman Catholic metaphysics. She's always been drawn to end-of-life care, and she's not quite sure why, except, she laughs, it's her need to stay as far out of hospitals as possible. She's not into high-tech nursing. She's into what she calls "the okayness of death," where there's no sense of fear or defeat. She thinks it's not so much death that we're afraid of, but the process of dying—the physical suffering and the emotional pain of leaving behind loved ones, especially if we're leaving them with a burden.

Daphne's directness is a gift when you're dealing with death, a subject hidden behind euphemisms. There's no tiptoeing around what's happening; it's all out in the open.

The way hospice works, Daphne would pop in maybe twice a week with as little as ten minutes' notice or no notice at all to size things up, from the patient's physical condition to the surroundings and how the family is coping. I remember feeling a bit threatened at first, like I was getting a home inspection to see if I was up to the task. But it's okay. I need the guidance. And Daphne is never judgmental. She'd been living in San Francisco the past couple of years and has a welcome air of counterculture about her. Her hair is very close-cropped, she favors jeans, and her favorite lunch is vegetarian squash soup from Whole Foods. She takes copious notes and explains in matter-of-fact detail what is happening, taking away the mystery and along with it the fear.

I was surprised to learn there would be no doctor visits—Daphne is the highest-ranking medical professional we will see—and that Tom's care will be almost solely in my hands. That was pretty terrifying at first, but I got over it. After all, what could I do wrong? Going into hospice meant giving up the fight and accepting Tom's fate. We weren't trying to cure Tom; we were helping him die.

Given the choice, most people would prefer to die at home, and hospice provides the support that makes that possible. Tom's hospice team includes Daphne, a health aide, a social worker, and even a chaplain, a young Asian woman whose ministrations Tom tolerates well given his hostility to organized religion. These figures appear intermittently with the understanding that the services of the nurse and the health aide in particular will increase as Tom's needs increase.

I was amazed at how quickly I embraced my new role as caregiver, measuring out and dispensing powerful medicines around the clock, stocking the fridge with Popsicles and Swedish meatballs, the foods I knew Tom would eat. The situation he found himself in in the last few months of his life was something he would have done anything to avoid. But by the time he was plunged into that hell, where he could no longer think clearly and needed assistance with the basic chores of living, his well-being was in my hands, and I was determined to give him as graceful and dignified an end to life as I could. I was the field commander in this new war, and I found it enriching and empowering, just as I'm sure Terri's parents did. In Tom's case, there was no choice but to let his body decide when the end had come, and to let the physical processes play themselves out.

This evening, my oldest son, Eddie, reads to Tom from Mitch Albon's *Five People You Meet in Heaven*. Eddie says that Tom stops him at various points and conveys the thought that although he can handle what is happening, his dying, he is worried that the ordeal is hard on me. Whether he said that or not, I don't know, but people project what they want to believe, and hear, which is why the Schindlers are so convinced their daughter is communicating. When a friend visits—we call her the pudding lady because she always brings Tom tapioca or chocolate pudding, his favorites—she asks how he is, and he responds, "Untroubled."

On Tom's hospice chart, it says, "Aware of diagnosis, accepting of prognosis, understands prognosis, family communicates honestly with each other." Daphne's notes quote Tom saying, "I've difficulty sometimes distinguishing between a dream, thoughts, reality ... what really happened." She goes on to note, "Wife reports pt [patient] thought he might not be in his home as he was, and that he was in Paris.

Patient says his orientation to time is the most compromised right now. Patient possesses a good sense of humor."

"This place is like a waiting room," Tom says, referring to our living room, with newspapers and magazines strewn on the coffee table. When he sees my consternation, he says, "No problem, I haven't been here that long." It has actually been more than two months since that January day when he could no longer navigate the stairs from our bedroom to the living room. The hospital bed had been brought in much earlier, awaiting the day when it would be needed. For a long time, it was the elephant in the room. We treated it like another piece of furniture to pile stuff on. When the time came to make the transition, Jeff Wright, a physical therapist sent by hospice, asked Tom how he would feel about being carried down the stairs. "Not good," Tom said. So we rented a wheelchair, and with Tom strapped into the wheelchair and with the help of a football-player-size friend, Jeff turned the trip down the stairs into a joyride.

Illness is beginning to rob Tom of his ability to speak, but on this day he still manages to call me Lovey. I know the word is precious. I write it down and date it, 3/18/05.

3.

SATURDAY, MARCH 19, 2005

A National Obsession

Being a Stage IV cancer patient (there is no Stage V) is like being on the 90th floor of one of the towers in New York. You don't know whether you can make it out, but you're sure going to try.
—Tom Brazaitis in a column dated October 14, 2001

I MET TOM soon after moving to Washington in December 1976, when I was fresh off covering Jimmy Carter's presidential campaign. We were introduced to each other as neighbors. We were both married to somebody else, and it would be several years before we connected as more than friends. His marriage dissolved in 1981, and my husband left for California that summer, ending our marriage. The old days of sticking it out for the sake of the children were over.

A full year passed before Tom asked me to lunch at the Old Ebbitt Grill and we plotted how we would attack the singles scene together. I hadn't done anything proactive about finding a new mate. Between my job and caring for three children, my life was full enough. Tom regaled me with his experiences answering personal ads. He had gone about it methodically, as though he were researching the acquisition of a new appliance.

I welcomed his company, thinking he would help guide me through the unfamiliar thickets of life as a divorced woman. We began spending more time together, attending professional events and then our first movie date, *The Night of the Shooting Moon*. It was as though a switch had been turned, and this man I leaned on as a friend had suddenly become much more. I was in love. But love is not simple the second time around, and it would be six years before we married. There were children, his and mine, to consider, and he was in no hurry. "It's a long life," he would tell me, and I wanted to believe him. My first husband was twenty-one years older than me, a gulf in time and experience that was hard to bridge. Tom and I were thirty days apart in age, and I loved the fact that he carried around a tape of "Let the Good Times Roll" and knew the lyrics of every rock-and-roll song. When he proposed, we were at a dinner in eastern Europe in the midst of a reporting trip that I had tagged along on. He leaned over and said he didn't think he would ever find anybody who loved him as much as I did. I'm sure he thought that was romantic, but it was one of those things that when I turned it over in my head made me worry that I was more convenient than beloved.

It was not until after he died, when many friends, personal and professional, told me how much he cared for me, how proud he was of my standing up for our shared beliefs on *The McLaughlin Group*, how his eyes would brighten when he talked about me, that I fully understood the extent of his love. I also discovered correspondence that underscored the depth of his feelings as he confided in others and sought approval for our impending marriage. Tom was not demonstrative. He didn't like holding hands in public or any of that goopy stuff. He was a product of his generation, a manly man who'd been brought up believing displays of passion are for private moments. After we had been inseparable for three or four years, a psychiatrist friend we were visiting one weekend inquired, "What's up with you and Eleanor?" "What's this, group therapy?" Tom shot back.

Tom liked to quote Woody Allen that 90 percent of life is showing up, and he was always there for me. On our tenth wedding anniversary, he surprised me with a trip to Niagara Falls, where he had booked the classic honeymoon package. Tom brought romance and adventure to my life. We built houses one summer alongside former president Jimmy Carter for Habitat for Humanity, and we went to running camp in North Carolina, bunking with other fitness fanatics, or body Nazis, to use Tom's term. Still, like an adopted child seeking reassurance, I couldn't get enough of Tom telling the story of when he first saw me walk down the street in our northwest Washington neighborhood and thought to himself, now there's a woman I'd like to know better.

Tom arrived in Washington the summer of the Watergate scandal, a first-rate reporter who'd proven himself on the police and city hall beats for his hometown newspaper, the *Plain Dealer* in Cleveland, Ohio, and was now reaping the reward of a coveted spot in the Washington Bureau. He was so new to national politics that he couldn't always identify the members of Congress in the press scrums on Capitol Hill, but he was a quick study and always made deadline. Nobody could turn around copy faster than Tom. I envied his alacrity. "They take what I give 'em," he would laugh, the key point being that what he gave them was worth taking.

I valued his judgment first as a colleague and friend, then as a lover and husband. The first time I did national television, it was *Meet the Press*, and Secretary of State Cy Vance was the guest. I was so nervous I didn't sleep much the night before. I felt like toothpicks were stuck between my eyelids. Tom took pity on me and helped me craft my questions. His rules were no softballs, no grandstanding, and avoid questions that invite a yes or no unless that's what you're looking for. Those were the days when a panel of journalists took turns grilling the guest, and I had many more questions prepared than I could ask. Moments before we went on the air, the reporter seated next to me, Chris Wallace, who was then with NBC, leaned over and whispered, "Don't be nervous—there are only millions of people watching." I'm sure he doesn't remember that long-ago stab at gallows humor, but I've never forgotten it.

When I started doing *The McLaughlin Group* regularly in the mid- to late '80s, I would always go over the issues with Tom, whose liberal instincts and fondness for the memorable phrase served me well. He liked to joke that he would get me ready to tape the show by shouting "WRONG!"

After we were married on September 30, 1989, we wrote two books together, a venture that tested both of us and underscored our respective strengths and weaknesses. Tom was the big-picture guy, while I was the obsessive collector of information wanting to jam in every factoid. He was the master procrastinator with shelves full of books on how to gain control of your life, get things done, and free yourself from clutter. He slept soundly at night, while I lay awake listening to his even breathing, seething with frustration at the inequity of our sleep patterns. He accused me of not being satisfied until he too was waking up with anxiety in the middle of the night. These moments, though very real, never threatened our relationship. We agreed that it wasn't as bad as remodeling the kitchen.

When I started writing a Web column for *Newsweek*, Tom was always my first editor. He was never harsh, but he was rigorous. He caught every dangling participle and spelling error, and, more important, he challenged my thinking when it was fuzzy. "This is not your best work" were the words I dreaded to hear because I knew he was right.

I loved Tom in large part because he had such a good mind, yet he didn't have the advantages of so many of our peers in the newly credentialed world of journalism. He often felt like an outsider coming from Cleveland, and he lamented growing up in a "broken home," a phrase I told him was outdated and wished he would banish from his thinking. He was the only child of a devoted mother who worked for years as a salesclerk in a department store and played the organ in the Catholic church. His parents divorced when he was eight, and his father struggled with alcoholism and diabetes, never amounting to much, as the saying goes, and dying in his early fifties. His grandparents on both sides emigrated from Lithuania, and his mother was steeped in the culture of that tiny Baltic nation even though she'd never been there.

Tom and I had become pals after discovering we had something in common as fellow ethnics in a profession increasingly populated by Ivy League–trained elites with easy-to-pronounce last names. My maiden name was Roeloffs. My parents came from the tiny island of Föhr in the North Sea off the coast of Germany and Denmark. My father owned a delicatessen, first in Brooklyn, then in Queens, and I had grown up in an ethnic neighborhood much like Tom's in Cleveland. We were so much alike it was scary, working-class in our backgrounds, liberal in our politics, traditional in our values, down-to-earth in our lifestyles. We even shared the same eating habits, bland and blander.

Now, AS TOM LIES in the living room, his life ebbing away as it must, the Republican-controlled Congress is marshaling its power to defy death. Ken Connor is in the middle of the legislative negotiations. It was his February 6, 2005, op-ed in the conservative newspaper the *Washington Times*, titled "Ominous Implications for Handicapped," that attracted the interest of Florida representative Dave Weldon, a physician and strong pro-life conservative. Connor establishes the link between opponents of abortion rights and proponents of disability rights, noting in his column that the U.S. Supreme Court's decision to deny federal review of the Schiavo case occurred on the thirty-second anniversary of its decision to legalize abortion rights in its *Roe v. Wade* ruling. "That case effectively held an unborn child is a 'non person' entitled to none of the protections of the U.S. Constitution. The case paved the way for abortion on demand and allowed an unborn child to be killed, if it was inconvenient, unwanted or imperfect. Opponents of Roe have argued the case rationale threatened others who may be deemed inconvenient, unwanted or imperfect. Bush vs. Schiavo has proved them right."

Connor met with Weldon's aides to brainstorm about what approach they might take to "save" Terri that would warrant federal involvement and produce a consensus in the highly fractious Congress. They decided on a modification of the habeas corpus act with the argument that convicted capital serial killers like Ted Bundy in Florida get the benefit of protections that Terri Schiavo, who is innocent of any wrongdoing, doesn't get. "Whether you're liberal or conservative, Republican or Democrat, black or white, people of good will and common sense ought to agree that before the state was able to take the steps necessary to produce the death of a person, especially an innocent person, that they ought to be accorded at least the same kinds of due process protections that a convicted capital felon has," says Connor.

The idea gained immediate traction across party lines. The Congressional Black Caucus, all Democrats, affirmed the concept, as did Democratic senator Tom Harkin, a longtime champion of disability rights. Connor also heard from Florida Republican senator Mel Martinez, who wanted to help. Martinez, who had run for lieutenant governor as Connor's running mate in the '94 Republican primary and was a good friend, chewed out Connor for not calling him. "I told him flat out, 'Mel, the governor was savaged by the Florida media over this issue, and I didn't want you to feel burdened on my account.'"

Unlike Jeb Bush's experience in Florida, federal intervention is looking like a political winner. There is even talk of President Bush interrupting his Easter break in Texas to re-

turn to the White House to sign legislation, a powerful in-
centive for Congress to find a compromise between what
the House and Senate have passed. A death row inmate has
more legal rights, says House leader Tom DeLay. "All we're
doing in Congress is giving Terri Schiavo an opportunity to
come to the federal courts and review what this judge in
Florida has been doing, and he's been trying to kill Terri for
4 years." Whatever DeLay's real motivation for taking up
Terri's cause, he does stand to gain politically. The brou-
haha over Terri has driven news accounts of DeLay's involvement in an expanding corruption scandal off the front
page and highlighted pro-life values in a way that DeLay
believes helps Republicans. Appearing before the conservative Family Research Council, where no press is permitted,
DeLay lets down his guard and calls Terri Schiavo "a gift
from God" for their cause. A few days later, the liberal
group Americans United for the Separation of Church and
State obtains a tape of DeLay's remarks. The overtly political nature of his words taints whatever altruistic impulses he
and his party might have.

Growing suspicion that the GOP is using the Schiavo
case to rally the religious Right is driven home by reports
on ABC and in the *Washington Post* of a one-page memo circulated among Republicans explaining why they should
vote to intervene in the Schiavo case: the "pro-life base will
be excited," and it's a "great political issue" that will energize the party's Christian conservatives for the 2006 congressional elections. The memo will later be exposed as
talking points prepared by an aide for Senator Martinez.
Martinez, thinking the sheet of paper handed to him on the
Senate floor was a standard checklist of arguments, passed it

along to Democratic senator Tom Harkin, who was working closely with the GOP to pass legislation to preserve
Schiavo's life. Harkin leaked the memo to the press but
wouldn't come forward as the source until a week after
Terri died. He kept quiet as Democrats assailed Republicans for cynically exploiting a tragedy, while Republicans
who, except for Martinez, had never laid eyes on the memo
said it had to be a Democratic dirty trick. After Harkin
went public, Martinez interrogated his staff, and the aide
who drafted the memo was flushed out and fired. But the
damage was done.

Connor watches with dismay as the broadly drawn bill he
envisioned mutates—his word—into what is essentially a
special pleading for one person. On the House side, James
Sensenbrenner, the obstreperous chairman of the Judiciary
Committee, worries the bill as originally drawn will open
the door to convicted capital felons seeking relief, and insists on modifications to scale back the bill. Few people
cross Sensenbrenner and live to tell the tale, and the Schiavo case was no exception.

On the Senate side, Oregon senator Ron Wyden, a
Democrat, takes the lead in objecting to the expansive bill
first sprung upon the Senate, and then drafts the narrowly
focused version that will pass. "If the original version of the
Schiavo bill had prevailed, Congress would have turned itself into a medical court of appeals," he tells me. "The halls
would have been filled with people wanting their member
of Congress—all 535 of us—to step in and try to produce a
remedy for them."

Wyden recalls how the Republicans planned to railroad
through a bill without any hearings. Early this morning,

senators were alerted over the congressional hotline that if no one objects, the GOP majority will pass the Schiavo bill by unanimous consent. Nobody pays much attention to these advisories, which are usually routine and not newsworthy, but an aide who had been following the Schiavo issue was at her post and alerted Wyden.

He's an expert on end-of-life issues as a senator from Oregon, the first state to pass an assisted suicide law. Although he had qualms about the 1997 state law, he defended the legality and constitutionality of Oregon's two ballot measures against federal interference and says his fears about potential abuse have been dispelled. Oregon has fewer assisted suicides than states that don't have a law, and there's a huge increase in people spending their last days at home with hospice care. Wyden is also learning firsthand about the wrenching decisions associated with the end of life. His mother has an advanced case of Alzheimer's. "She left tons of notes about what she wanted—to make sure we pull the plug. She has a master's degree from Yale. She's incredibly smart and certain about not being left to live if she couldn't make decisions. I'm the only one left, and I find it very hard to even think about it—even though we walked through how she would want it handled early on."

Democrats do not want to vote on Schiavo. They buy the conventional wisdom that this is a political windfall for the GOP, and a vote against "saving" Terri will once again put them on the losing side of the cultural war. Florida Democrat Bill Nelson, who is up for reelection in '06, is especially adamant about not voting. He was singled out in the Republican memo as potentially vulnerable in a state President Bush had won handily. For nervous Democrats, the

GOP plan to pass the bill by unanimous consent is their gift from God, allowing them to continue their Easter travel and skirt accountability. There was never any serious thought given to stopping the federal government from interfering in the Schiavo family tragedy.

Iowa senator Tom Harkin, a traditional liberal with a 100 percent rating from NARAL-Pro-Choice America, is almost alone as a Democrat in pushing for broader protection. For him, the issue is personal. His profoundly deaf brother, Frank, was sent away as a child to a residential school for the "deaf and dumb," a phrase that reflects an outdated attitude about the nonhearing. Observing the discrimination his brother experienced turned Harkin into a lifelong advocate for people with disabilities. He speaks for those who bring another dimension to the debate, who fear that the decision to withdraw Terri Schiavo's feeding tube is a slippery slope that could ultimately affect them in a negative way if others judge their existence too marginal to continue living. "So they all wound up weighing in on our side," says Connor, who met with representatives of more than a dozen disability groups who understood the implications of what happens to people if they're not deemed to be sentient or they cost more to maintain than they produce.

It's Easter break on Capitol Hill, and most Democrats have left Washington, expecting Congress to stay in recess through the holiday. With only three members present, the Senate convenes at 5:00 in the afternoon to pass a resolution that empowers House speaker Dennis Hastert to call the House back into emergency session. In addition to the Republican leader, Tennessee senator Bill Frist, the other two stalwarts are Democrat Tom Harkin and Pennsylvania

Republican Rick Santorum, who is closely aligned with the Christian Right.

Santorum offers a prayer at the start of the session since the Senate's usual chaplain is not there. Frist speaks to a nearly empty Senate chamber at 6:15 to report Congress "has been working nonstop over the last three days to do its part to uphold human dignity and affirm a culture of life." He assures the country that this legislation will pass "and give Terri Schiavo one last chance at life."

The two-page bill petitions the federal court in Florida to remove Terri Schiavo from the jurisdiction of Judge Greer, who has withstood enormous pressure within the state and now from Washington to repeatedly rule to remove Terri's feeding tube. The congressional action is at odds with the GOP's historic position of support for states' rights.

A confident DeLay appears on CNN to express confidence that Schiavo's nutrition and hydration will be restored while the federal court reviews the case. The protesters gathered outside Terri's hospice in Florida take their cue from DeLay and applaud Congress's quick action. But the Reverend Pat Mahoney, the antiabortion activist brought in by the Schindler family to organize the demonstrations, knew that victory was not at hand, and that his side was in trouble, because there was no provision in the bill to reinsert the feeding tube while the court action was under way. Everyone around him was celebrating as Mahoney cautioned, "We're not out of the woods yet."

Mahoney is a self-described "sixties-type person," though he was barely a teenager at the time. His wife says he never met a demonstration he didn't like. Physically compact and supercaffeinated on Red Bull, his drink of choice, he is a man in perpetual motion, the majordomo of what is turning out to be a huge event. He decides to go on a hunger strike until Terri is fed. Mahoney has fasted many times in support of various causes, so he knows how to do it responsibly, abstaining from food but taking fluids. Still, this experience will test him more than any other in his twenty-nine years of ministry. The Florida heat and the unpredictability of the crowds add to the pressure.

Everybody wants the story reported their way, and Mahoney is generally satisfied with the media coverage the protesters are getting—with one exception. He says it's a mistake to characterize the movement to keep Terri alive as monolithically right-wing Republican and religious. "I'm not a conservative Republican, I'm a Democrat," he says. "I've slept in Dumpsters with the homeless. I think we have a responsibility to reach out to the most needy and broken in our society, which is why I'm opposed to the death penalty. I'm a pacifist—I'm against war. This is a continuation of my commitment to the dignity of life. I'm opposed to the death penalty like I'm opposed to racial injustice like I'm opposed to abortion—it's all connected."

Mahoney knew the Schindlers through Randall Terry, the antiabortion activist and founder of Operation Rescue who lives in Florida and has taken up Terri's cause. Mahoney and Terry had teamed up in 1991 to found the Christian Defense Ministry, which most recently had been in the forefront of the battle to keep the Ten Commandments in an Alabama courtroom.

Mahoney had traveled to Florida weeks before Judge Greer's ruling to meet with the local police departments and scope out the upcoming protests. He put a specific chain of command in place and assured the police there would be no surprises and no violence. "If somebody comes in that we don't know, who seems to be acting out, we'll come tell you."

There was what Mahoney calls "a little rumble" over who should act as the spokesperson for the Schindler family. He didn't think Randall Terry was the right public face because his radical antiabortion activities made it too easy for the media to paint the protesters as religious-Right zealots. Mahoney lost the internal battle, and the fiery Terry was in the news every day. Determined to show that support for Terri was more diverse, especially in the black community, Mahoney reached out to the reverends Jesse Jackson and Al Sharpton, civil-rights leaders aligned with the Democratic Left, urging them to show their support. Jackson is criticized for being a publicity hound when he shows up in Tallahassee to lobby the Florida legislature to intervene, but he is there at Mahoney's invitation.

The protests are done with military precision, down to the number of Porta Potties ordered. A snow fence encloses a small area where protesters are permitted to gather. A commercial area across the street with a parking lot houses twenty-four satellite trucks. The street outside is barely wide enough for two cars. The people showing up have differing agendas, which has the potential of leading to violence. When you have television cameras in America today, there's no telling who might show up, says Mahoney. "There were people there that scared me to death," he says. Those people would be monitored in an extravigilant fashion.

Mahoney catches flak from the media when it is apparent that people bringing food and water to Terri are part of a staged photo-op. In his defense, he argues that to let the event unfold spontaneously would have meant people attempting to cross the barricade and taking the police by surprise, which would have violated his agreement with the police. Still, some twenty people are arrested, including a man who claims he is a priest and tries to enter the hospice to administer Holy Communion to Terri.

Mahoney has high praise for the Pinellas police officers who take the insults hurled at them daily and maintain their professionalism. They are called Nazis, and their guarding of Terri is likened to guarding concentration camps. "Every group, liberal or conservative, if they don't like you, you're somehow linked to the Nazis," says Mahoney. "They were the unsung heroes—there was no act of violence, no property was destroyed, no one was injured."

It is a huge marketing ploy meticulously choreographed with the close cooperation of the police and local shopkeepers. The Schindlers use a thrift store just a few feet from the media as a command center. Michael Schiavo has been living at the hospice in a residence room, which is not uncommon for relatives whose loved ones are at a critical stage. He controls the visitors' list, which is also not uncommon for a spouse, but this is a constant irritant to the Schindlers and their entourage of supporters and advisers. Terri's room is next to the nurses' station, which is next to a visitors' waiting room. The distrust is so great that the Schindlers are forbidden to be anywhere on the hospice premises, including the waiting room, for fear they will break into Terri's room. During the limited times they are permitted entry, they go through four security checkpoints where they are searched for cell phones and cameras. Once inside Terri's room, an armed police officer stands guard at her bedside. Knowing the value of keeping Terri's image before the public, Mahoney proposes that a family member or close adviser go into the hospice wearing a pair of glasses embedded with a camera. The James Bond maneuver is rejected for fear that any photo released to the media will invite Michael's wrath, and he could cut off all visitation rights.

4.

Palm Sunday Compromise

> *New members signing on to the Internet site for cancer patients*
> *are greeted with this sardonic message: "Welcome to the club that*
> *nobody wants to belong to."*
> —Tom Brazaitis in a column dated October 14, 2001

FOR ALL THE RESEARCH Tom had done about his illness, he isn't quite sure what hospice means, or maybe he was so focused on keeping the cancer at bay, he thought he could elude the stark finality that the word alone evokes. When I explain that hospice provides a support system for people who are terminally ill and are at home, he bursts out singing, "You'll Never Walk Alone."

I would later discover the tape of an interview he did in late May 1999 with the administrator of a hospice in Cleveland for a story about this still unfamiliar but growing phenomenon of a place where people could go to die. I was struck by the innocence of Tom's questions. He was just weeks from being diagnosed with a life-threatening disease himself, but there was no sense of foreboding. He was a reporter working to extract information, and he wanted to

understand the point at which a person reasonably concludes "no heroic measures" and opts for an end free of
tubes and hi-tech hookups.

Then that day came in mid-January when I could no
longer safely get Tom down the stairs from our bedroom to
the living room. We had still been sleeping in the same bed
as his illness advanced. Some friends found this amazing,
but I didn't. "This is the closest I've ever felt to you," he
would say as we settled down in the king-size bed we shared
for more than fifteen years. I feel protective, more like a
mother than a wife, and sad, because I know I'm losing my
husband bit by bit. One Saturday morning as I left for the
gym and he was going to be alone in the house, I made him
promise to stay in bed. I didn't want to risk his falling while
I was gone. He smiled mischievously. "How many husbands
have a wife that tells them that?"

He was increasingly shaky on his feet. We had taken up
all the carpets to smooth out the terrain, but I worried he
could slip and hurt himself, compounding his health problems. The hospital bed provided by hospice and delivered
weeks earlier has not been slept in except by our two cats. It
sat empty at one end of the living room, a place to stack
newspapers and magazines. Neither Tom nor I had wanted
to take that next step of moving him into what we knew
would be his deathbed. Now the moment was upon us.

There would be benefits despite the psychological discomfort of abandoning the marital bed. Tom would be
more comfortable on the ground floor, where he could feel
like he was participating in life instead of being confined to
a sickroom.

Jeff, the physical therapist sent by hospice, volunteered

to transport Tom—pick him up in his arms for the trip down the stairs—but backed off when Tom recoiled. At six feet tall, Tom typically weighed 180 pounds, but after the ravages of chemotherapy, he was easily 15 or 20 pounds lighter, down to where he was in high school, he told me with some pride. With Tom in a wheelchair, Jeff maneuvered him down the stairs and into the hospital bed, treating the descent like an adventure and maintaining a respectful tone for this man he has come to admire. Jeff's occasional visits brought joy to Tom. They talked sports and ragged on each other like two jocks in the locker room. Jeff installed a bar over the bed so Tom could pull himself up and keep in shape, a bit of foolery that played to Tom's image of himself as an athlete. Tom never left the bed after Jeff set him down that day.

The decision that Tom and I faced to forgo further curative care was far more straightforward and therefore easier than anything the Schindlers and Michael Schiavo had to deal with. We had run out of treatment options. Our challenge was to admit to ourselves and to others that the fight was over. It required a radical shift in thinking. I had said so often that cancer is not a death sentence, it's a chronic disease that can be managed, it had become my mantra. I had lulled myself into thinking Tom could go on almost indefinitely. The suggestion that he enter hospice, voiced by the oncologist right after Thanksgiving in 2004, shattered my false hopes and shook loose my fragile hold on normalcy. But I regained my bearings and even felt a measure of relief. I could stop kidding myself; the worst had happened, and my job now was to make the best of the worst. I needed to bear up not only for Tom, but for me. There were dark days ahead. Tom had always kept careful track of his medications and doctor appointments, and when it was time for his regular Tuesday chemotherapy infusion, he was dressed and ready to go. This had been his routine. I hated explaining that it was no longer necessary. You'd think somebody would be relieved at getting out of chemotherapy, but that's not the case when you think it's extending your life. And Tom wanted more time. I thought about driving him over to the doctor's office to chat with the nurses, so he could get a sense that life as he'd known it now for years hadn't come to a screeching stop. But he was getting so unstable on his feet that leaving the house was a major undertaking. He had a routine dental cleaning scheduled for the end of December. I agonized before canceling it. Somehow giving up on his teeth meant giving up on him.

Cancer had hovered over our lives for more than five years, which is when the first symptom appeared. I remember the day well because it was the weekend and I had been traveling and I thought Tom was out of sorts because I'd been away. He finally revealed his worry, that he'd seen blood in his urine. We went to our big book of medical symptoms where we learned cancer was a possible culprit but that there were benign causes as well. Tom made an appointment with our primary-care doctor, who seemed unconcerned. "Well, you're a runner. This happens sometimes with runners." He gave Tom a sterile cup and told him to come back if it happened again. Tom's urologist wasn't as sanguine. When Tom mentioned during a routine checkup having had blood in the urine, he scheduled a scan for the following day. That afternoon, Tom had a call from Ginger, the nurse, wanting to schedule an appointment concerning "the large mass" on his left kidney. It was the first he'd heard of a large mass, and Tom mustered a memorable quip, "I'd prefer you use the term *nodule*."

He had surgery to remove his kidney within a week, after first being scanned head to toe to determine whether the cancer had spread. When the scan came up clear, he called me with the results, cheerily declaring, "I don't have cancer—my kidney does." It was a line borrowed from President Reagan, who insisted after surgery to remove a cancerous polyp from his colon that he didn't have cancer, his colon did. Press secretary Larry Speakes urged reporters not to challenge the president, explaining the importance of maintaining Reagan's signature optimism.

Tom went into the hospital on July 1 with an upbeat attitude, and the surgeon, who was usually deadpan and didn't give away much, seemed almost exhilarated after the operation. Everything had gone well. We thought this was behind us and kidney cancer was never going to darken our door again. Tom was up and walking the day after the operation. The nurses all marveled at his athleticism. Life got back to normal pretty quickly, and the three-month scan and six-month scan both showed no evidence of cancer. It was in the one-year checkup in August 2000 that the doctor spotted what he called a nodule in Tom's lung. "If this is cancerous," he said, "it's not lung cancer. It's kidney cancer metastasized—or spread—to your lung."

Tom reacted like a reporter and headed for the Internet. He plugged in "prognosis" and "kidney cancer." He wanted to know everything because now he had to decide what kind of treatment to pursue and where to go, which doctor, which hospital. This was a major investigative effort, and in the modern world of competitive medicine, he was on his own. The urologist's last words to Tom were, "Good luck, man." He gave him a couple of names to consider, but that was it.

Of the fifty-one thousand cases of kidney cancer diagnosed in the United States each year, 70 to 75 percent who have a kidney removed are home-free and don't experience a spread of the cancer. Tom fell in the smaller percentage that accounts for twelve thousand kidney cancer deaths every year. Why somebody like Tom who otherwise enjoyed good health would get this relatively uncommon form of cancer is unknowable. One doctor said it was the equivalent of getting hit by a safe falling from a window: it was random, and Tom happened to be in the wrong spot. There is a link to smoking, as there is to so many diseases. Tom had spent about fifteen years as a smoker, beginning with his army days stationed in Germany when the PX practically gave away cigarettes, they were so cheap. Then as a journalist and weekly newspaper editor, he was certain he couldn't write without a cigarette. But it had been years since he had smoked; he was fit and healthy, and there was no history of cancer in his family.

After much research, Tom settled on a course of treatment known as immunotherapy that would be administered on an outpatient basis at the Cleveland Clinic, a world-class medical center where Tom had the added advantage of being a hometown boy. He would chronicle for readers of the *Plain Dealer* the cutting-edge therapies keeping him and countless others alive to battle another day. A combination of drugs—interferon, interleukin, and a third drug mysteriously labeled GMCSF—would induce flulike symptoms, with the goal of summoning the body's reserves and boosting the immune system. Tom stayed with relatives, and I flew in on weekends. I remember how we shopped for clothes he could easily wear and wash during those months. It was like sending him to cancer camp.

The side effects of the treatments were horrendous at first, fevers that reached 105 degrees followed by bone-rattling chills. Tom called them "the shakes and bakes." I was terrified when I first witnessed this. I'd never seen a fever so high, but after watching the cycle a couple of times, I gained confidence that the fever would come down, and that we could handle what happened at home on our own. We got quite practiced at symptom management with the help of a stack of ice packs and an electric blanket.

This regimen kept the cancer stable for eighteen months, and the side effects eased with time. We got to the point where Tom was able to inject the drugs himself, and when he ran out of easy-to-reach sites on his body, I would do the injections. The drugs arrived in an iced package via FedEx, and Tom would fill the syringes. He used to inject himself with allergy shots, so he was familiar with the process. But when we told people about our home health care, they often would recoil and look squeamish. I would then explain that you don't have to find a vein. These are subcutaneous injections into a fatty area of the body. People who've had aged animals are familiar with the procedure, and in fact we were injecting our diabetic cat with insulin twice a day during this period. We were quite the team. The refrigerated medicines went everywhere with us. I remember pulling off a golf course into the rough once to give Tom an injection. The unimaginable becomes the routine. It's a lesson I would learn over and over throughout the course of Tom's illness.

Tom was the poster boy for immunotherapy, so he was unhappy when a tumor in the soft tissue of his buttocks ("of all places," as he used to say) that had been dormant showed growth and he was taken off the treatment. This was a clinical trial that required those enrolled to show continual improvement or stability. The doctor put a happy face on things, explaining that kidney cancer is typically slow growing, and no one could know if the treatment had anything to do with the period of stability Tom enjoyed. Maybe it was his immune system doing the work. There were new drugs coming online. We would wait and see.

THE SUNDAY NEWS SHOWS are full of talk about the "Palm Sunday Compromise," a two-page bill called "An Act for the Relief of the Parents of Theresa Marie Schiavo," and poised for passage in the House and Senate. President Bush says he will return from his ranch in Crawford to be available to sign the measure the moment Congress acts. "Hours do matter at this point," White House press secretary Scott McLellan tells reporters aboard *Air Force One*. This is the quickest the government has responded to anything since the immediate aftermath of the 9/11 attacks when the president and both houses of Congress joined together to pass national-security legislation.

Schiavo's brother, Bobby Schindler, is visiting the Capitol, escorted by an official of the National Right to Life Committee. He's become a featured speaker at evangelical gatherings around the country. He says he's there "to help save my sister's life." Various members of Congress are holding forth in the House Press Gallery, and Schindler is there when Virginia Democrat Jim Moran declares the Schiavo bill sets "a very dangerous precedent that will come back to haunt us." Schindler is polite but passionate and hands Moran a video disk that he says proves his sister is functional. The same video had prompted Republican leader Bill Frist to announce on the floor of the U.S. Senate three days earlier that Terri Schiavo is "not somebody in persistent vegetative state." Since Frist had said he was speaking as a medical doctor, not as a politician, more than a dozen of his colleagues from Yale Medical School signed a letter saying his license should be revoked for making such an impetuous and ill-advised judgment about Schiavo's condition. Moran refers to the encounter with Terri's brother when he addresses his colleagues in a speech later that day on the House floor, saying, "I don't know who's right and who's wrong. But that's the point: neither do my colleagues. Ten courts and nineteen judges all have reached the same conclusion."

The Senate passes the bill by voice vote on Sunday afternoon, an arrangement that Senate Democrats signed off on. Democratic leader Harry Reid, a pro-life Mormon from Nevada, is especially sensitive to social issues, given his religious orientation and his opposition to abortion. He tells Democrats to stay out of the Schiavo debate, that it's a political loser for them. With Reid's blessing, they worked behind the scenes to narrow the scope of the bill so that only Schiavo would be affected, but Democrats don't want to make a public display of their opposition.

Under Senate rules, a single senator can stop action on the bill, but none choose to do so. Democrats stay silent, fearing any objection will leave them vulnerable to the charge that they killed Terri Schiavo. Florida senator Bill Nelson, a former astronaut and political moderate, faces re-election in '06 and doesn't want to fuel religious-Right activism against his candidacy in the state that is ground zero in the Schiavo fight. "I don't want to vote," he tells his fellow Democrats. Schiavo's slow death from lack of hydration coincides with the holiest week on the Christian calendar, timing that infuses the debate with a level of emotion that can fairly be described as fanaticism.

House Democrats are less malleable and force the Republican leadership to scramble well into the evening hours on Sunday to assemble 218 colleagues, the minimum for a quorum, because so many members are traveling and taking advantage of the two-week Easter break. Freshman Republican Joe Schwarz got the message on his Blackberry calling him back to Washington. He wasn't happy about it. As a moderate in a party that had moved far to the right, he didn't think this was an issue Congress should be voting on. "But I was not going to run away from it," he told Edward Sidlow, author of *Freshman Orientation*, an account of what turned out to be Schwarz's single term in Congress. (He was defeated in the GOP primary by a right-to-life minister backed by the Club for Growth, conservative Republicans dedicated to defeating Republicans they dubbed RINOs—Republicans in Name Only. The radical shift right away from the centrist Schwarz allowed a Democrat to capture the Republican-leaning seat in Battle Creek, Michigan, in the '06 midterm election, one of many so-called swing districts that brought the Democrats back into power on Capitol Hill.)

A physician who had treated patients for thirty years

before getting elected to Congress in 2004, Schwarz believed that some end-of-life issues might rise to the level of
a congressional hearing or investigation, but the focus on a
single individual such as Schiavo was misplaced. Still, when
majority leader Tom DeLay rallies Republicans, Schwarz is
among those who vote with their party to intervene on the
side of saving Schiavo's life. He would later tell Sidlow:

> This issue was before us because some of our most
> zealous members, particularly Mr. DeLay, wanted to
> make a public display on something that they could
> define as a right-to-life issue. To say that this was not
> being done because some in our party were looking to
> gain politically would raise disingenuousness to an art
> form. ... I would not have chosen to vote on it, and I
> suspect that three or four other physicians in the Con-
> gress would say the same thing. But there it was and as
> a physician, I saw no other way to vote. This person
> had robust brain-stem activity, spontaneous respira-
> tion, spontaneous cardiac activity, was in no imminent
> danger of dying, she wasn't on life support, not on a
> respirator, and she was being given nourishment
> through a feeding tube ... along with at least 15,000
> other people in this country who at one level or an-
> other have decreased clinical abilities. So, what do we
> do now? Take the feeding tubes out of all 15,000? I
> don't think so.

The House sets the vote for one minute after midnight,
and a three-hour debate gets under way on Sunday evening.
Barney Frank, a Massachusetts Democrat known for his

sharp intellect and wit, says the caption for the House floor debate should be, "We're not doctors. We just play them on C-Span." On a more serious note, he says what a lot of his colleagues are thinking: "This is a terribly difficult decision which we are, institutionally, totally incompetent to make."

Dr. James Bernat is a neurologist and an expert on what he calls "vegetative state." He doesn't use *persistent* or *permanent* because he says it confuses a person's prognosis—whether they will improve—with the diagnosis, which is vegetative. Prognosis is predicting, and it has a certain degree of error. However, with Schiavo, he says, "If anyone was not going to get better, she was that person. It was so obvious to everyone. She had been like that for fifteen years—flat EEG, brain scan showed extreme atrophy. Nobody comes back from her type of vegetative state. But in some cases it isn't that clear and we need to admit that."

The term *persistent vegetative state* was coined in 1972 by two neurosurgeons writing in the medical journal *Lancet*. They chose the adjective *vegetative* because its definition in the *Oxford English Dictionary* captured the essential features of the patients: "a merely physical life, devoid of intellectual activity or social intercourse ... an organic body capable of growth and development but devoid of sensation and thought." Unlike a patient in a coma, whose eyes are closed, PVS patients lie with their eyes open while awake and closed while asleep. They breathe on their own, they blink, and they have facial expressions, behavior that misleads others into thinking they are sentient and acting with intention. But it is wakefulness without awareness, which careful bedside monitoring reveals.

I met with Bernat in his Vermont farmhouse. In addition

to a busy private practice, he chairs the ethics committee at the Dartmouth-Hitchcock Medical Center. He told me about attending his fortieth high school reunion in Cincinnati the summer Terri Schiavo died, and his classmates, knowing he had testified before the Senate Committee on Health about vegetative state, pressed him for his views. "You try to divine what the person herself wanted," he told them. "Is she the sort who would want to continue? Or would she refuse life-prolonging procedures that didn't improve her quality of life? I think the courts did that to the fullest. There was a financial conflict and a romantic conflict that complicated the decision, and the churchgoing Republican judge was vilified for ruling on clear and convincing evidence. The parents also had conflicts," he continued. "Even if she had made clear her wishes that she didn't want to live like this, they still wanted to keep her alive—so they were not as focused on following her wishes as she was their daughter and meaningful to them. They said even if she were ten times worse, they still wanted to keep her alive."

Bernat had been asked by Michael Schiavo's attorney to be an expert witness, but he declined after hearing about the various conflicts in the case, which is how the Schiavo side turned to Dr. Ronald Cranford, with his long history of testifying in right-to-die cases. Where Cranford tends toward the combative and colorful, Bernat is soft-spoken and determinedly cautious. He disagrees with Cranford on the use of the term *persistent* in describing vegetative state and recalls a case in Minneapolis, a policeman who Cranford had said was PVS, "and twenty-two months later, the guy woke up. There was a lot of publicity that this famous doc-

tor had made a mistake," says Bernat. In fairness to Cranford, the man's faculties were still greatly impaired, but the
incident was a reminder that assessing a person's awareness
is tricky business.

Cranford readily admitted he made a misdiagnosis.
David Mack, the police sergeant who'd been shot, was presumed in a vegetative state until a nurse noticed his eyes
were not randomly moving, they were tracking, and he
could communicate with a sign board, a clear plastic board
with the alphabet on it. Cranford brought in Father John
Paris, a Jesuit priest, to visit with the man. "His eyes would
just move around and you point to the letter and his eyes
indicate yes or no," recalls Father Paris. "Do you know
what this guy says to me? H E L P M E D I E . ... Here was a
man who was fully alert. He was in what we call a 'locked-in
syndrome.'"

Paris was reminded of David Mack in the wake of the
Schiavo case when the journal *Science* published an article in
September 2006 titled "Detecting Awareness in the Vegetative State." It reported that a twenty-three-year-old
woman, unconscious for five months after a traffic accident,
showed brain activity when she was put into an MRI brain-
imaging scanner and told to imagine playing tennis at
Wimbledon, and then to pretend she was in her house
walking from room to room and thinking about what she
would see. The images produced by the MRI showed her
brain "lighting up" in the same way as the brains of a
healthy control group of volunteers. Typically, such patients
are asked to respond to words, or a baby's cry, or they're
shown a picture. These tasks were sufficiently different
that, combined with some sophisticated programmatic

technology, they detected unexpected mental activity. Several months later, the woman was able to fixate on a small mirror and track it from right to left, a response that meant she was not in a persistent vegetative state. Whether this is good news depends on your perspective. "This is worse than being in a PVS, where you have no awareness," says Father Paris. "Imagine being trapped, fully aware, hearing every conversation and, if they catch your eyes, able to communicate, and able to do nothing else."

Physicians are always concerned with neurological status because if there is no awareness, that's reason enough to stop treatment. But Paris points out that for some people, the possibility of being conscious while trapped is worse, yet that doesn't change the ethical propriety of stopping treatment. Technology can detect little islands of neuron activity in the brain, as they did with this woman in England, upgrading her from PVS to locked-in syndrome or, the more scientific term, minimally conscious.

Dr. Bernat, a leading expert on PVS, calls the report "disturbing" because it challenges the notion that a definitive diagnosis of PVS can be made at the bedside by observing a patient. CNN touted its story with this lead-in: "A woman plays tennis even though she's in a vegetative state." The *Washington Post* quoted Bobby Schindler saying this kind of research could have helped his sister. That's not true, says Bernat. Terri Schiavo suffered anoxic damage, meaning her brain cells died for lack of oxygen. The American Academy of Neurology says that after three months with anoxic damage, the chances of recovery are nil. A brain damaged by trauma is a different physiology, and the time line stretches out to at least six months, where recovery is possible.

It was the job of Cranford and others who examined Schiavo to elicit any response that indicated she was acting with intention. The doctors enlisted by the Schindlers who testified she could respond to treatment were self-evidently not qualified to make such an assessment. One was a radiologist, Dr. William Maxwell, who was out of his depth. The other, Dr. William Hammesfahr, though he calls himself a neurologist, is not a member of the American Academy of Neurology and is regarded by his professional peers as an outlier.

There was no disagreement among the board-certified neurologists who examined Schiavo. Bernat says it was "cruel" of the doctors to tell the Schindlers that alternative treatments—hyperbaric oxygen and invasive dilators—could work for somebody with Terri's extensive brain damage. He points out that Michael Schiavo had sought experimental treatment, taking Terri to California in December 1990, nine months after her cardiac arrest, where they were doing work implanting electrodes into the thalamus to revive people in vegetative states. The thalamus is the gray-matter nucleus deep in the center of the brain that is involved in awareness. The California experiment didn't work, but the electrodes, with the juice turned off, stayed in Terri's brain. It would have required another operation to remove them, and doctors representing Michael Schiavo would later claim they didn't order more PET scans or MRIs done on Terri because the tests would have been dangerous due to the presence of the electrodes. The lack of recent tests on Terri's brain function fueled the suspicion among the Save Terri crowd that Michael was trying to usher her out of the world without giving her a fair hearing.

On the House floor, Republicans stand up one after the other to argue that in America, we don't let people starve an animal to death, we don't starve a prisoner to death, so how can we treat an innocent woman so barbarically? Chairman Sensenbrenner, a key player in crafting the legislation that would give Terri's parents the right to plead their case before a federal court, asserted without any factual basis that death by starvation "is one of the most cruel and inhumane ways to die."

Lack of hunger and thirst is a normal part in the dying process. In a survey of hospice doctors and nurses, more than 90 percent say there is no suffering from the lack of eating and drinking. But Terri wasn't dying—she didn't have metastatic cancer—she was in a somewhat stable physiological state. If she continued to get hydration and nutrition, she could live a long time. Bernat says he wouldn't cite the hospice data to refute the hysterical claims that Terri is suffering an agonizing death from lack of food and water. The more important fact is that she was in a vegetative state, which means she had no awareness of pain or any other sensory stimulation. "She had no capacity for suffering. Whatever you do to her, that's the relevant fact," says Bernat. "She was cared for in a hospice, and hospice nurses are very tuned in to dying. She was given opiates when the feeding tube was removed. They err on the side of alleviating her pain even if there's one zillionth of a chance she would experience discomfort or pain. That's what hospice nurses do. The reality was misrepresented for political purposes."

THE PERIOD OF "WAIT AND SEE" ended for Tom when headaches signaled that the cancer had advanced to his brain. Over the next year, he would travel periodically to the Cleveland Clinic for a gamma ray knife treatment, which is targeted radiation to the brain to zap the tumors. He wrote about how he would lie perfectly still in an isolated room listening to classical music as the targeted rays blasted away. It was painless except for the metal frame that had to be screwed into his forehead. Tom had me take his picture with the large screws prominently displayed while he grinned as though to say, what's to worry? He gleefully e-mailed it to friends and family. I hated the picture, or rather I hated what it represented. I keep it turned against the wall. Once you're getting your brain radiated, you're getting near the end of the line. But I loved his impulse to taunt the demons. He was like a kid on Halloween.

It was his custom to line up a golf game whenever he was in Cleveland. With the prognosis getting dire, he once played more than thirty-six holes, leaving his golf partner begging for mercy. His physicality was important to him. He had attended John Carroll University on a basketball scholarship and decades later fell asleep at night imagining sinking one graceful basket after another. We ran marathons together, and I took up golf in an effort to share that activity, a misreading on my part. He much preferred the guys. Tom charted his decline from the late-summer day he had to walk off the golf course because he couldn't keep up. It hit me when he had trouble navigating the single step on the stoop of our house. He called me at the office to say he had fallen and how humiliated he felt in front of the yard crew mowing our lawn.

Now, after a catheter has been installed and his mor-phine doubled, Tom says quite clearly, "What do you want to do this summer?" I say, "I want to take a trip with you," and then I go into the kitchen to fix his cream of rice cereal and fight back tears.

5.

The Hard, Honest Road

*I will continue to stand on the side of those defending life for all
Americans, including those with disabilities.*
—A pajama-clad President Bush signing the Terri Schiavo bill at
1:11 A.M. at the White House

WE LIVE IN A DEATH-DEFYING CULTURE even though,
by age eighteen, the average American has witnessed thousands of deaths on television. These are fantasies that shield
us from the reality of dying. For baby boomers who've
made a fetish out of extending youth, it's embarrassing to
succumb to terminal infirmity. Boomers have transformed
every stage of life, and the final one will be no exception.
Donald Schumacher, president of the National Hospice
and Palliative Care Organization, says only half-jestingly
that "death trainers" will become commonplace along with
belowground lattes.

At some point in the arc of existence, we all have to move
from challenging death to embracing it. But that is not
what is happening with Terri Schiavo. America's political
leaders are making a mockery of her last days, actively

working to forestall her demise, turning this young woman into an iconic figure and raising the hopes of those gathered outside the hospice in Florida. A pickup truck arrives pulling a trailer with ten-foot-high stone replicas of the Ten Commandment tablets along with a version of the Liberty Bell that looks so authentic it could be on loan from Philadelphia. A man with a trumpet plays "Amazing Grace." Some fifty people stand behind signs that say "Let Terri Live" and "President Bush Please Save Terri." They pray and sing while twenty-four-year-old Will Svab of nearby Seminole, Florida, holds a six-foot plastic foam spoon with the words "Please Feed Terri." To their credit, the mood is reverent even as the surroundings take on the trappings of a carnival.

It is 12:42 A.M. Monday when the House vote is recorded at a lopsided 302-58 in support of the legislation. President Bush signs the measure at the White House twenty-nine minutes later. With Schiavo entering her fourth day without a feeding tube, every moment counts. The news coverage notes that Bush was in the residence and was dressed for bed when an aide handed him the bill for his signature.

Republicans like to be known as the party of states' rights, so legislation that orders federal intervention over a state court decision is quite a departure for Bush. There would be accusations of hypocrisy, but that's not unusual in Washington when self-interest is involved. In Bush's case, he is responding to a very vocal minority in his party that opposes abortion and views all issues related to when life begins and ends as a violation of pro-life principles. Before his presidential ambitions put him under the microscope,

Bush had taken a more practical approach to end-of-life issues. As governor of Texas, he signed a bill allowing medical professionals to refuse or discontinue the use of ANH, or artificial nutrition and hydration, including a feeding tube, if a patient has no hope of recovery and does not have the financial resources to pay for the care—even if the patient's family members disagree. The law allows a ten-day grace period for the family to find treatment elsewhere before the plug is pulled. But that's it. The taxpayers should not be expected to pick up the bill, Bush said. Now that he is president, Bush chooses political grandstanding over the hard choices that are made every day in this country by families and medical professionals.

Whereas the Schiavo case got everybody's attention, another case unfolding almost simultaneously in Texas received little notice. Sun Hudson was four and a half months old when doctors at Texas Children's Hospital went to court in late February '05 to seek approval to remove him from the machines sustaining his life. The baby had been born with a form of dwarfism that is typically fatal soon after birth. Allowing him to linger on life support would lead to painful suffocation as his rib cage and lungs failed to develop. Under the Texas Advance Directives Act, which Bush signed in 1999, the hospital had the right to discontinue the life-sustaining treatment even though the baby's mother insisted he be kept alive. Realizing the sensitivity of the case—an infant born to a single mother who had no resources and no health insurance—the hospital went the extra step of paying for a lawyer for the mother, Wanda Hudson, to take her case before a judge. Hospital officials also say they contacted some forty other medical institutions with newborn intensive care units to see if any would agree to treat the baby. None would take the case.

Sun Hudson was not quite six months old when he died on March 15 dressed in a blue teddy bear outfit and cradled by his mother, just moments after a breathing tube was removed. His death marked the first time the courts allowed a hospital to discontinue an infant's life-sustaining care against a parent's wishes. There was legitimate concern about Wanda Hudson's grasp on reality; she claimed her son had been fathered by the sun and would live forever. She never named a biological father. The Texas law worked like everybody hoped it would and is held up as a model by medical ethicists. It even won the support of the Texas Right to Life and National Right to Life committees, which were given a seat at the table to help craft the bill after then-governor Bush had vetoed a similar measure two years earlier because of opposition from the religious Right. Known colloquially as the "Texas futility law," it codifies an area of agreement that even the most zealous advocates of the "culture of life" support, and that is that a physician is under no obligation to provide futile medical interventions.

There was an expectation that other states would follow the Texas example, but so far only California has a similar law. The issue is too raw politically, and once the political stakes are raised, there is less room for compromise.

Despite its stand in Texas, the National Right to Life Committee is helping lead the fight to keep Terri Schiavo on life support. The video of Terri keeps her plight before the nation, and her fight becomes our fight. Everyone asks themselves what they would want if they were in her situation, and what they would do if they had a loved one living in such a compromised state. This conversation is played out in a variety of venues, with more people making their wishes known in advance directives and assigning someone they trust to make decisions for them if they are no longer competent. In an episode of the HBO series *The Sopranos*, Tony Soprano, a Mafia kingpin with a sensitive side, is talking to his therapist about Uncle Junior's declining mental faculties. He describes a scene that clearly disturbed him of a nanny with a baby crossing the street while another caretaker crosses from the opposite side pushing a wheelchair with a woman staring vacantly. "The circle of life," the therapist observes amiably. "Circle-jerk life—I'd rather put a pillow over my head," says Tony.

How many of us have airily declared we would drink hemlock or put a gun to our head when the time came? We wouldn't want to live that way, whatever way it is. But life endings don't typically play out that way. Terri Schiavo had no capacity to act on her own behalf. Tom was among those who would have done anything to avoid these last months of dependency, but he accepted the hand he'd been dealt and played it out with gallantry.

"If you're lucky in the end, you can give up your dignity and let your loved ones take care of you," says the therapist.

In a shocking twist that seems to belie the wise words from the therapist, a paranoid Uncle Junior shoots Tony in the chest, thinking he's somebody else. Sister Janice had wanted to put their uncle into assisted living, but Tony refused, saying the family will take care of him. In a subsequent episode, visitors to Tony's bedside include two members of the religious Right, one wearing a T-shirt that says "Terri Schiavo Vigil 3/31/05." They're protesting the firing of the hospital pharmacist for refusing to fill prescriptions for birth control pills. Tony frets about whether the pharmacist will supply him with Viagra. "I'm going to need plenty in my condition." He's assured God has nothing against procreation. "But it's not for procreation," he protests. Undeterred by Tony's taunts, they offer to pray for him on the eve of his surgery, telling him there are 11 percent fewer complications if a patient is prayed for.

That's untrue, according to a $2.4 million federally funded study on the medical effectiveness of so-called intercessory prayer. The results, released in April 2006, found no difference in recovery rates between patients told that strangers were praying for them, a second group told that strangers might or might not be praying for them, and a third group that was not prayed for at all. Raymond J. Lawrence, an Episcopal priest who directs pastoral care at New York–Presbyterian Hospital and Columbia University Medical Center, wrote in the *New York Times* that this was welcome news because if it could ever be persuasively demonstrated that such prayer works, "our religious institutions and meeting places would be degraded to a kind of commercial enterprise, like Burger King, where one expects to get what one pays for." Doctors should also be pleased, Lawrence wrote, because if prayer could be scientifically shown to help, "every doctor would be obligated to pray with patients, or at least provide such service, and those who declined to do so would properly be subject to charges of malpractice."

Tom wasn't a religious man and learning he had terminal cancer did not shake his conviction that he had himself to rely on, and his loved ones, not what he viewed as some made-up God. He believed that this life is it, and he worried sometimes that this distance he imposed upon himself, living life as a journalist trained to observe rather than participate, prevented him from living life fully. Raised Catholic, he attended Catholic high school and college. His mother was deeply religious and for fifty years played the organ in a Catholic church in Cleveland. Tom drifted away from his faith and in recent years called himself an atheist. He became openly hostile to organized religion at the same time the country became more overtly religious and the Christian Right became synonymous with the Republican Party. Tom wrote a column questioning whether an atheist could ever be elected president. He knew the answer was no.

When Tom underwent open-brain surgery to remove one stubborn tumor that the less invasive gamma ray knife couldn't get, I worried about how healthy brain tissue could be affected. But I knew he was okay when he asked as he came out of the anesthesia, "Is Bush still president?" It was our running joke ever since the contested 2000 election.

The last book Tom ordered from Amazon.com arrived today. It is a small philosophical tract called *On Bullshit*.

TOM POSSESSED A HEALTHY SKEPTICISM and a wry wit, so it didn't surprise me when the therapist he'd been seeing told me with some amusement that Tom's presenting complaint on his first visit in December 2000 was, "I'm more morose than usual," and that he would prove an elusive patient over the next four years as he fought cancer. Dr. Stephen Hersh specializes in treating people with life-threatening illness. "Welcome to the land of input over-load," he said as he ushered me into his small office and asked if I'd like some chocolate to go with the Diet Coke I'd brought along with me. A fit-looking man with white hair and a beard, he was the same age as Tom, born just three days later, two Leos. "You could say we were litter-mates," he says. He's pulled out his records on Tom along with his notes and invites me to put on my journalist cloak and squeeze information out of him that might be useful to my understanding of Tom's thinking during this period. I rattle on for a bit about how I sometimes felt closer to Tom, and sometimes he would push me away—but then again maybe I was the one who was running away. I didn't want his illness to swallow me up. I didn't really know. He was so clear-eyed about what he was facing and so willing to take responsibility for his illness that he spared me from much of the day-to-day stress. Kidney cancer affects more men than women, and I could see from the Listserv on the Internet that a lot of men let their wives take the lead in pursuing treatments, making appointments, handling their medica-tions and diet. It was a gift to me that Tom took charge and always urged me to continue with my life and career. Some people imagine that if they were given a limited time to live they would travel the world over, or go on vacation indefi-nitely. Tom would always say, no, I just want to live my live as normally as possible, which is what I wanted to hear.

"And as far as I know, it's what he wanted to do," Dr. Hersh says. "He was extremely private with me too and worked quite hard, I felt, to keep me at a distance except when I was useful, which kept him in control. That was consistent."

Control, it's gotten a bad name—witness the phrase "control freak"—but it's important in dealing with catastrophic illness for both the patient and the caregiver. I found with every new setback that once I found my footing and felt a measure of control that I could settle into a routine that incorporated whatever had happened. It's amazing what the human spirit can endure, and that was true for Tom many times over. When he first went to see Dr. Hersh, Tom was moderately depressed, scoring twenty-five on a test where anything above ten signals depression. He was ruminating a lot about death and hopelessness. But as his disease progressed and he knew he was terminal, he was no longer depressed. This seems counterintuitive, but by going public about his disease, Tom had created a major support system for himself and much of his time was spent connecting with and counseling others via e-mail. He would marvel at how many people were praying for him. Being an atheist, he didn't put much stock in it, but he liked having a following, and it buoyed his spirits knowing that many people cared. He felt it was too late for him to get better, but it wasn't too late to keep going.

He was very businesslike in terms of what he believed in—ashes to ashes, dust to dust. He didn't want to suffer while dying. He feared the dying process more than death. He believed death would be like before he was born, nothing, oblivion. Some people find the prospect of eternal oblivion terrifying; Tom found it soothing.

Hersh's notes from early 2001 say, "Working on spirituality." Tom had talked about his strict Catholic upbringing and his drift away from the church, but what Hersh was encouraging him to do was find meaning beyond himself—

with other people, nature, African violets, whatever, he explained. Tom proved deft at imagery. "Everything feels right when I'm getting things through the net in jump shots from a semicircle," he said. The golf course was his church as he imagined everything from how the ground felt under his feet on the first hole to how the wind felt on his skin. Tom was thrilled that he could still play golf, and about his illness, he said, "The disease is still lurking there. What it has on its mind is not known."

What's interesting is he gave his disease an identity. It was a constant in his life, bringing fatigue and queasiness with only periodic respites to regain what strength he could. He was about to begin his sixth round of immunotherapy, which meant the return of "the shakes and bakes." "Can I afford to live any longer?" he asked Hersh, suddenly anxious about the high cost of his illness, and what must have seemed diminishing returns. He was beginning to have what's called "chemo brain," a side effect of the treatments where it's hard to concentrate for more than an hour at a time. Yet Dr. Hersh noted in their next visit, some six weeks later in May of '01, that his patient's color was good, his eyes were sparkling, and he was energetic and in a good mood. "Eleanor is not fretting so much anymore," he reported. And then Tom disappeared for three months, says Hersh, a familiar pattern as the cancer waxed and waned, and Tom would feel more or less need for his counsel.

Tom reappeared in Hersh's office on August 13, 2001—he was tan and firm-muscled, his handshake was powerful, and he was very upbeat. "Doing brilliantly," Hersh wrote in his notes. He was about to start an eighth cycle of IL2, the principal drug in immunotherapy for kidney cancer. "I feel like shit for several hours and into the next day, and then I get better," he told Hersh, who noted that his patient's eyes were incredibly bright. "You know how intense he could be, and he said to me, 'I might as well participate in life.' So that was a good moment, a very good moment."

Tom was driving back from his regular checkup at the Cleveland Clinic when two jetliners took down the World Trade Center, a third flew into the Pentagon, and a fourth crashed on an empty field in Pennsylvania. The horrific events kind of energized him, he told Hersh. He was a journalist and it was a big story; cancer would have to take a backseat. Hersh noted how well he was managing the cancer, and he added in parentheses, "Is this a patient response?" In other words, is Tom's relative health "just him," or is he responding to the immunotherapy? "He had quite a will, so my bias is it was him," says Hersh.

In mid-November 2001, Tom took the self-rating scale that less than a year earlier had revealed he was chronically depressed. He was not at all depressed. If only the story could end there. A month later, relieved to have completed a tenth cycle of immunotherapy, he talked with Hersh by phone. "Hey, I'm still alive," he exulted, telling the therapist he would make appointments as needed. "I'm going to engage in life."

More than a year went by before Tom contacted Hersh again. It was January 2003, and he had a specific purpose in mind. Despite the long absence, he wanted to secure an agreement that Hersh would be available to him when he became terminal. "By the way, I still have cancer," he said. "I kind of gathered that," the doctor replied.

By then, Tom had been without active treatment for several months, since March 2002, when scans showed growth in the soft-tissue tumor in his buttocks. "The treatment failed me," he said. He had endured a record number of cycles and kept the cancer at bay; now he was without a life raft in the medical world, and there was only so much his phenomenal will could do. "I feel pretty damn good," he told Hersh. But as someone who's worked with terminally ill people for more than thirty years, Hersh noted that the muscles at his temple were losing their bulk. This is a telltale sign for people with cancer that they're losing their battle. After extracting a commitment that the doctor would be available to him when his condition worsened, as he knew it would, Tom once again disappeared.

By November 2003, Tom's cancer had spread to his brain. After the neurosurgeons at the Cleveland Clinic were done with what Hersh calls "all their mucking around," Tom was back for counseling about the promise and perils of whole-brain radiation. Hersh spent some time educating him about the effects; they weren't pretty. Short-term memory loss topped the list, making it one of the more awful treatments for someone like Tom who uses his mind a lot. He was already experiencing memory gaps and having trouble writing in longhand and typing, and this was before the whole-brain radiation regimen he was about to undergo. "You know, I'm diminished," he told Hersh. Looking at his notes, Hersh told me that he came on strong to Tom, telling him, "You are not yet terminally ill; you have advanced disease. The dominoes are falling; they have not yet fallen." He urged him to think about his definition of himself at that time of his life and his quality of life, and to talk with me about it. I remember sitting at the dining room table one evening not long after and Tom said, "I have descended into old fogeydom overnight." It was true; that's what happens. Maybe that was my opening to explore the loss that he was experiencing, but the best I could do was reassure him that his core self was there, and that's what mattered.

It was just days before he checked into Sibley Hospital as an outpatient for brain radiation therapy that we appeared together on the Diane Rehm show. "How are you feeling about the prospect of that, Tom?" she asked.

"I feel about it like I do about most things connected with this illness. I'm approaching it as a reporter. It's the one thing, keeping this sort of distance from the disease has helped me immeasurably in being able to live with it. I've examined the downsides to this ... and the upsides and made a decision that overall it's better for me, even though there are some side effects that will diminish me."

Tom saw Hersh only a couple of times after that, which Hersh told me he rationalized as, Tom needs control, leave him alone. Actually, it was the disease gaining ground. The entire year preceding his death was a decline, but it wasn't a straight line. Some days were better than others; some days Tom didn't get out of bed. I would return home in the evening some nights and the house would be dark and Tom laying there in the bed just as I had left him in the morning. I would beg him not to leave me before he had to. I didn't know whether it was the disease or depression that had finally gotten ahold of him. "It was the disease," Hersh told me later.

He explained that what happens with brain tumors and metastases to the brain is there's a problem of space.

There's increased pressure that drugs try to control, but people essentially get squashed. Since we're a water-based electromagnetic system, things start functioning slower and slower. Whole-brain radiation didn't buy Tom a lot of time, and it stole his energy and cognitive ability. It's really a form of palliative care. Tom realized he wasn't going to get better but he wanted more time, and he pushed it very far. He was an intense fighter who could summon vast amounts of energy that he focused where he wanted when he wanted. It made him a maddening person to live with at times because he had all this focus and ability and sometimes seemed to hoard it, or didn't share it, or didn't use it in the way that I wanted. "There are some people who are intense and have incredible energy and survive longer than all the medical curves, and others who are not intense in that way go quickly and quietly," Hersh said.

Even in those months of decline, it was not all grim. There were long stretches when Tom seemed mostly himself, and there were moments of hilarity as Tom's brain underwent chemical and electrical changes that short-circuited and confused his thinking. He couldn't always distinguish between what he saw on television and what was happening in our more mundane daily existence. He imagined himself in Paris holding court among who knows who and telling me to give him a heads-up when I called the cab to take us back to our hotel. One night he elaborately outlined a wedding ceremony down to the order of speakers. When I asked whose wedding, he said, "Ours." As we were eating dinner one night, he exclaimed, "What kind of an establishment is this? I didn't get a fork!" He called for the maître d'—whose name was Patrick. Where that came from, I had no idea. I usually played along. Once when I corrected him, he laughed, and said, "Oh, I knew that."

My son Eddie, who was visiting and helping care for Tom, devised a little game that made it easier for Tom to accept his assistance. "I'm your aide-de-camp," he told him. When Eddie left to fly back home to California, Tom was still ambulatory, but we knew where this was heading. "Enjoy it," Eddie said, quickly amending the phrase when he saw my expression, "Well, not exactly enjoy—but *experience* it—because this is life." Even though seeing a loved one sick and near death is gut-wrenching, it opens up possibilities for spiritual growth and yields life lessons you can't get any other way, says Susan Apollon, a psychotherapist who treats children and adults traumatized by illness and death. "Surrender, and pay attention," she says. "Even if you ultimately lose your loved one, don't lose the lesson."

MICHAEL SCHIAVO on *Larry King Live* tonight says, "There is no happy ending. When Terri's wishes are carried out, it will be her wish. She will be at peace. She will be with the Lord." He's probably right when he says Terri doesn't feel pain or hunger because her brain function is so compromised. Once her feeding tube is disconnected, he says she will "drift off to a nice little sleep and eventually pass on to be with God."

Friends and family of Michael Schiavo say he is driven by loyalty to the woman who was his college sweetheart, and that he genuinely believes he is carrying out her wishes, however casually they might have been expressed. In a *Nightline* interview, he says he sympathizes with the

Schindlers. "I have children, and, you know, I couldn't even fathom what it would be like to lose a child. ... [But] they know the condition Terri is in. They were there in the beginning. They heard the doctors. ... Fifteen years—you've got to come to grips with it sometime. ... And to sit here and be called a murderer and an adulterer by people that don't know me, and a governor stepping into my personal, private life, who doesn't know me either? And using his personal gain to win votes, just like the legislators are doing right now, pandering to the religious Right, to the people up there, the antiabortion people, standing outside of Tallahassee? What kind of government is this? This is a human being. This is not right."

Michael Schiavo is a hulking presence on or off the television screen. At six foot two and with the physique of a football player, he radiates bitterness and belligerence. The experience with his wife and his in-laws and the political meddling have left him with a very large chip on his shoulder. "I'm not the warm-and-fuzzy type," he says, stating the obvious as though to dare anybody to think otherwise.

A year after Terri's death, at a symposium on bioethics at the University of Pennsylvania, he lashed out at the media for expecting him to be the one to "move forward and be positive" when the right-wing bloggers call his two children "bastard children" and their mother, whom he had since married, "a concubine," and say that he was responsible for breaking Terri's bones. "Yet I'm supposed to be thoughtful and spiritual and insightful," he said sarcastically, "and I've endured years of that." He recalled the memorable scene in the 1987 movie *Moonstruck* when the character played by

Cher commands Nicolas Cage to "Snap out of it!" "I'm not sure I'll ever snap out of it," he said.

What people saw was only the final third of an ordeal that began for him fifteen years earlier. After Terri's collapse, the doctor took his brother, Brian, aside and told him she was gone, and that he should explain that to Michael. Her EEG was essentially flat in 1990. It took years for Brian to pass along that information. He thought it was a cop-out by the doctor; he didn't think that should be left to him. Michael is somewhat more forgiving. "I guess he thought it would be better to hear that from your brother than a guy in a white coat who calls himself doctor." Either way, though, Michael says he would not have accepted that grim diagnosis from his brother, or anybody for that matter. He had never heard of PVS and subscribed to the "Where there's life there's hope" school of doctoring. But as the years went by and hope faded, he embraced a different scenario, one rooted in the practicality of Terri's situation, and what he believed would have been her wishes.

Addressing a roomful of bioethicists, he noted that "most people with that title were on my side," but the divisions elsewhere, particularly within the Catholic Church, inflamed the debate along with cable television. Every day outside the hospice between five and six in the afternoon and ten and eleven at night, the television lights would go on and the demonstrators would begin chanting or praying as if on cue. Everybody was there for the live shot. Schiavo couldn't compete and mostly absented himself from the public debate, seething over the inequity of television's presentation. "I had plenty to say, and in retrospect, I should have spoken out from the beginning. I had no idea the case would get so big, and the other side would run away with it." He thought a handful of people in the print media got it right, "but TV was a joke," he said. "They're in the entertainment business, and Larry King is no different than Sean Hannity and Bill O'Reilly, and none of them are fair and balanced." He will always carry a grudge against Larry King for having Terri's sister, Suzanne, follow him on the broadcast to say she had evidence he abused Terri. People believed it because they heard it on *Larry King*.

6.

Two, Three Days at a Time?

In the movie 28 Days, *Sandra Bullock, who plays a recovering alcoholic undergoing treatment, says, "They tell us to live one day at a time—as if we had a choice. Two, three days at a time?" Of course, all of us live one day at a time. Some of us are just more aware of it.*

—Tom Brazaitis in a column dated March 24, 2002

We have a fair amount of control over some things, such as how long we can keep a body alive in some circumstances, and far less control over others, including how long we can keep someone's mind functioning. In this situation, can anyone really claim to be playing God or not playing God?

Tom knew his time was limited, and he lived his life as best he could in the face of mounting physical limitations. He belonged to the Gridiron Club, a group of journalists who each year stage a musical roast of politicians and the press. He had performed before presidents Clinton and Bush, produced numerous skits and twice served as music chairman. He loved the Gridiron, and the Gridiron loved him. In the spring of 2004, just months before he enrolled in hospice and already greatly weakened by cancer, he got up onto the stage and belted out the rock-and-roll tune "Tutti Frutti," in a parody tribute to former New York mayor and 9/11 hero Rudy Giuliani. I sat in the audience terrified for Tom that he would just keel over, but he pulled it off with spirit and style.

Those watching did not know he had spent the previous night retching, ending what he referred to as his thirty-year record. It was the first time he had thrown up since he was in the army. This was new. He suffered from low-grade nausea and a lack of appetite, but until now he had been spared the worst of that particular side effect. He consulted with his doctor, who advised he get his electrolytes checked before risking anything strenuous. There was no time for that. Tom's solution was to not eat anything all day Saturday and grit it out.

He came back the next day for the traditional Sunday reprise for friends and family. The Gridiron gave him a standing ovation. For those who didn't know otherwise, he looked almost robust. Steroids prescribed to reduce swelling in the brain gave him a rosy glow to his face along with a sense of well-being and an increased appetite. He actually gained a few pounds, which created an artificial look of health. When people would tell him how good he looked, he would respond with the Billy Crystal line from *Saturday Night Live*, "Better to look mahvelous than feel mahvelous."

Later that same year, even after enrolling in hospice, Tom made the heroic effort of getting into his tuxedo to stand and sing with the Gridiron chorus at the winter dinner. I drove that night, and when I had trouble getting the car started in valet parking with a line of cars behind us, Tom got out, came around and took over the wheel—tricky maneuvers for someone with cancer cells in his spine. "I may have cancer, but I can still drive," he said, waving me over to the passenger's seat. That was the last time he drove.

The toll the evening took was obvious to all. Tom moved slowly and shakily and he was paler and thinner. Even his wedding ring had gotten too big. Everyone greeted him with gusto, telling him how they needed his talents for the spring dinner. It was a big lie, and we all knew it. Tom wouldn't perform in another Gridiron show. When the spouse of one journalist told me how great he was doing, I snapped back that he really wasn't. I felt bad about my reaction, and she later apologized, explaining she was a nurse and knew better. She meant that it was great that he could be there. And it was.

Tom arranged for his cremation a full year before he died. The package was called "pre-need," a phrase I came to recognize watching *Six Feet Under*. He handed me the envelope, which I stubbornly refused to open until I had to, and then I was grateful to have it. He also gave me a program from a memorial service that had been held at the National Press Club that I could use as an outline. The widow later sent me her exchange of e-mails with Tom in which he said he would like a memorial "celebration" like she had had for her husband. He wanted to know whether he could prepay the costs so I wouldn't have to deal with that. The word *celebration* did not come easily to me, but knowing that's what Tom wanted made all the difference.

AFTER THE EUPHORIA of winning the vote on Capitol Hill and having the president personally intervene in Terri's case, the Schindlers are unprepared for what comes next: one loss after another in the federal courts they have looked to as a last resort. In the federal lawsuit they file against Michael Schiavo and Judge Greer, the Schindlers claim among other things that their daughter's religious liberties are being infringed on because Pope John Paul II has adjusted and updated Catholic doctrine to say it is unacceptable for Catholics to refuse food and water. That argument doesn't hold sway in the courts, but it has roiled the medical community by reopening ethical issues that it thought had been settled. Hospice physician Carlos Gomez has been to the Vatican twice to give his views on end-of-life care, in 2002 and again in March 2004. He was there when the pope, who was suffering from Parkinson's disease, haltingly read from a document that seemed to reverse decades of Catholic doctrine by declaring "the administration of water and food, even when provided by artificial means, always represents a natural means of preserving life, not a medical act. Its use, furthermore, should be considered, in principle, ordinary and proportionate, and as such morally obligatory."

As he watched the pope wheeled in by attendants, Gomez thought that he was "sick as stink," a phrase used to describe a person who is so sick he belongs in a hospice program. Though palpably ill, Pope John Paul was still able to project the enormous warmth and charisma that characterized his reign. "But then this is the part that blew me away," says Gomez. "They gave him a document to read that had nothing to do with ethics, morals, saving souls. It was all about politics—the internal politics of the Vatican and which faction would gain control after the pope's death." Where did this come from? Gomez wondered. The advisory group he was part of hadn't reached a consensus, much less endorsed such a sharp turn from established church doctrine. The Vatican had convened the 2004 conference in conjunction with the World Association of Catholic Physicians to discuss the ethics of caring for patients in a persistent vegetative state. Gomez stood about five yards from the pope, who he thought was incapable of putting a sentence together, he was so ill—immobile, pale, having difficulty enunciating, and with trembling hands, exhibiting all the symptoms of end-stage Parkinson's. This new statement, Gomez thought, had Ratzinger's hand all over it, signaling the conservative shift of the church. Cardinal Ratzinger was the Vatican's enforcer when it came to stymieing any moves toward liberalization. A favorite of John Paul's and his eventual successor, he was already putting his stamp on the Schiavo case. This was a full year before Terri Schiavo's story became a national obsession in the United States. Still, the Vatican was well aware of its power on the "culture of life" issues that Pope John Paul had singled out as a focus of his papacy.

The pope read the statement without any inflection, which is typical of Parkinson's disease. He stumbled over the words, Gomez recalled. Then the visiting physicians were allowed to come up for a blessing. Each person's name was called out along with where he's from. The fellow in front of Gomez was a physician from Ukraine. He kneeled and kissed the pope's ring, and the pope held his hand and started speaking to him in Ukrainian. However sick the pope was, Gomez thought, there was a real intellect in there. Gomez was next, and when he went up to receive the blessing, the pope ad-libbed in Spanish, and then in English with the doctor behind him, even cracking a joke, "So far from home, just to see me?" Three blessings, three languages—however slowed by illness, the pope was lucid and mentally sharp.

Born Catholic in Cuba, Gomez came to America as a toddler in 1960 with his parents, who were fleeing Fidel Castro's regime. His father was a doctor and the family settled in Atlanta. He has a photo of himself and his siblings in front of a theater with a sign reading, "Colored to balcony," an early lesson in the disparities of America. His father was a classic Latin patriarch and Carlos rebelled, grew his hair long, had a beard, and hated medical school, too scientific, too cut-and-dried. "I'm more of an artsy type," he explains. What saved him was a PhD in public policy that allowed him to indulge his love of language and literature and to ponder the existential questions of life and death. From there it was a natural progression to hospice work, where caring for the sick and dying includes helping people make peace with themselves and their loved ones. The photo of him bowing before the pope is one of his prized possessions, though he no longer considers himself a practicing Catholic. "I just can't do it anymore," he says. "I can't do it on lots of levels. For example, it was thought the fetus in the womb wasn't quite a 'soul' until there was fetal movement after the first trimester—and there have been differing opinions all throughout—and all of a sudden we come out with this hard-and-fast rule. Believe me, I'm not a fanatic, but life is a little grayer than that."

Gomez found the pope's 2004 allocution on vegetative state and artificial nutrition and hydration "confused and confusing," and when the Schiavo case went national, he was on television saying "No, this isn't murder, these are not bad people—yes, it's a tragedy, but it's not black-and-white." He argued the case that the feeding tube should be removed, but he understood the anguish of the parents. The church bungled it badly, he thought, and revealed an underlying hostility to hospice that added to Gomez's discomfort as a hospice physician. "They think we're in the business of hastening death," he says.

The pope's allocution muddled the church's position by giving ammunition to the growing fundamentalist wing that opposed any compromise on issues of life, from its nascent beginnings to endings that could be extended far beyond what we once considered natural. The pope sought to redefine a feeding tube as a natural occurrence and not a medical intervention since it delivers something so basic and natural as food and water. This contradicted a string of court rulings but allowed a chorus of conservative commentators such as Pat Buchanan on *The McLaughlin Group* to declare feeding tubes are not extraordinary means. Cardinal McCarrick, nearing retirement as head of the Catholic diocese based in Washington, D.C., went so far as to declare that once you insert a feeding tube, you can't remove it. "Where did that come from?" Gomez wondered. "But that's what he said."

People of goodwill can disagree about whether a feeding tube constitutes life support in the same way that a ventilator assists breathing. Turn off the ventilator and the patient dies. At least that's what Karen Ann Quinlan's parents thought in 1975 when they filed papers with the supreme court in New Jersey that would allow her father as guardian to remove what they considered extraordinary means, which was a ventilator. Karen Quinlan became the first right-to-die icon when at age twenty-two she stopped breathing after consuming a combination of alcohol and Valium at a party. She was not going to recover; there was no disagreement about that. The attending doctor said it was his duty to do what was best for his patient, and that was preserving her life as long as possible. He had no real reason for coming to that conclusion except that's what doctors do—and this was at a time when challenging the medical establishment was even harder than it is today. Julia and Joe Quinlan wanted their daughter off the ventilator. When they visited her in the hospital she seemed to be in pain, writhing around in a way that didn't fit their expectation of somebody who was unconscious. In fact, Karen Quinlan was doing many of the things we would see Terri Schiavo do on a videotape thirty years later—grimacing, twisting, appearing agitated. The Quinlans thought the ventilator was causing her discomfort. It was the newest technology in 1975, and it was big and invasive. Karen Quinlan couldn't have experienced pain because she was in a persistent vegetative state, but her parents didn't know that—and the term *PVS* did not yet exist. A diminutive and frail-looking Julia Duane Quinlan speaking at a bioethics conference thirty-one years after her daughter's accident recalled how her family's quiet suburban life was transformed when their case was thrust into the public eye. "Overnight, Karen, Joe and I became celebrities. Her high school picture was on every front page in this country, and in Europe and Asia. We had the press on our lawn day and night. We never sought glaring publicity. We never allowed her picture to be taken. We protected her privacy until the end of her life."

There was no video of Karen Ann Quinlan and the family barred photographs, yet the case packed plenty of emotional punch and marked the beginning of a right-to-die movement against modern technology. Three decades later, Julia Quinlan marvels that it's almost impossible to find someone who does not recognize the name Karen Ann Quinlan. "She will always be remembered as that sleeping beauty that thousands of people all over the world prayed for. Her life served a purpose far beyond what she could have suspected." Together with her husband, Julia Quinlan founded a hospice in their daughter's name. Joe Quinlan was a patient in the hospice program and died at home in his wife's care.

The New Jersey Supreme Court ruled in their favor, yet Karen Quinlan lived for eleven more years after she was taken off the ventilator. She lived for that length of time because she had a feeding tube and was supported by antibiotics and blood pressure medications. When it was suggested to Joe Quinlan as his daughter's guardian that for the same reason he objected to a ventilator, he might want to oppose antibiotics for an infection, "He was rather appalled," recalls Dr. Robert Veatch, a scholar who specializes in religion and ethics and was the family's ethics adviser. "His instinct was that big machine was awful but something as simple as an antibiotic or feeding tube, he could never stop." Veatch was at the Hastings Center in New York, a nonprofit research center that examines ethical questions in health care, when he got a call from a young lawyer named Paul Armstrong, a recent graduate who was working in a storefront legal aid clinic in New Jersey. "I've got this case—you won't believe it," he told Veatch, who was managing Hastings' death and dying research.

This was the Great Society era, and free legal services were readily available to people like the Quinlans who were not wealthy and needed a lawyer. This was a big case with constitutional implications, and Armstrong knew he was in over his head. He called a law school buddy who was a new hire at a big Wall Street firm to enlist his help. The firm was under some pressure because it hadn't been doing enough pro bono work, so the Quinlans lucked into some first-rate legal counsel.

By 1975, the right to refuse treatment had been well established, but there was ambiguity about how to handle medical decisions for an incompetent person like Quinlan. Jehovah's Witnesses who refused blood transfusions established the right to refuse medical treatment for religious reasons. That in turn opened the door to a broader right to refuse treatment for whatever reason as long as a person is rational and understands the consequences. The harder question occurs when a person is incompetent and has not made his or her wishes clearly known, and the family is at odds, which is what happened with Schiavo.

There is irony in the fact that religious refusal set up the whole right to say no since the Schiavo case turned that tradition on its head, with the Schindlers citing their beliefs as practicing Catholics as a reason they could not remove their daughter's feeding tube. In 1975, the Quinlan family's parish priest testified in support of the family's decision to take their daughter off the ventilator. End-of-life decisions were not yet intertwined with the abortion issue, which would gain political velocity in the coming decades. The backlash provoked by the 1973 *Roe v. Wade* ruling peaked during the Schiavo case with antiabortion demonstrators and the Catholic Church driving the protests and pressuring the politicians.

Armstrong was a graduate of Notre Dame and Georgetown, Catholic institutions, and he drew on Catholic clergy and scholars to build his case. John J. Paris, a Jesuit scholar and teacher of ethics, says the supreme court of New Jersey quoted liberally from the materials that he and the late Richard McCormick, founder of the Kennedy Institute of Ethics at Georgetown, provided to Armstrong. The judge cited the accepted distinction between ordinary and extraordinary means, but he didn't want to rely solely on Catholic doctrine as the basis for his ruling in a secular court, so he said he presented it because it influenced how the family reached their decision. "And then he argued the decision was legitimate because that's what a rational person would do," says Paris. "He said if you polled, a majority of people would make a similar decision, and therefore it's legally appropriate."

The judge was speculating, but not by much, says Paris. He and McCormick had gone before a hundred audiences over the years and asked the question, "If you were in a well-diagnosed persistent vegetative state, would you want to be maintained?" Of the thousands of people they asked, exactly two said they would want to be kept this way, and both happened to have been presidents of their local right-to-life community. "Then I say, 'If nobody would want this for himself or herself, why do we have the idea we should impose it on everybody else?'" says Paris.

With the right to refuse medical treatment well established, the question with Quinlan was whether you could remove life support from someone who was incompetent even with her family's permission and not be charged with euthanasia, or murder. The New Jersey Supreme Court said if you have the right to refuse treatment, you don't lose it because you become incompetent. Quinlan's parents testified that she had said when watching television, "I don't want to be a vegetable," and they knew she wouldn't want to be kept alive on a ventilator. It was the first case where family members got permission to stop lifesaving care for an incompetent person who once was competent. It's known as the "rational person standard."

The next case to capture national attention was that of Nancy Cruzan, who in 1983, at age twenty-five, drove too fast on a country road, lost control of her car and went through the windshield, landing facedown in a ditch. It was a rainy night, so her head was in a puddle and she didn't breathe for a long time. The highway patrolman first on the scene thought she was dead; he checked for vital signs and couldn't find a pulse. But paramedics managed to restore her heartbeat, and her family held out hope that she would recover. Her eyes were open and an electroencephalogram (EEG) measuring her brain waves indicated she was not brain dead. Brain death means total irreversible loss of all brain function, and in most states it's the same as being dead. But the longer the brain goes without oxygen, the cells die from the outside in, and the thinking part—the cortex—goes first. The inner part of the brain acts like a thermostat that controls things such as temperature, breathing, and automatic reflexes like crying. By the time the rescue workers resuscitated Cruzan, the cortex was gone, dead. Four to six minutes without oxygen will cause extensive damage, and Cruzan was without oxygen longer than that. What the paramedics saved was the thermostat of her brain, the part that controls reflexes; her consciousness had been destroyed.

"Think of a TV set," explains Dr. Arthur Caplan, a PhD in philosophy specializing in bioethics at the University of Pennsylvania. "If the picture is rolling or you can't make it out but there's a picture there—that's a coma. There's something going on but it's not on right. With brain death, something is unplugged; there's nothing there. In PVS, there's white snow only on the screen. Something's really shot inside the set; probably the picture tube is blown out." Caplan finds this analogy useful when talking to families when a loved one has suffered brain damage. He adds that for people who get their medical information from the tabloids while waiting in line at the supermarket, a typically provocative headline is "Coma Cop Wakes Up." Coma means unconscious, prognosis unknown, so these "miracles" are not really surprising. Nobody comes back from brain death, which can be documented with a flat EEG. Perhaps cruelest of all is PVS, where the brain stem lives but a person's consciousness, the thinking self, dies.

By the time of Cruzan's accident, the medical community recognized PVS, and they also had a CT scan machine, which over time showed the shriveling of her brain's cortex. Cruzan was one of the first people to get a diagnosis of PVS. Her family agreed that she wouldn't want to be kept alive this way, but the nursing home in Missouri refused to withdraw her feeding tube, arguing that a feeding tube is not a treatment. So this was a battle about nourishment, and lining up on the side of the nursing home to argue the case were Missouri governor John Ashcroft, Attorney General William Webster, and every right-to-life group in the state. Ashcroft and Webster would go on to become national figures, their politics honed in the red-hot antiabortion climate of Missouri. Even Randall Terry, the founder of Operation Rescue, the most extreme of the antiabortion groups, was on the scene in Missouri outside Cruzan's nursing home, just as he would be years later in Florida outside Schiavo's hospice.

The difference between Cruzan and Schiavo is there was no cable TV yet, and there was no family dispute, but the Cruzan case still triggered an absolute war, because the state was lined up to protect her and the family was lined up on the other side. Neurologist Dr. Ronald Cranford made the PVS diagnosis on Cruzan, just as he would with Schiavo.

The Cruzan case went all the way to the U.S. Supreme Court—the only right-to-refuse treatment to reach the high court—and it got there because state officials, that is, Ashcroft and Webster, who were building their political careers on right-to-life politics, intervened and turned it into a constitutional question: What right did the state have to compel treatment? The Missouri Supreme Court ruled that tube feeding could be stopped only if whoever speaking for her, including her parents, could produce "clear and convincing" evidence that is what she would want, a standard the Cruzans had been unable to meet. The Supreme Court in a five-to-four opinion sided with the State of Missouri and against the Cruzans. In the words of then chief justice Rehnquist, it was not unconstitutional to "err on the side of life." William Colby, the attorney representing the Cruzans, wrote later that he felt sick to his stomach over the ruling until he read the opinion closely and found eight words tucked in near the end of Rehnquist's opinion, words so inconspicuous he felt he'd almost stumbled upon them: "discovery of new evidence regarding the patient's intent." The Missouri Supreme Court eventually granted Cruzan the right to die based on new witnesses, friends of hers, who came forward. Her grave marker has three dates: Born, Departed (the date of her accident) and At Peace, the date of her death nearly seven years later.

A FRIEND, columnist Katy Burns, comes to visit Tom, and writes about it in the *Concord Monitor.* "He is increasingly curling his once vigorous athletic body into a fetal position. He's emaciated, his body ravaged by a cancer that has spread from his kidneys into his bones and his brain. And he's doped up with more and more morphine. But he, the essential 'he,' the quick and curious mind, still seems to be there. As Eleanor told us in a warning email before the visit, his ability to communicate is seriously compromised. But he smiles, and his eyes follow us as we talk, especially when the subject turns to politics, his passion."

Tom's wide-eyed look at times is the result of pressure on the optic nerve. As the cancer continues its relentless march, his body becomes so drenched with perspiration that the bedding soaks through. Daphne explains that the area of the brain that controls temperature is affected by the cancer and is causing the profuse sweating. Daphne explains everything so straightforwardly that this awesome transition into the next life, or the unknown, or nothingness, whatever you believe, becomes almost matter-of-fact. Life is narrowed down to its absolute basics—fluids in, fluids out.

7.

Politics vs. Morality

I'm a little nervous, but I think this is what God wants me to do.
—Josie Keys, fourteen, arrested for attempting
to carry water into the hospice for Terri

CABLE TELEVISION SHOWS the escalating civil disobedience outside the Florida hospice. A dozen people are arrested. Among them are Josie Keys and her brothers, Cameron, twelve, and Gabriel, ten. The children are with their parents.

The day does not start well for Terri's supporters. An appellate court decision was issued at 2:30 in the morning upholding the judgment of the nineteen state court judges who had considered the case. "Theresa Schiavo's life and liberty interests were adequately protected by the extensive process provided in the state courts," U.S. District Judge James D. Whittemore wrote in a thirteen-page ruling that acknowledged the "gravity of the consequences" while refusing to grant relief. Managing the protesters is getting harder as hope slips away, and Rev. Mahoney is furious at the callousness of the judge in waiting a full day and into the wee hours before issuing his ruling. In the countdown of Terri's life, she is in her fifth day without food and water and rapidly reaching the point of no return. The needless delay, which Mahoney sees as judicial whimsy, means valuable time lost in the escalating legal maneuvers.

Florida governor Jeb Bush adds to the frenzy with a press conference in which he declares Terri may have been misdiagnosed and it is more likely she is in a state of minimal consciousness rather than in a persistent vegetative state. Bush is relying on a neurologist retained by the Adult Protective Services team in Florida's Department of Children and Families. Dr. William Cheshire spent ninety minutes with Terri and concluded that her neurological signs are ambiguous enough that if he were her attending physician, he could not in good conscience withdraw her feeding tube. "To enter the room of Terri Schiavo is nothing like entering the room of a patient who is comatose or brain-dead or in some neurological sense no longer there." Although he could not document a single instance of conscious awareness or intentional behavior during his time with Terri, he reported in an affidavit filed with the State of Florida that as a visitor, he had "the distinct sense of the presence of a living human being who seems at some level to be aware of some things around her." He introduced into the debate the phrase "minimally conscious state," which is meant to distinguish patients who are brain damaged but can follow objects or people with their eyes and occasionally seem able to respond. The phrase has been in use as a diagnosis only since 2002.

Cheshire's credentials to reach this judgment are questionable. After completing his residency in neurology years earlier, his career veered away from the kind of clinical expertise needed to determine the status of a patient like Schiavo. He heads a laboratory that focuses on unconscious reflexes such as digestion, and he is affiliated with a group founded by Christian ethicists called the Center for Bioethics and Human Dignity. He notes in his affidavit that he believes it is "ethically permissible" to withdraw artificial nutrition and hydration from a person in a permanent vegetative state but that the diagnosis of PVS has a high error rate.

Governor Bush seizes on the new diagnosis to urge the Florida legislature to take up Terri's case, and to announce that he has asked the Department of Children and Families to intervene based on this supposedly new and compelling evidence. "I'm doing everything within my power to make sure that Terri's afforded at least the same rights that criminals convicted of the most heinous crimes take for granted," an emotional Governor Bush declares at a press conference in Tallahassee. "If a prisoner comes forward with new DNA evidence 20 years after his conviction, suggesting his innocence, there is no doubt that the courts in our state or all across the country, for that matter, would immediately review his case. We should do no less for Terri Schiavo."

Bobby Schindler is there to watch the press conference, and he thinks Bush seems frantic, that the pressure is really getting to him. When an aide to the governor asks him to leave, that the press conference is for press only, he doesn't protest. As he makes his way out, a second aide stops him and says, "The governor wants to meet with you." Bobby doesn't know what is going on, but he says, "Great," and when the press conference ends, he is escorted to the governor's office, where he finds Florida senator Martinez waiting with Bush.

"Bobby, we're doing everything we can to try to get your sister hydrated," Bush tells him. The governor's lead counsel comes in to brief them on the latest legal maneuvers, and Bush keeps saying, "Whatever needs to be done, get it done." At the end of the meeting, as Bobby prepares to leave, Bush offers one final reassurance: "Your sister should be getting hydrated very soon." As Bobby remembers the conversation, Bush doesn't waver. There is a certitude about what he says, and his bearing, how he says it. Bobby is so relieved he feels like crying. He says later he must have thanked the governor a hundred times. But he does not call his parents, phoning his sister Suzanne instead, and telling her to hold off telling Mom and Dad in case something goes wrong. It isn't long before one of Bush's attorneys calls to say they are having a problem. "It might take us longer than we had hoped to get your sister hydrated."

Back at the hospice, word has filtered through to Rev. Mahoney about Bush's alleged promise to Bobby that he will intervene. "Don't leave the hospice. There's going to be fireworks," Mahoney is told by a religious-Right person who was in the room when Bush gave his evidently heartfelt assurance to Bobby that everything will be okay. Police cars are streaming up the long road leading to the hospice, and the cops are taping things off like they are preparing for crowd control. The rumor is that the FDLE is on the way. That's the Florida Department of Law Enforcement, which is under the direct authority of the governor and functions like Bush's private police force. Word spreads that Bush has ordered the FDLE to take Terri to a local hospital to have her feeding tube surgically reinserted.

If that was Bush's intention, his plan was thwarted when he said in his press conference that he would consider taking Terri into protective custody. Michael Schiavo's lawyer, George Felos, immediately went to Judge Greer and got a court order saying Terri could not be moved. Greer rules against a request by Florida state welfare officials to take protective custody of Schiavo and reattach her feeding tube. He also rules against a second motion that would have allowed Jeb Bush to intervene on an emergency basis.

That's when Bush backs down. If he had gone ahead, there would have been a confrontation between his police force and the Pinellas Park police. Rev. Mahoney has a good relationship with the Pinellas police, and he goes to them after the much anticipated clash fails to occur. They tell him they "absolutely" would have prevented Terri from being moved, honoring Greer's court order as opposed to Bush's executive order. Brandi Swindell, a twenty-eight-year-old right-to-life activist from Idaho who is on a hunger strike at the hospice, believes Bush could have gone in and gotten Terri if he had acted immediately. There was a three-hour window while Judge Greer was reviewing Felos's filing when Bush's executive authority would have gone unchallenged. "I have to tell you," she says, "George Felos and Judge Greer seemed more committed to taking Terri's life than Governor Bush was committed to saving it."

In the eyes of the protesters, the battle to keep Terri alive has turned into a power struggle between two elected officials. A banner flying over the hospice from a small aircraft taunts: "Who's Gov? Bush or Greer?" Terri Schiavo has been without food and water for six full days and according to attorneys and friends of the Schindlers is showing signs of dehydration—flaky skin, dry tongue and lips, sunken eyes. "It's very frustrating. Every minute that goes by is a minute that Terri is being starved and dehydrated to death," says Bobby. Seeing her is like looking at "pictures of prisoners in concentration camps."

Bush is unwilling to stretch the limits of his executive power. "It is frustrating for people to think that I have power that I don't, and not be able to act," he tells reporters. Sitting in his office and waving the new affidavit from the neurologist, Bush gets emotional as he quotes from Cheshire's report recounting how Schiavo in a videotape three years earlier made a crying sound, grimaced and pressed her eyebrows together allegedly in response to hearing a doctor say he was going to turn her over. None of this is firsthand observation; it is more like recycled propaganda. Bush is playing it to the hilt, claiming Terri Schiavo "signals her anticipation of pain. Just like you would, or just like I would. Now is it perfect? Is she responding with the same eloquence that you would respond to? No, she's severely, profoundly disabled," he says, but that shouldn't disqualify her from life. Bush refers to the series of court decisions as a "lockdown." "You know what I hope for first and foremost?" he tells reporters. "That Mr. Schiavo would say 'I'm going to let Terri be with her parents. I'm going to move on with my life. I've made my point.'"

Right-to-life protesters are demanding Bush go in and seize Schiavo. In an afternoon interview with the Associated Press, Bush attempts to set some boundaries. "There's a point past which I can't go, irrespective of what my views are. We have 90,000 abortions that take place in our state. That troubles me equally because I believe that is the taking of innocent life. But I don't have the ability to prohibit that."

Bush is seen as well meaning but ineffectual, caving to Florida circuit court judge George Greer. In the eyes of the Schindlers, Greer is the real villain in their family drama. He first ruled in favor of Michael Schiavo's request in February 2000 to have his wife's feeding tube removed. Another judge ordered it reinserted two days later. The case went back to Greer with new medical testimony, but he said there was no evidence Schiavo had any hope of recovering and ordered the tube removed a second time. Under pressure from the religious Right, the Florida legislature granted Governor Jeb Bush emergency powers to intervene, and in October 2003 the feeding tube was reinserted. The Florida Supreme Court struck down the law that allowed Bush to intervene, and Greer for a third time, on February 25, 2005, ordered the tube removed with three weeks to comply, setting the stage for the extraordinary clash we are witnessing between the religious Right, aided and abetted by the full force of the federal government, and the U.S. judiciary in the person of Judge Greer. "This man was even more committed to his principles than the people who opposed him," says Rev. Mahoney. "This man stood up to the president, to the governor, the House, the Senate, the Florida Department of Law Enforcement. It's hard to say I admire that, but there's a certain grudging respect I have for his commitment to principle, that Governor Bush didn't have, that Congress didn't have. In the showdown over Terri, Judge Greer didn't blink; Governor Bush did."

In Florida, judges are elected, and although the race is nonpartisan, Greer's views as a Republican and a Christian were well known. He was expected to rule on the side of saving Terri, and when he didn't, his supporters on the Right felt betrayed. Jim King, a Florida Republican legislator, knows Greer well and describes him as "kind of a melba milquetoast sort of a person," not somebody with the fortitude to stand up to the criticism being dumped on him. But Greer stood his ground. Judges don't get to pick their cases. They're assigned, King explains. "So in this situation, it's George's turn. He reaches in and he gets the Schiavo case, and he's got it as a load around his neck forever."

Suddenly Greer is in the media spotlight, and people he thought were his friends have forsaken him. His personal security is so perilous that he is whisked away each evening and taken to places where nobody can know where he is. "All George was doing is what we the people have empowered him to do, which is make a judicial opinion and stick to it," says King.

Christian conservatives vowed to defeat Greer, but he was reelected in 2004 to a second six-year term, which a spokesman says will be his last. The vocal minority that inflamed the media coverage around Terri doesn't have the same muscle at the ballot box that they have on the cable television shows. Republicans like Greer and King saved their party from sinking deeper into the embrace of the religious Right in Florida while Democrats stayed on the sidelines, much as they did in Washington.

The controversy over Terri Schiavo flared in Florida long before it captured national attention. Social conservatives, angered by narrow court rulings that decide hot-button issues in a way that could never win a legislative majority, are waging war on judges. The buzzword is *activist judges*, those who impose their views from the bench on a society that is unwilling or unprepared to accept them. Abortion rights, affirmative action, gay marriage, even *Brown v. Board of Education*, the 1954 ruling that desegregated the schools, are on the conservatives' list of grievances. Opposition to activist judges is part of what conservative commentator and former presidential candidate Pat Buchanan labels "the culture war." Despite the raw emotion and the 24/7 news coverage, the judiciary is unmoved, and late today, running out of options, the Schindlers reach out once again to the U.S. Supreme Court. The high court has refused three times before to hear their case, and will once again quietly turn down the request.

Bobby Schindler had never heard of Randall Terry, the radical Christian antiabortion protester, before a cousin called his father to suggest getting Terry involved in the fight to save Terri's life. It was the fall of 2003, and Michael had successfully petitioned for the second time to have Terri's feeding tube removed. The lawyer handling the Schindlers' case told them she had run out of legal maneuvers. Their last chance was somehow getting the governor involved. They'd already been putting pressure on Governor Bush, and they were told Terry could attract the kind of media attention that would force Bush's hand. Terry helped lead the protests surrounding the removal of Nancy Cruzan's feeding tube in 1990. He has been arrested more than forty times for his activities on behalf of the pro-life cause, beginning in 1986 when he chained himself to a sink at an abortion clinic. For the Schindlers, desperate to save their daughter, Terry was the perfect cable-news bait.

They met at the Schindlers' condo on the Sunday before Terri's feeding tube was going to be removed. Terry laid out a blueprint on how best to pressure Bush through the news media. He told the family they had to get an R.V. and station it at the hospice as a kind of command center. "And then he articulated a plan, a strategy, and off we went," says Bobby. It worked. So many things fell into place that they took to calling these coincidences "God-Instances." For example, the Florida legislature was called back for an emergency legislative session. It had nothing to do with Terri, but there they were, all assembled and accessible, there was an election coming up, and intervening to reinsert Terri's feeding tube was a convenient way to court the far Right conservative vote. Terri's Law was passed, the governor signed it, Terri's feeding tube was reinstated, and the Schindlers said publicly that the credit belonged to Randall Terry and the media attention he had generated.

But this time events are spinning out of the family's control. The lawmakers in Tallahassee are complaining about intimidation, and they are less inclined to help than they were before. A group headed by Jim King that had supported Terri's Law eighteen months earlier now stands firm with the Democrats in refusing to back any kind of reprieve for Terri Schiavo despite multiple entreaties from Bush. Dubbed the Republican Nine, their faces are plastered on "Wanted" posters, and they have to be escorted by security guards into and out of the state capitol because of the irate protesters.

King had been president of the senate in 2003 and, under pressure from Bush and pro-life activists led by Randall Terry, had fashioned the compromise legislation giving Bush what amounted to the right to pardon Terri Schiavo the way he might spare a prisoner on death row. King had to call in chits to get the votes because many of his colleagues felt this was not what government should be doing. When the bill passed giving Bush the authority to order Terri's feeding tube reinserted, King didn't sound like he'd just won a major legislative victory. Speaking from the podium in the well of the senate, he anguished over whether the senate had done the right thing, and in interviews soon after said he regretted his vote and if anything resembling Terri's Law came before him again, he would vote against it.

As fate would have it, the issue came roaring back eighteen months later with the governor pushing harder than ever and a compliant Florida House dutifully passing another stopgap version of Terri's Law. At a luncheon with the Republican Senate caucus, King reminds his colleagues he is on record saying he would never vote for this thing again, "And I'm not," he declares. "I don't care who's in favor of it. It's wrong; we shouldn't be involved in this; the courts have acted. Terri's tube should be taken out. I've been raised as a Christian, and I was taught that no matter what your life was on earth, heaven was going to be better. And here she is, trapped in a horizontal prison. I'm not voting for it."

It was a casual luncheon, and King didn't intend his remarks as a policy directive. His term as president of the senate had ended the previous year, so he is surprised when, one by one, his fellow Republicans come to his office to ask, "Jim, are you serious? You're not going to vote for it?" He repeats his pledge: he won't vote for another iteration of Terri's Law. "I don't care if I'm the only one," he declares. "Well, you're not going to be the only one because I'm not voting for it either," his colleagues tell him. Soon there are nine Republicans ready to derail Bush's quest to save Terri. King is thought to be the mastermind, but in truth, the Republicans who stepped up are a cross-section of the caucus. "Some of them don't even like me," says King. "But yet on this issue, they all felt the same. It wasn't because we were all moderates because there are some conservatives in there too. And it wasn't just because we were all Christians— there was a Jew and there was a Catholic. It had nothing to do with anything except we all felt that Terri deserved to have her [wishes]—and we presumed those were her wishes, or would have been—honored."

The fight that follows gets ugly. Today, the GOP-led body rejects Bush's pleas, voting down the legislation to restore Terri's feeding tube twenty-one to eighteen. The nine renegade Republicans are denounced as murderers. The computers in the capitol crash with the volume of e-mails from all over the world. Some say the legislators did the right thing, but most are critical, saying Terri isn't being treated as humanely as the family dog. The federal appeals are failing as well, and a distraught Mary Schindler outside her daughter's hospice says, "When I close my eyes at night, all I can see is Terri's face in front of me, dying, starving to death. Please, someone out there, stop this cruelty. Stop the insanity. Please let my daughter live."

King never hears from the governor. They had worked closely together the first time Terri's case had come before the legislature in 2003, but Bush knew where King stood this time around. He didn't even try to sway him.

Both of King's parents had died of cancer, his father at seventy-eight, his mother at eighty-three, "and like a deathbed wish granted," he says, their end-of-life experience made him an advocate of "no heroics, no add-ons, no keeping me alive at all costs." In the mid-1990s, as a member of the Florida House, he had offered legislation three years in a row before it finally passed to become Florida's Life Prolonging Procedures Act, which is known colloquially and more accurately as the "Death with Dignity Legislation." It recognizes the fundamental right of competent adults to make their own medical decisions and establishes procedures for written directives, so that when death is imminent, "you should have the rite of passage rather than to be kept Herculeanly alive," says King. "There are some things in the medical profession that are actually worse than dying, and some of those things are the methodologies and the protocols that they suggest you go through if you have cancer." When the Schiavo issue came up the first time, he saw it as an end run around the law he had crafted. "But we got trapped," he says. The legislature was already in a special session, and both the governor and the Speaker of the house were ardent defenders of saving Schiavo at any cost. With the Speaker, it was largely political; he was running for the U.S. Senate and thought he could capture the far-Right conservative vote (it didn't work; he lost the primary). With Bush, it was more complicated, King thought, attributing

Bush's ardor less to politics and more to "a deep-seated feeling that anything that deals with any kind of avoidance of care is criminal."

King's defiance of Governor Bush, even though belated, earned him hero status among the dwindling band of Republican moderates in the country. Former New Jersey governor Christine Todd Whitman called him at the height of the standoff. "Jim, I know exactly how you feel. I've been a Republican all my life and I feel as if the party has been stolen." King didn't know Whitman before that phone call, but they were kindred spirits. Like Whitman, the GOP was in King's DNA. He wasn't a Johnny-come-lately to the party like so many Republicans in the South. "My folks were Republican, and people who were change coats that came in under the Reagan Open Arms umbrella to sit at our table are now questioning whether we should even be allowed in the room." When Randall Terry announced he would challenge King for the Republican nomination in his Jacksonville district, King was unperturbed. He figured having Terry as an opponent was the next best thing to getting a free ride. "It should be a slam-dunk," he said (and it was).

The legal efforts to forestall Terri Schiavo's death are coming to an end. Asked about the failed intervention, President Bush uses language that signals he's still at one with his party's base. "This is an extraordinary and sad case, and I believe that in a case such as this, the legislative branch, the executive branch ought to err on the side of life, which we have," he says.

THE HOSPICE WORKERS who shave Tom leave a mustache (it's too hard to shave there), and he looks handsome, like a silent-film star. Maybe it's all those Turner Classic Movies he's been watching these many weeks. There are worse things than dying young, Tom had e-mailed a friend, a piece of wisdom that he was reminded of on his visits to his mother in a nursing home, "seeing the barely living wheeled from place to place, conscious but not really alive." I knew what Tom wanted, but for people like Terri when the picture is not so clear, the interplay of religious belief and governmental action will dictate the outcome. The cluster of issues around the beginning of life, abortion and stem-cell research, and the end of life, when the most personal and painful decisions must be made, often with little guidance or compassion, is fair game for politicians, but those who guess wrong about which way the political winds are blowing will pay a price.

8.

Arc of Human Existence

When the diagnosis is cancer, a man or woman has a choice to make: Learn as much as possible about the attacker and try to defeat it or pretend that life will go on as always if you ignore it.
—Tom Brazaitis in a column dated October 14, 2001

I'M LINING UP Tom's morning medicines, and I remark to the hospice caregiver that I might as well give him everything that's available. "Yes, please," he says, his voice strong.

The fear of pain and loss of dignity is what worries people as they contemplate their final days. There are moments during Tom's last weeks of life when I thought you wouldn't keep an animal alive in this condition. He has to be moved every three or four hours to guard against pressure sores, and he cries out each time in obvious pain. There's an art to turning a bedridden patient that involves putting a "draw sheet" under the body and using it to pull and gain leverage. In the morning when the caregiver is here, I am sometimes upstairs on the phone or the computer, and I hear his cries. I steel myself, wanting to believe the hospice nurse, Daphne, when she says he's startled by the sudden movements and can't comprehend what's happening. It's not that he's in pain. But then again, how can she be sure? She suggests giving Tom an added dose of morphine a half hour before the caregiver arrives.

Morphine is the drug of choice, and hospice provides generous amounts in a quick-acting liquid and in longer-acting pills. I learn to "premedicate" with extra morphine to prepare Tom for when he's being cared for or moved. Morphine is tricky—it's the best painkiller there is, but it can also kill, or hasten death, which is why it falls under what is known as the "rule of double effect." According to this ethical principle, it is morally acceptable to treat a terminally ill patient with high-dose opioids if the intention is to relieve pain even if the side effect of the medication is death. "That's very different from giving somebody a prescription and saying take this and wash it down with a fine Bordeaux so you don't wake up in the morning," says Daniel Sulmasy, chief medical ethicist at St. Vincent's Manhattan Hospital and New York Medical College.

Sulmasy is a Franciscan friar in addition to being an internist, so his thinking is heavily influenced by Catholic doctrine. But his aversion to deliberately drugging someone into a premature death is shared by those with a more secular background who care for the terminally ill and dying. Still, there is wide latitude within the framework of easing pain to hasten what we think of as a natural death, though it is rarely discussed openly.

As for loss of dignity, the hospice health aides I encounter range from caring and competent to near-Gandhi-like figures in the way they minister to Tom. Any qualms I might have had about tending to Tom's personal needs vanish as though I were trained to do this. The tug I feel is no less strong than when I first became a mother. This is a human being entrusted to my care. I'd like to believe he is mostly free of pain, but I do know he is in familiar surroundings, and that is a gift I can give him. A friend asks, "Eleanor, how far are you going to take this?" I am taken aback by the question, which suggests I have some choice in the matter. To me, there is no choice but to let death come as naturally as life. The alternative is a hospice facility, or a nursing home. I might have felt differently if we were looking at years instead of months, but this is something I can do, and will do.

The last movie we went to see was *Sideways*, and I parked the car while he waited at the theater. A small thing but a huge role reversal, and I could see he hated it. I e-mail a friend, "Tom is leaving us little by little—losing his cognitive powers, losing weight, losing his ability to enjoy life at its most basic level. I feel like I'm hanging on by my fingernails on the edge of a cliff."

She responds, "Part of the peace will come in knowing how to prepare for it and how to say all you want to say in the time you have. But the truth is—it sucks." She has just been through hospice with her dying mother.

TERRI SCHIAVO'S ROOM looks out on flowers and fountains, a tranquil setting that seems far from the turmoil surrounding her case. The Florida Suncoast hospice where she has been for five years sits on ten acres of land and is huge, with well over two thousand patients. It is newly renovated, and although the rooms are not large, there are family rooms where patients and visitors can congregate and dining areas where they can have a meal together. Michael Schiavo comes and goes unseen through a back entrance to avoid protesters and the media. Terri's parents and siblings enter the facility through the front entrance, thanking well-wishers who line the sidewalk and embrace their cause as "the passion of Terri," a suffering akin to Jesus as Easter approaches. Schiavo, media-shy and angry at his in-laws and at his plight, is virtually living at the hospice, but thanks to careful scheduling, the two sides are never in Terri's room at the same time.

Mary Labyak, administrative head of Florida Suncoast hospice, has been through the removal of Terri's feeding tube twice before. The first time, the tube was reconnected at the hospice; the second time, in 2003, Terri was taken by ambulance to a hospital for the procedure. Protesters charged the ambulance when it came for Terri, jumping on it and breaking beer bottles. Most of the protesters wanted the tube feeding restored while others shouted, "How can you make this suffering go on?"

Remembering how quickly the violence erupted, this time Labyak wants to be prepared. She works closely with law enforcement and professional protesters like Rev. Mahoney to anticipate what might happen. The FBI is brought in to track people attracted to the demonstrations who are found to have significant criminal backgrounds. The protesters run the gamut from religious types who sit in silent prayer to people who just happen to be in the area and want to be part of the action. One man is arrested at a pawn shop trying to buy a gun and saying he intends to do a commando raid. It turns out he was acting on his own, but the threat he posed had to be taken seriously. Labyak struggles to keep calm at the facility, telling law enforcement she doesn't want anybody hurt if the worst happens and the protests get out of control. She tells the armed guards brought in to escort visitors into the hospice to "behave like southern gentlemen and not like law enforcement doing a snatch and frightening people." A Web site pops up with directions to Labyak's house saying she should be "taken care of," which is scary enough but when added to numerous other threats prompts Labyak to change her daily routine to the point that she rarely shows her face at any of the four main facilities at the hospice. "It just seemed prudent," she says. Right-wing bloggers portrayed her as a Nazi, and when articles inside her home showed up pictured on a Web site, she feared someone had gained entry to her house. Labyak is not one to scare easily, but she takes reasonable precautions, not going out at night alone and trading in her navy blue Chrysler convertible for a less flashy sedan.

She and others at the hospice are served subpoenas by Governor Bush and the U.S. Congress but never have to testify because the legal maneuvering moves so rapidly that the subpoenas are nullified with the next action. In the almost thirty years Labyak has been associated with the Florida Suncoast hospice, first as a volunteer, then as program director and finally as its CEO, she has never had a situation where the family had to go to court. There are people admitted to hospice every day who haven't made a firm decision, or where there's family conflict. "We'd always found some middle point people could live with. That's what we do," she says.

Google "Mary Labyak" and the first reference that comes up is "The Death Factory," which is the way Terri's most fervent supporters portray hospice and the work they do. Labyak stayed out of the public fray, declining to refute the negative image on the theory that hospice had one role, and one role only—to provide care for Terri. The decision about the feeding tube was not in their hands; they were carrying out a court order, and they weren't taking one side or the other. In retrospect, it was a huge missed opportunity to educate the general public about the work of hospice, and to allay the widespread fears generated by one side of the debate that hospice actively kills people.

For these two weeks in March, Americans were confronted with a heightened sense of mortality. It wasn't only about Terri Schiavo. It was about ourselves, and what we took from the debate about dying and disability that will inform our decisions when it is time. Tom wrote of the chill that would occasionally overtake him—"the dreads," he called it, "a reminder that I've got an appointment with fate." But then he wrote, "It is comforting to know I am not in this alone."

A poll released last night by CBS News shows that an overwhelming majority of those interviewed—82 percent—think Congress and the president should not have intervened in the Schiavo case. What was even more startling to the politicians and the pundits were the "internals" of the poll that measured the reaction of various subgroups of the electorate. Among conservative Republicans, 76 percent opposed the government's actions; among all Republicans, the figure was 72 percent; and among white evangelical

Christians, it was still an astounding 68 percent. Those were the folks the politicians thought they were pleasing.

A massive exercise in pandering to the conservative base turned out to be a massive, misplaced overreach by the Republican-controlled Congress and a president eager to score points with his right-wing supporters. On MSNBC tonight, Keith Olbermann, one of the most thoughtful talk show hosts on cable television, asks the elemental question. How did a single case out of the estimated thirty thousand cases of people in a persistent vegetative state get elevated—and funded—into international prominence? And why wasn't a neutral observer appointed who could act on Terri Schiavo's behalf, other than the courts, which the Schindlers believe rightly or wrongly are biased against them? The answer, as with everything in this case, has many layers. The court on two occasions appointed a disinterested third party to act as Terri's "guardian ad litem," which means guardian at law. The first was Richard L. Pearse Jr., a local attorney from Clearwater, who was named in 1998 when Michael Schiavo first petitioned the court to have his wife's feeding tube removed. Pearse's report cited obvious conflicts of interest and recommended Michael's request be denied, which it was. In addition to the trust fund for Terri's care that Michael would inherit, Pearse wrote that it was clear to him that Michael had given up all hope for Terri's recovery and wished to get on with his life. Since only Michael believed Terri wouldn't want to remain alive in her condition, that was not sufficient to determine her wishes, Pearse concluded. The Schindlers felt vindicated by the report, but the victory would be short-lived. Michael's brother and sister-in-law came forward to back up Michael's assertion that

Terri would not want to live this way, and the Pearse report was filed away, overtaken by events and the passage of time.

Jay Wolfson, appearing on Olbermann's show this evening, was named Terri's guardian ad litem in 2003 after her feeding tube was reinstated for the second time. Judging by the thirty-eight-page report he filed, he was professional and thorough. Given a month to examine thirty thousand pages of legal and medical documents and to make recommendations to Governor Bush, he tells Olbermann that as the father of three sons he can't imagine what it would be like to have any one of them no longer capable of interacting and dying by pulling a tube. He has kind words for all the players in this drama, calling the Schindlers wonderful people, the protesters outside the hospice decent people, and Governor Bush wise and conscientious, and noting that although Michael Schiavo is not a warm-and-fuzzy man, "that doesn't make him a bad person." But it's not about any of them, he says, and it's not about the Florida legislature, the courts, or the U.S. Congress. This is about Terri, and what her intentions might have been. "And if you don't believe what Michael and others have said about what she expressed after two funerals of her family members—which would have been in context, who were on respirators and who died, and she said, 'I don't want to be like that'—if you don't believe that, then nothing is going to change your mind. But if the evidence is credible, and it was deemed so through the legal process. ... How do we resolve these terrible things? I just pray that in the end, Terri's interests will be served best through this process."

A wonkish academic with a mustache and a goatee, Wolfson had no idea who Terri Schiavo was when he got a call in

October 2003 asking him to serve as her guardian ad litem.
He had just gone through the dying of his father, his father-
in-law, and his best friend's father, and his mother, in her
nineties, had fallen and broken her hip, and he was watching her decline. There was no mystery with any of these
loved ones or their expectations; deciphering a stranger's
wishes was another matter. A professor of public medicine
at the University of South Florida, Wolfson also has a law
degree, and still he wondered why he was recruited for this
task, which he equated with "parachuting" into the lives of
people he didn't know. Summoned a few weeks into the
guardianship to meet with Governor Bush, Wolfson told
him he'd never before heard of Terri Schiavo because he
didn't watch television or read the local paper. Bush smiled
and said, "Oh, you're just like my brother." He also said
something else that stayed with Wolfson as he immersed
himself in the intricacies of Terri Schiavo's legal and medical saga. Bush said, "I need your help to get through this."

Wolfson spent the better part of twenty days with Terri
Schiavo, sitting by her bedside sometimes for as long as
four hours at a stretch. He played music, talked to her and
held her hand, searching for some spark of responsiveness.
He cradled her head in his hands, looked in her eyes and
pleaded with her, saying, "You've got to help me help you,
please." He tried not just to understand the medical file and
the legal proceedings but to find some flicker of something
that might give him a clue about what this woman might
have wanted. It wasn't so much that he wanted to err on the
side of life but to see if he could find some consistent pattern of response that was more than a reflex. She made
noises, some of which sounded like cries, some like laugh-

ter, some like groans, but hard as he tried, and as long as he stayed, there was nothing to indicate anything other than the reflexive behavior of someone in a persistent vegetative state.

His then four-year-old son asked him, "How old are people when they die?" The question jolted him. He had to think for a moment before replying, "As old as you're going to get." He was reminded of *Dante's Inferno*, which he read in high school, where a sign on the Gates of Hell reads, "Abandon all hope ye who enter here." As if to liken Terri's existence with a living hell, Wolfson asks rhetorically, "Can you imagine life without hope?"

Wolfson's report was due on December 1, 2003, and at 11:50 P.M. on the thirtieth of November, a Sunday night, Michael's attorney, George Felos, called to say he was challenging the constitutionality of Terri's Law, the emergency legislation that called for Wolfson's appointment. Felos was apologetic; he and his client had gone along with the notion that compromise was still possible. Wolfson proposed that Terri be given additional tests to determine her cognitive state, and whether it was true, as the Schindlers say, that she could recover. There would have been a swallowing test to see if she could eat and drink on her own, which the Schindlers maintained was possible if somebody were patient enough to help her. Wolfson wanted both sides to agree to abide by the outcome of the tests, which almost certainly would have favored Michael's side of the case. So although Michael, counseled by Felos, was the first to pull out of the deal, it's equally certain the Schindlers never would have gone along with it. What Wolfson came to understand about Terri's parents is that their hope knew no bounds. And that fiercely felt hope had transitioned into belief, and that belief had become in their minds a fact. "How do you separate what you know and what you believe?" Wolfson mused. "When you want a response from somebody so badly, belief creates false hope not just for them but for everybody around them." The Schindlers were not going to let Terri die no matter how bleak her medical prognosis. Maybe they were fooling themselves about her getting better, but even if she didn't, they loved her anyway. For the Schindlers, this is what unconditional love means. They couldn't understand Michael's perspective, and shared with Wolfson what they believed was evidence of Michael's abuse of Terri. Wolfson looked into it and concluded in his report that the charge of abuse was baseless.

Asked by Olbermann what he thought of the "bona fides and goodness of Michael Schiavo," Wolfson pointed out that in fifteen years, Terri hasn't had a bedsore, which is a tribute to the quality of care she received. Wolfson noted that Ken Connor, who represented Governor Bush in his effort to intervene in the Schiavo case, made his reputation taking on nursing home injuries. He of all people should know the significance of keeping a bedridden patient free of bedsores for that length of time. At one point, the nursing home staff tried to get a restraining order against Michael because he was so demanding about his wife's care. As for Michael's other relationship with the woman he was living with, Wolfson said he wasn't going to pass judgment. But then he sort of did, speaking for himself, saying that just because he loves his mother doesn't mean he can't love his wife, that relationships he had with people that were intimate years ago don't preclude his continuing to care for them.

Daniel Sulmasy, the medical ethicist from St. Vincent's Manhattan Hospital, is a much sought-after guest on the cable shows because of his nuanced approach to the Schiavo case. "I don't want to rip feeding tubes out of people or take treatment away from people that seems to be working," he says. "I certainly wouldn't want to be kept on a feeding tube myself, but I don't want to say that I have a right as a physician to trump the family's wishes. Where I think I do have a right is when I say this isn't going to work—this isn't going to even do what you're claiming." If Michael Schiavo and Terri's parents all agreed they wanted to continue treatment for her, Sulmasy wouldn't override their wishes. From the Catholic perspective, as long as Michael is truthful about Terri not wanting to be kept alive this way, then it is morally permissible to discontinue the feeding tube, says Sulmasy, adding, "I'm not his confessor."

In our society, the courts are his confessor. Sulmasy makes a distinction between a biomedical determination of futility and a subjective determination about quality of life. The feeding tube kept Terri in a minimal state of being, and if the courts had agreed with her parents, that this is what she would have wanted, Sulmasy would have no problem keeping the tube in place. Whether this would meet the definition of "extraordinary" care depends on whether it is more burdensome than beneficial, and in his thinking that judgment is reserved for the patient or the patient's family, not the physician. *Extraordinary means of care* is an old theological term. It never meant how many whistles or bells; it meant whether you had an obligation to do this to preserve your life, or whether it was optional. *Extraordinary* is another word for *optional*—you can do it, but you don't have to. And it applies to a feeding tube, a ventilator, or even antibiotics. It depends on the circumstances. The people agitating to keep Terri alive say that a feeding tube is different—it's cheap, it's not invasive once it's in place, you don't have to do anything more—and it's delivering the basics of life, food and water, to which every human being is entitled. As technology makes medical advances more accessible, the decision making gets more complicated. In the Quinlan case, the parents wanted her taken off a cumbersome respirator they believed was causing her pain. Now people can be on ventilators at home that are small, not that costly, and they raise the question, does everybody who can't breathe have to be on a ventilator at home?

Sulmasy spends a good bit of time reassuring Catholic nursing homes and hospitals that the papal statement of a year ago shouldn't be interpreted as meaning everybody who's dying should be kept on a feeding tube. "A huge number of people, good people, Catholics in the United States, now think the Catholic Church teaches that no one can die without a feeding tube," he says. If you follow closely the final days of Pope John Paul, you will discover that his doctors put in a feeding tube through his nose, not a peg into the stomach like Schiavo, and he apparently asked them to take it out. It wasn't in very long, though it's murky as to whether it was reinserted in the last few minutes as he was dying. In any event, it was stopped the last few days at his request. He refused to go back into the hospital; he was dying of Parkinson's disease and he refused extraordinary means, so that remains the teaching of the church. The pope was able to make his wishes known. What about a patient who is in a persistent vegetative state? Here Sulmasy says the papal statement is best interpreted as meaning there should be a presumption in favor of a feeding tube, unless there is good evidence that it is more burdensome than beneficial, the key phrase, elastic enough to accommodate a variety of circumstances.

Sulmasy says his interest in end-of-life issues dates back to when he was an undergraduate at Cornell in the late 1970s and attended a moot court at the law school where they were discussing the case of Karen Ann Quinlan. He was fascinated by the theoretical questions surrounding the brain-damaged Quinlan's right to die. Then as a medical student, he found himself drawn to patients who were dying, taking a special interest in caring for them and their families. His skill in this unexplored arena won him letters of commendation written to the chief of medicine. The defining experience that set him on his life's work occurred when he was a fourth-year med student caring for a woman with advanced breast cancer. She complained of weakness in her legs, and he suspected she had cord compression, meaning a tumor was pressing on her spinal cord, which could lead to paralysis if not treated immediately. The diagnosis was confirmed by a special test. Sulmasy was feeling quite proud of himself when the attending neurologist arrived with his entourage, all men in white coats. With no preliminaries and with eight strangers standing around the bed staring at her, the neurologist said, "Lady, you've got a big fat tumor stuck on your spinal cord, and we've got to give you some radiation so you don't get paralyzed, okay?" Then the great doctor turned and walked out, leaving

Sulmasy, a mere student, "with this weeping mess this woman was left in."

Most of us will get a bad medical report at some point in our lives. How we get that news, and how we will react, is unknowable. If we're lucky, we'll have a doctor who is attentive to the emotional side of things. With the demographics tipping toward the elderly and baby boomers starting to obsess about old age and death, pop culture offers clues about what lies ahead. When Tony Soprano, the fictional HBO Mafia kingpin, is in the hospital recovering from a near-fatal gunshot wound, a visiting pastor brings him a copy of Chuck Colson's book. Colson worked for President Nixon and served time for his role in the Watergate cover-up. In prison he found Jesus and became a different man, says Pastor Bob, hoping to inspire in Tony a similar conversion.

"Salvation is about saving yourself from yourself," says the pastor, who represents the Church of the Open Door of the Redeemer.

"It must be nice to have something to hold on to," Tony muses.

"Evolution is Satan's way of denying God," Pastor Bob offers, dropping in that the earth is only six thousand years old.

This gets Tony's attention. "You're saying there were dinosaurs back there in the Garden of Eden with Adam and Eve!" he exclaims, adding with exquisite logic, "No way— they'd be running shitless—and it's supposed to be the Garden of Eden."

Coming to grips with one's impending mortality is a terrifying event and one that most of us face only when we

have to. For all the touches of mordant humor, Tony Soprano, Mister Tough Guy, is groping his way toward spirituality. He recalls a dream where he felt he was being pulled
toward something. "It makes you wonder about heaven and
hell," he says. "My wife [the long-suffering Carmella] said I
woke up and said, 'Who am I? Where am I going?'" But
then Tony reverts to form. If he can't be restored to his full
manhood, and he's not talking spiritual here, enough of this
introspection: "Do me a favor and—what's the term—
whack me," he says.

The creator of the HBO series *Six Feet Under*, Alan Ball,
says if the show, which is set in a funeral home, is about
anything, it's that everything ends. He wanted to provide
people with a sense that they're not alone, because we all go
through this. Knowledge is power, and coming face-to-face
with death, thumbing our nose at it, even laughing about it,
however vicariously, removes the mystery, and therefore
much of the fear. Each episode of *Six Feet Under* began with
a random death that reminded Tom and me of the fragility
of life as we watched throughout his illness, grateful for the
conversation that the fictional drama prompted between us
when the television light flickered out.

9.

Hey, Good-Looking

I promise you, if she dies, there's going to be hell to pay with pro-life, pro-family, Republican people of various legislative levels, both statewide and federally, who have used pro-life, pro-family, conservative rhetoric to get into power and then when they have the power they refuse to use it.
— Randall Terry, Operation Rescue

DEMONSTRATORS CARRYING PLASTIC CUPS of water solemnly step up to the police line at the hospice, crossing over one at a time into the waiting arms of police officers who lead them away to be arrested. It is so orderly and choreographed with camera crews alerted that when a ten-year-old boy approaches, nobody deviates from their assigned roles. The reporters shout their questions: How do you feel? Are you afraid? The boy murmurs something back. He's not sure how he feels; no, he's not afraid. Then he's staring up into the faces of two police officers, each with a hand under his arm as they lead him toward a police cruiser. Never mind he's a child and a third their size. They have their orders. The boy's father looks on proudly; his son just became a man.

Among the protesters is a slender blonde woman, Brandi Swindell, who stopped eating the day Terri's feeding tube was removed. She spends her days in front of the hospice praying, with lots of breaks to do media, and to sit in the shade. It's hot and muggy, and she's slowed down quite a bit, with the headaches and all. She drinks water, and in the afternoons she'll sip a cup of Pedialyte to keep her electrolytes balanced. It was designed for babies and looks like pale apple juice. Her intention is not to hurt herself, but to make the point in the most sacrificial way she knows how that what is happening to Terri is barbaric and savage, her words. It's a grueling schedule. She's up at six, at the hospice by seven, and never in bed before midnight. When she did *Fox & Friends* and *Scarborough Country*, they identified her on the screen as "Brandi Swindell on a hunger strike," a label that gives her presence purpose. "People think, oh, she must have grown up in a pro-life Christian home, and I didn't," she says. Her parents are people of faith, but they didn't go to church every Sunday and they struggled with alcoholism, and now they're separated, she says, adding, "They're wonderful people. We joke that we put the fun in dysfunctional."

A purposeful life is what this young woman had been seeking since the summer of 1997 when she was twenty and working a summer job at Yellowstone. One of her roommates got pregnant and had an abortion. It was a traumatic experience for everyone, and the fun-loving friend Brandi knew was lost forever, or so it seemed at the time. Brandi had always been pro-life because of her concern for the fetus, but now she had a new lens to look through, that abortion is psychologically damaging for women. A fourth-generation Idahoan, she returned home with a mission, to research and gather data to understand the impact of abortion. She discovered that members of her family, including her mother, had had abortions, and years later, there were regrets. Brandi was fourteen at the time of her mother's abortion and had no idea it had happened. Her mother opened up about the experience, and how heartsick it left her. She now attends pro-life events and is an activist like her daughter.

Brandi sees the fight to save Terri as far more than a pro-life crusade. She considers herself a modern, independent woman and is the proud owner of a button that says, "Another pro-life feminist." She felt compelled to join the protest in Florida once she realized Terri was not terminally ill. "I felt Terri was being treated like a rag doll" and stripped of her constitutional rights "just because she didn't eat with a spoon and fork like everyone else." A protégé of Rev. Mahoney, Brandi had interned in Washington at pro-life organizations, where her leadership skills were recognized. She has an easy rapport with everybody, not just her allies, and with her blonde hair piled high, large hoop earrings and spike heels, she looks like she could have stepped off the set of *Sex and the City*. In 1999, she founded Generation Life, a youth-oriented group whose mission it is to mobilize the post-*Roe* generation, people like her born after the 1973 Supreme Court decision legalized abortion. "A lot of us think we could have been aborted," she says. Her newest project is a "life-affirming medical clinic" in Idaho that would reach out to women with unplanned pregnancies. She is a feminist who identifies with early suffragists Susan B. Anthony and Elizabeth Cady Stanton, as opposed to what she calls "modern-day feminist thought."

How did a brain-damaged woman at the end of life become so entwined with the pro-life movement? The Schindlers file another flurry of legal appeals based on dubious new evidence that Terri tried to vocalize her will to live to one of their lawyers. The mammoth legal effort is made possible by contributions from national right-to-life-associated groups and pro bono work by lawyers sympathetic to the pro-life cause. This latest claim is based on an assertion from a lawyer who says she told Terri on the day the feeding tube was removed that this whole controversy could end if she could express one sentence: "I want to live." The motion filed with the court says Terri "attempted to verbalize the sentence. She managed to articulate the first two vowel sounds, first articulating 'ahhhhhh,' and then virtually screaming 'waaaaaaa.' She became very agitated, but could not complete the vocalization attempted." It's a pretty shaky proposition at best, but word quickly spreads among the protesters that Terri tried to speak and placards pop up, "Terri: I want to live" and "Terri asks Mom for food."

Michael Schiavo's attorney, George Felos, says the question of whether Terri can communicate has been addressed countless times, and that the sounds Terri makes are a reflexive reaction to touch and not an attempt at communication. Dismissive of the so-called experts, the Schindlers persist in deceiving themselves about their daughter's true condition and their prospects for a legal victory. They were told years ago, back in 2000, by J. Wesley Smith, a noted bioethics critic, that they couldn't win their case as long as the PVS diagnosis stuck. "Because people have generally said that's a life not worth living," says Smith, who by his own description is a gadfly who typically doesn't back away from controversy. He recalled to me his initial encounter with the Schindlers, how he had just concluded a lecture, and was told these people were in the lobby wanting to talk with him. He knew who they were. "I wasn't planning to get involved, but the Schindlers put up such a powerful fight for their daughter's life, I felt that I had to ride into the Alamo. I knew the outcome, and when one knows the outcome, one is reluctant to give his heart to it, but I saw this, and still do, as a noble struggle." Smith signed on as an informal adviser and used his celebrity as a prolific author and public advocate—Ralph Nader was his mentor—to generate op-ed pieces and advise the legal team on how to try the case. Smith says he never pushed Nader to take a stand, but the legendary consumer activist weighed in on the side of keeping Terri's feeding tube in place. Nader's mother had died recently, and he felt the hospital hadn't treated her respectfully enough and with enough care for her life because of her advanced age. Politics aside, it's often personal experience that affects our perspective on public policy. Wesley Smith's epiphany came when a friend committed suicide influenced by literature from the Hemlock Society. The experience became the introduction to his best-selling book *Forced Exit*, and moved him from working with Nader fighting tort reform to fighting assisted suicide.

What made the Schiavo case big, he says, is the Internet, where the Schindlers—without talking to him, he notes—posted videos of Terri on their Web site. Critics rightly charge that the sequences were cherry-picked from among hours of footage, but viewers didn't know that, and the haunting images elevated Terri into the nation's consciousness. "What people saw was a human being—and in our culture, if you don't see somebody, it's an abstraction. The one that got to me was when she's asked to open her eyes—her eyes are closed for a while, then they flutter, then they open, then she opens them so wide, she wrinkles her brow in an apparent earnest attempt to please. ... I remember going to the Chicago O'Hare Airport and the front page of the *Tribune* had a picture of her smiling—it was the smile that changed the world. She became human, and for a lot of people, many in the pro-life community but also disability rights activists, that made her a cause worth fighting for. That's what caused a critical mass, which I never expected—and I think everybody was caught completely by surprise."

The impact was international. In the United Kingdom, a man with a form of Lou Gehrig's disease, a motor-neuron disorder, was so afraid his feeding tube would be taken away that he brought a lawsuit against the national health system to ensure it wouldn't.

Denial is a natural human response when confronting the loss of a loved one. The Schindlers, empowered and enabled by a network of true believers and hangers-on, carried their crusade far beyond where anybody would have imagined possible. They enlisted a significant fraction of the country, the Congress, and the president in their efforts to save their daughter's life, and to imagine their daughter was capable of a life far beyond what responsible medical professionals were saying. We can look at the Schindlers' actions as the ultimate extraordinary measures to save life, and set aside questions about the quality of that life. Or we can judge them more harshly, and ask whether they're saving Terri the person or what remains of life in her body, and is there a difference?

Friday is the day we tape *The McLaughlin Group*, and I know Schiavo will be an issue. My instincts are on the side of hastening death, but I don't have the heart to take too firm a stand, knowing I am living an end-of-life drama in my living room.

Brenda Stewart, a licensed health care worker I hired through a private agency, is a key figure in Tom's care. She greets him each afternoon with a spirited, "Hey, Good-Looking," and is amazed when he responds by singing several verses of the song. Tom's memory for song is extraordinary. I swear he can remember every lyric he's ever heard.

Brenda is outraged that they have pulled Schiavo's feeding tube. I don't really agree, but I am comforted by the fact that the person caring for my loved one feels so strongly about preserving life. Brenda is a gift to me, and to Tom, whom she treats with great respect, even reverence. They watch Turner Classic Movies in the afternoon and vie with each other to identify the stars of yesteryear. The truth is that Brenda spends more quality time with Tom than anybody, including me. She's planted in a chair by his side for four hours every weekday from three to seven, and she brightens the mood from the minute she walks in the door. She's become my confidante, the person who has seen the dying process up close countless times and has a sense of the rhythm of these final days.

As Tom loses his ability to communicate, Brenda gets protective and thinks the time for visitors is over, except for immediate family. She doesn't want him remembered this way. She's heard visitors extolling his talents, and she doesn't want those memories replaced by the image of a dying man in a hospital bed. The much younger hospice nurse, Daphne, thinks there's no reason to discourage anybody from coming as long as they know what to expect. This isn't *Tuesdays with Morrie*, the best-selling account by Mitch Albon of his conversations with a former professor of his who was stricken with Lou Gehrig's disease. Tom's ability to converse is vanishing. Sitting by him, holding hands, something he didn't do easily when he was well, letting him know you're there, being quiet, maybe reading to him is what's meaningful.

The cameras are rolling, and John McLaughlin in his booming Jesuitical voice wants to know, "What accounts for this steep plunge in the approval and the steep climb in disapproval?" President Bush's poll rating is the lowest of his presidency—45 percent, down seven points in just the last week, while his negatives are up five points. Conservative commentator and two-time presidential candidate Pat Buchanan gets first crack, as always. He's the beadle, an Anglican Church term for the person who follows behind the bishop with the incense. He's first among us lesser equals, and he doesn't disappoint, telling John that the change in Bush's polls "occurred coterminous" with the Terri Schiavo case. But he says the president did the right thing by intervening. "This is an important milestone this country is crossing," he says, his hands chopping the air and his passion evident. "An innocent woman, guilty of nothing more than severe brain damage, has been sentenced to death by starvation and dehydration." Buchanan harks back to World War II and says that German doctors who did the same thing to severely retarded and senile people were charged with crimes against humanity. "This country is changing in a way a lot of folks who grew up in it would not recognize," he says.

John turns to me next, and I say there's a big difference between severely retarded and disabled and somebody who has no cognition, who is not capable of feeling pain or expressing herself. I point out that the term *brain-dead* is commonly accepted, and is acknowledged as a form of death. I would learn later that Terri Schiavo is not brain-dead because her basic reflexes are working, but I'm right in the sense that the thinking part of her brain is gone. And I say that the president, by interfering in this most personal of family decisions, flying back to the White House, grandstanding in the middle of the night in his pajamas, has meddled in individual lives in a way that most Americans find repugnant.

"What about the pajamas?" John demands. "Was it a stunt?"

"Well, he was woken up. I'm assuming he sleeps in pajamas," I reply, claiming literary license. As for the stunt part, I cite a memo circulated among Republicans last weekend that said the Schiavo case is a great political issue to energize the party's conservative base. Instead, it's backfired, revealing a party driven by social conservatives who want to impose their beliefs on the government. And they're blaming "runaway justices" when twenty-three federal judges have looked at the Schiavo case, a majority of them Republican appointees, all came to the same conclusion.

McLaughlin tries to steer the conversation back to politics and chides Buchanan for "giving his personal view about whether or not this woman is required to have extraordinary means to keep her alive. ... We don't want to get into that. We want to know what the political impact is of a plunge of seven percentage points. It looks like a backlash against the Republicans, correct?"

The McLaughlin Group is a public-affairs show, but it's really more like a televised food fight. Tony Blankley, a droll British-born conservative, is quick to pounce. Defending his political kin, he says the Bush brothers, Jeb and George, are "practicing Christians who believe in the right to life." Democrats can claim their actions are cynical, but he thinks most Americans, whether they agree or disagree, know this is a sincere position held by these two men. Tony is certainly free to hold that view, but regardless of motivation, healthy majorities even among conservatives say Congress and President Bush should not have gotten involved in the Schiavo case, period.

McLaughlin rattles off the lengthening list of Bush's woes: mounting casualties in Iraq, the impending defeat of his Social Security plan, a gay marriage amendment to the Constitution, Iran and the bomb ...

"Gay marriage is a winner in there, John," Buchanan interjects.

Undeterred, John continues, "And finally, the Republican Congress and the president playing politics with the

Schiavo case. ... Are these things coalescing into critical mass, and is the president in danger of becoming a premature lame duck?"

Buchanan dismisses the notion of Bush as a lame duck. He says Bush is a leader because he takes a stand and that he and his brother "believe in things. And presidents that become famous, like Reagan, are people who stand up against the tide and don't go with the polls."

"The problem is that leaders can be wrong," counters John.

"They can be right, too," says Pat, returning the volley. It's hard to get in the conversation when these two get going on conservative dogma, but I see an opening.

The common thread with the list of ills that John recites is that Bush and Company think they can spin their way out of anything. A senior administration official once told the *New York Times* that Bush and his top aides create their own reality and we mortals in the media merely react. It's worked pretty well for them until now, but it's beginning to unravel with the Schiavo episode and with the continued carnage in Iraq. The Bush spinners think they can put a gloss on everything and people won't notice the facts. The credibility gap is catching up with them.

I'm willing to grant the point that Pat and Tony are making, that President Bush and Governor Bush are sincere. But there was never any realistic hope that the federal government was going to be able to make Terri Schiavo whole again. And the more they say it's not about politics, the more people think it is political. And the polls reveal that. The American people are smart.

Midway through my miniperoration, Tony Blankley is

apoplectic. "Let somebody else get into this," he yelps. McLaughlin ignores him, which is what he does when he disagrees with what's about to be said. "Eighty-two percent of the people feel there was no reason to do what was done," McLaughlin concludes with an air of authority, as if to say, "End of discussion." But Tony will not be squelched. He says John's list sounds like John Kerry's critique of Bush, and he lost the election. Blankley's list: "Iraq going better, democracy breaking out in the Middle East. ... You could write that list up, too," he says.

Denigrating John's analysis inflames the good doctor, who holds a PhD and never backs down even when he should. He dares Tony to answer my point about people feeling manipulated by this president and the Republicans. "You saw the memorandum that went out to the Republicans," he says.

"It wasn't a Republican memo," Tony says flatly, not knowing he would soon be proved wrong when an aide to Florida senator Mel Martinez admits writing it.

Now Pat jumps in to defend the GOP's honor. Just because some character wrote a memo saying, "This might help us," is that why hundreds of congressmen flew back to Washington? "John, there are people here who believe in this life issue deeply."

"I didn't say there were not," says John.

"Then what is all this talk about politics?" Pat counters.

"There are also people out there who feel there was manipulation," John says.

"Jeb Bush has been fighting this for years," says Pat. "And it is unfair and unjust to suggest—"

"Jeb Bush can be wrong," John interrupts.

"I know he can be," Pat agrees, "but he's not political on this."

Once again, I see an opening, and I say what I believe should be obvious to all, that however heartfelt Jeb Bush is, "every Republican adviser thinks there's political benefit in this. You energize the base."

Tony pounces. "How many Republican advisers have you talked to?"

"I'm a reporter, Tony. I talk to ..." Before I can finish, Tony says snidely, "And the top Republican advisers confide in you?"

The jabs continue. It's the kind of car crash that makes *The McLaughlin Group* memorable, and the gender imbalance of the guys bullying the lone liberal female is part of it. Lots of it I toss off, figuring I'll get my turn in the debate. But this time I feel Tony is challenging my credibility as a journalist, and it incenses me, especially since until he took the job as editor of the editorial page of the *Washington Times* he had no claim to being a journalist. He used to say he only played one on TV. "I would appreciate your not getting so personal," I say not once but twice in an effort to shut him down. It doesn't work.

"I'd like to know who they are ... your top Republicans," he says. I feel like I'm before the House Un-American Activities Committee, which had its heyday hunting down alleged Communists during the height of the cold war.

"I'm not going to be naming names," I say.

Tony responds with disgust and heavy sarcasm. "Oh, you're not going to give away your sources? Your top Republicans ..."

Recognizing the tit-for-tat is getting out of hand, John intervenes on my behalf. "Let Eleanor continue," he says. "We don't want mob rule here."

With the path cleared for me, I make the point that the Republicans believe they have to energize their base so they'll turn out in the midterm election and defend the Republican majority. "To pretend this isn't about politics is to pretend you're not living in Washington," I declare, getting the last word in the exchange.

What follows is the exit question, John's signature. "Is this low approval rating of the president going to get worse, stabilize, or get better?"

Buchanan, a loyal Republican, hates to say it but he does: Bush's rating could drop to 40 percent.

McLaughlin presses, "Could he drop into the 30s?"

Buchanan hesitates, and decides with a laugh that 44 percent "is about where he'll be."

Sensing blood, McLaughlin says, "By the way, don't forget what I said about the Catholic Church and extraordinary means." He's only touched on this debate on the air, but when the red light is off, indicating the cameras are not rolling, he and Pat have argued about whether a feeding tube qualifies as extraordinary means, and whether the church has changed its position. Each knows where the other stands, and each regards himself as the last word on Catholic scholarship and doctrine. John is a former Jesuit priest and Pat, a devout churchgoer, is the product of Catholic education. "The Catholic Church is right on this," says Buchanan, adding with a mischievous grin, "Its former noble son is wrong."

His religious standing challenged, John says some Catholics may believe as Pat does, but that's not the church's position. "The church has taught that extraordinary means may not be required by anyone who wishes to die."

"Explain it to the pope," says Pat.

"Explain it to the pope? He hasn't said anything about this," says John.

"He certainly has," says Pat, referring to the statement read a year earlier by the ailing Pope John Paul that was taken by some as a presumption in favor of keeping a feeding tube in no matter what.

"The Vatican press is not speaking for the pope," John says.

"Look, the pope has spoken about the culture of death, and that is what this is right here in America," says Pat.

"That is your extrapolation of this case," says John, his frustration mounting at this challenge from his friend of almost forty years. The two served together in the Nixon administration when John was still in the priesthood and working as a speechwriter in the White House. "Come on, Pat, get off it," he says.

Watching this from the sidelines, I say, "There's something odd about a party that worries about people before they're born and then really after they're dead. What about the time in between? That's when we need government involved."

Reading the transcript later, I see that I ducked the question about Bush's poll rating, saying only that the Republicans are in danger of losing their libertarian wing because of the overreaching on Schiavo. I leave the field free to Tony, who predicts Bush will stay between 45 and 55 percent for the next three years, which would take him to the end of his term. Tony says there's a Republican base that's in the mid-40s that will stick with Bush.

Pat chimes in, "He's got a base. He's got a bottom. He's got a floor. ... People have bonded with this president. ... He's like Reagan. He's got a base beneath which he will not go."

John is dubious. "The answer is it's too close to call," he declares with his signature booming certainty.

"Despite the political travesty imposed on Terri Schiavo, will the good exceed the bad?" John asks. Among the panelists, there are two yesses, me and Pat, and two nos, Tony and *Chicago Tribune* editor James Warren. John's the deciding vote: "Living wills—more good than bad. Happy Easter. Bye-bye."

10.

Living Corpse

I chose to spend my final days in a hospice because it sounded like the most painless way to go, and you don't have to take a lot of stuff with you.
  —Humorist Art Buchwald in a column published after his death

Why not let Terri's parents care for her? That refrain sums up the view of many Americans who, exhausted by the acrimonious debate, wonder why the simplest, most obvious solution can't be achieved. The *New Yorker,* in an editorial on the affair, asked what harm would have been done if Michael Schiavo had agreed to let the Schindlers maintain Terri indefinitely on life support. Certainly this would have satisfied Randall Terry, Tom DeLay and Bill Frist. But is it truly respectful of life to keep a mindless body alive as a kind of living corpse? Wesley Smith, the attorney who advises the Schindlers and calls himself a Martin Luther King liberal, says it is wrong to withhold sustenance from a person based on cognitive capabilities. Even if the means of delivering that sustenance is a feeding tube, which the courts have defined as a medical treatment, he thinks nutrition and hydration merit their own category, apart from a ventilator or antibiotics or even an aspirin, because of the heavy symbolism—feeding is nurturing—and because their discontinuance can have only one outcome, which is death.

Smith makes a distinction between somebody like Tom, who is dying from cancer and whose body is shutting down, and Terri, who is otherwise physically healthy and could live a normal life span. "It didn't matter to me that Terri was in a persistent vegetative state or minimally conscious; to me she's a human being and we shouldn't judge somebody by their capabilities." In Smith's view, it's a slippery slope. If we look at Terri and conclude we wouldn't want to live like that, that she has a poor quality of life, then what's to stop that attitude from spilling over and victimizing people who are seen as a burden to themselves and society—the poor, the elderly, minorities? The growing emphasis in hospitals is on what's called "medical futility," where ethics committees weigh life-sustaining treatment against other factors such as cost, which nobody likes to talk about, and quality of life, whether it meets a certain standard. How do you measure a life worth living? Not everybody has the same standard.

Smith has a reflexive dislike for the bioethicists who ruminate about these issues and who populate hospital ethics committees. They're philosophers, he says with disdain, and they're dealing in issues of right and wrong where nobody has a monopoly on wisdom. He regrets that the fight over Terri Schiavo deteriorated into a media narrative of "the religious Right versus reasonable people," losing the nuances of what is at stake for public policy in an aging society with dwindling resources. You can count the number of Schiavo-like cases on one hand, he says, where family disagreements get pushed into the public arena. Most families settle their differences at the bedside. "The big fight is going to be over refusing wanted treatment—and that's where I think a lot of the bioethicists want to take it. And that's where a lot of us are going to draw the line and fight tooth and nail."

Should society draw a line based on ability to pay? The truth is that except for the lucky few, our medical system is driven by concerns about costs. In Terri's case, Medicaid pays for a big chunk of her care, including her medications, and Woodside Hospice, which is run by Hospice of the Florida Suncoast, a nonprofit chain, absorbs the remaining cost of her care, an arrangement that allows the Schindlers the luxury of pressing for unending care.

TOM HAD AN EXCELLENT insurance policy through his employer, and the medical team that treated him at the Cleveland Clinic is aware of the power of his pen. He writes columns describing his treatments, and in one he relates a conversation with his neurosurgeon about his uneasiness with the high cost of keeping him alive when there are so many unmet medical needs in society. The physician said his job is to treat patients, period. As long as a viable treatment exists and the patient is willing, he's prepared to try, he told Tom. In another country where the government controls who gets certain treatments, Tom wouldn't have gotten the high-tech gamma ray treatments that zapped the cancer in his brain. "It doesn't work that way in our society, thank God," the doctor said. "It's nice to live in a society where every life counts." Still, the meter was ticking. After Tom died, the bills arrived, bills I'm sure he assumed his insurance was covering, tens of thousands of dollars of uncovered medical expenses that nobody breathed a word about until Tom had drawn his last breath.

ETHICIST DANIEL SULMASY resists what the media circus has become—one expert declaring we're murdering an innocent woman, and another insisting it's the rights of a spouse that are being trampled. What he finds most annoying are the assistant producers who call and want to know the intimate details about what's happening to Terri's body. It strikes him as an invasion of her privacy to talk about her potassium level and the condition of her lips. He is amazed at the media's apparent refusal to recognize how people have died for the first fifteen thousand years Homo sapiens has been on the earth. "At the very end of cancer, at the very end of tuberculosis, people stop eating. This is what happens—and we haven't been guilty of murdering all of them because we couldn't figure out how to find a way to get snake intestine and mashed banana into a tube through their nose into their stomach as they were dying."

There haven't been randomized control trials to determine whether it's better to die with or without a feeding tube, but the wisdom of hospice nurses and what Sulmasy has observed with dying patients is that the body shuts down and makes endorphins, which produce a natural high. Anybody who's engaged in a serious fast knows that even twenty-four hours into it, the sensation of hunger starts to leave. In Terri's case, the feeding tube is a twenty-four-hour drip into the stomach, so it never gives the sensation of a full stomach. "And certainly the wisdom of hospice nurses is that it's better to die dry than to die wet. People think when somebody is dying, even if they're not eating, we should hydrate them, put an IV in and keep the fluids going. But that's not how people die naturally. What tends to happen is the lungs begin to overflow with fluid the body really can't handle, the person gets more saliva, and there's something called the death rattle," which Sulmasy demonstrates with a gasping wheeze. It's actually better if a person is a little bit dehydrated as he's dying. You can swab a person's lips with glycerin. If they're awake, give them ice cubes to suck on. Sulmasy recommends to family members "who feel the need to do this nourishing thing" that they take a demitasse spoon, put a little honey on it, and put it under the person's lip three times a day. He's found that very meaningful to families who feel strongly that feeding is an act of love, and the patient, if they're awake, gets pleasure from the taste of honey and the intimacy of being fed by mouth, probably for the first time since childhood.

It makes no sense to put feeding tubes into the vast majority of people who are dying, and nobody is anticipating that. But Terri wasn't dying. With the proper care, she could have lived a long time, which creates an ethical dilemma. Is Terri's condition an extreme disability, or does she have what Sulmasy calls "a lethal condition"? He says most people don't get into a persistent vegetative state unless they've already met the cardiopulmonary definition of death. When a person's heart stops and we rush in and do CPR with the hope of reviving them, and they suffer anoxia, meaning they are without oxygen for several minutes, they end up like Terri Schiavo. "The most common cause of PVS is incomplete rescue from death," says Sulmasy. The prognosis is often better for those who go into the PVS state from trauma, like an automobile accident. Most neurologists won't call somebody permanently vegetative from trauma for at least twelve months; for anoxic brain damage, it's six months. Schiavo has been in this state for fifteen years. In Sulmasy's view, she was snatched from the jaws of death to begin with and then left with a devastating neurological condition from which, but for technology, she could have died at any point along the way. There's one remaining technology left at the end, which is the feeding tube. And so it's become a matter of debate whether this is a disabled person or someone who has a lethal condition. Terri's condition is not progressive, which makes the decision harder, says Sulmasy. If she were not going to live very long anyway, then you could continue the feeding tube without having to take into account the burden on the patient, family or society.

Sulmasy is in the forefront of the broadening debate about futility laws that govern care at the end of life. Many hospitals have been quietly putting into place procedures that allow doctors and medical personnel to overrule families when they consider care futile, with the decisions subject to review by ethics committees. It's touchy terrain as hospitals and some state legislatures grapple with how to balance the competing interests. New York is one of the few states with a law that directly addresses resuscitation, making it mandatory to do CPR on a patient even if the attending physician feels it is pointless if the patient's designated representative wants it done. The 2003 decision handed down by Attorney General Eliot Spitzer, a progressive Democrat, is anything but progressive, says Sulmasy. Instead, it perpetuates the fantasy of television dramas like *ER* and *Grey's Anatomy*, where CPR is almost always effective. In real life, that's not the case. "It's bloody and invasive and not a very pleasant thing to do unless you think there's a purpose to it. If there is no purpose, then it seems almost like desecrating the person's body," says Sulmasy.

His views were shaped as a young staff doctor, when he had to crack the ribs and perform CPR on a man who had been in a vegetative state for fifteen years, and had developed pneumonia and gone into cardiac arrest. The man's relatives had insisted, and the rules determining who had the final say were vague. The statute that Spitzer clarified allowed physicians to write a DNR order with the patient's consent, but was unclear about how to handle a "medically futile" patient if the family insisted CPR be performed. Could the doctor's judgment prevail? Spitzer put the burden of proof on the physician, who now must get a court order to refuse resuscitation or do CPR if the family insists even if there is a high degree of medical certitude that it won't work.

This is where the decision belongs, says Wesley Smith, in an open due-process situation, not with ethics committees with quasi-judicial powers that can turn into star chambers. He has faith in families making the right decision if given the proper information. "People think with CPR you go push, push and Grandma's okay. That's not what it is. Doctors need to be blunt and clear. 'We're going to break her ribs. Is that what you want?'"

Listening to this, it strikes me that by the time everybody

jumps through all these bureaucratic hoops, the patient is likely to be dead anyway. And that's not far from the truth. Three-quarters of the ethics consultations at St. Vincent's are about end-of-life-care issues, and 80 percent of those patients are dead in six months—and 50 percent are dead in a week.

Right-to-life protesters are demanding Governor Bush go in and seize Schiavo. The alliance Bush struck with the protesters has shattered in the face of their increasingly shrill demands. Antiabortion activist Randall Terry complains that Bush has stopped taking their calls. Rev. Mahoney has ramped up the public pressure on Bush, stopping just short of stalking the beleaguered governor, whose good intentions have blown up in his face. A prayer vigil outside the governor's mansion in Tallahassee turns raucous when gardeners come out to water the plants and the protesters begin to shout the obvious comparison, that Bush is denying water to Terri. Bush, a devout Catholic, is scheduled to take part in a stations-of-the-cross ceremony on the campus of Florida State University. Mahoney and his band of protesters wait with placards, but Bush doesn't show up. Mahoney gets ahold of the station Bush was supposed to read and holds a news conference to denounce Bush for not having the strength of character to appear and follow through with his commitment to save Terri.

In the evening, Mahoney gets a vitriolic phone call from the governor's chief of staff. "How dare you do this; how dare you go against his character? Governor Bush has done more to help Terri. He's your friend. You're pathetic." Mahoney relishes every word. He likes to think of himself as speaking truth to power. He wishes he had saved the message; it is a badge of honor. When I remind him that Bush seems anguished by the turn of events and can be seen fingering rosary beads when talking to the press, Mahoney says, "Somebody did that in the Bible. His name was Pontius Pilate. He was washing his hands of the affair. He says he can't do any more. Sure he can. How about going in to see her and say a prayer with the family? How does that sound? They're both Catholic."

Sharpshooters are spotted on the roof of the hospice. The police guards have been getting death threats. Terri's father urges the crowd through a spokesman to go home and spend Easter with their families. Michael is spending most of his time at his wife's bedside, leaving the room only for those short periods when her parents are there. Michael's attorney, George Felos, emerges from the hospice after seeing Terri to stand before the media throng and report, "She is calm, she is peaceful, she is resting comfortably. ... Her lips are not chapped, they're not bleeding. Her skin's not peeling. Frankly when I saw her ... she looked beautiful. In all the years I've seen Mrs. Schiavo, I've never seen such a look of peace and beauty upon her."

The suggestion that what is happening to this young woman warrants the word *beautiful* provokes a visceral reaction from the other side. Mahoney goes into overdrive, mocking Felos, a longtime hospice volunteer, for romanticizing death by starvation and dehydration, and releasing to the press the hospice's own internal description of how the body shuts down when deprived of food and water. Bobby Schindler says his sister is bleeding from the eyes.

"I thought, 'Holy cow,'" says Wesley Smith, watching this unfold on television. "I asked him afterwards, 'Is that really true?' He said she had blood pooling in her eyes. When you're dehydrated, your mucous membranes will crack."

A hungry media devours it all, a willing accomplice in spreading half-truths and myths about what happens in the dying process. Richard Land, a prominent evangelical and head of the Southern Baptist Convention's Ethics and Religious Liberty Commission, tells the *St. Petersburg Times* that the Terri Schiavo case represents a "clash of two very disparate civilizations—the Judeo-Christian civilization, which is based upon the sanctity of human life, and the neo-pagan, relativist, quality-of-life civilization." Not to put too fine a point on it, this is the culture war played out with Terri Schiavo starring as Joan of Arc, a martyr to the cause, whichever side you're on.

I'm struck by the fact that Felos refers to Terri as Mrs. Schiavo, an appellation that contrasts with the media's familiarity in calling her almost exclusively by her first name. Joanne Lynn, a senior scientist at RAND who specializes in end-of-life issues, personally lobbied ABC and NPR to get them to address her as Mrs. Schiavo instead of Terri. It changes the way people look at the case, says Lynn. "As long as it's Terri, she's a little girl in pigtails and not someone who grew up. When she's Mrs. Schiavo, she grew up; she made choices; she made commitments. She's not just somebody's little girl. Why belittle a woman by calling her by her first name?"

TOM BEGAN NOTICING his loss of mental capacity soon after undergoing whole-brain radiation. He knew the risks associated with the procedure, but it was his only option to retard the growth of new tumors once the cancer had spread to his brain. He got so frustrated losing his glasses that he went to the drugstore and bought four pairs. They were all over the house. I remember one rainy night I was driving to the airport and he called me on my cell phone to say, "You won't believe this. I couldn't figure out how to send." He was talking about transmitting a column on the computer. He eventually got it, but the moment is etched in my brain like notches on a tree, marking the progression of his disease.

Years ago, Tom had a friend, Laurel Lee, who wrote a best-selling book about her experience with leukemia. When the illness returned, her publisher exulted, "A sequel!" We used to laugh about that. To the extent that he could, Tom viewed his cancer as material, a meddlesome intruder that could be turned into useful copy for his column and help serve others.

Tom wrote his last column right after the 2004 presidential election. He told me it took him ten hours to write; normally he could knock off the eight hundred words in two or three hours. However much he struggled, the result does justice to his grace and talent as a writer and thinker. He concluded the column by comparing President Bush to Stephen Crane's "Man with a Tongue of Wood."

> There was a man with tongue of wood
> Who essayed to sing
> And in truth it was lamentable
> But there was one who heard
> The clip-clapper of this tongue of wood
> And knew what the man

Wished to sing
And with that the singer was content.
What's more, the singer was re-elected.

Tom was a careful wordsmith. Phrases like "very unique" or a "new record" would set him off, and he was ruthless about split verbs. He was a student of writing, browsing the bookstores for the latest tips on creative nonfiction in case there was some secret out there that had eluded him. To lose the ability to think logically and form a conceptual thought is a cruel fate for anybody, and especially so for somebody whose life and career are defined by verbal expression. I kept assuring him that his core intellect was there, and who cares about the periphery, but the missed synapses couldn't be ignored.

The theme keeps emerging where Tom thinks he's in the wrong house and that we're visiting someone and he's ready to go home. Even as he's lying flat on a hospital bed in the living room, he wants to know when the cab is coming. "Who's going to be in charge of returning the cats to their rightful owners?" he asks.

"They're ours," I reply.

"But we don't live here," he says. Then he realizes he must be wrong and he recovers to say, "Aha! You've got me again."

Later in the evening, I hear him with the hair dryer going in the bathroom. He never used a hair dryer, preferring to shake his thinning hair dry, and now he's bald anyway from the radiation.

"What are you doing?" I ask.

"Brushing my teeth," he says.

How much of this to reveal? I try to observe it scientifically. The pathways in the brain are getting confused, reality intersecting with old memories and new imaginings. I mostly go along with his train of thought; I don't challenge him. He was always good at choreography, whether it was a family photo or an elaborate musical skit for the Gridiron Club. Now he drew on his imagination to complement his shrinking reality.

Dr. Mike Vogelbaum calls. He's the neurologist at the Cleveland Clinic. "The only comfort I can provide is that if the cause of the progression is in the brain, it's usually not painful," he says. The brain has no nerve endings and is uniquely oblivious to pain. Tom's cancer has also invaded his bones, so there is considerable pain, but that's why we have hospice. Their specialty is pain management. "If he gets agitated, it will be forgotten quickly by him," the doctor tells me. He speaks fondly and wondrously of Tom's sense of humor, and he writes me a letter to that effect as well. When he would tell Tom he shouldn't be driving home himself after gamma ray knife treatments and that he worried about him, Tom would just smile and say, "You just keep worrying," and be on his way. By the time we did the Diane Rehm show together in November 2003 to talk about living with cancer, Tom was joking about getting a good hairpiece. Later in a column, he revealed how self-conscious he was about his bald head until he sat next to an attractive woman at a dinner who told him he was a handsome guy, but what was with the hat? He shed it along with his embarrassment.

Tom's friend Phil Barragate e-mails me about visiting. He's troubled about seeing Tom like this, and whether he can handle it. But if he doesn't come, he feels he would be deserting a friend. After considerable angst, he and his wife make the drive from Cleveland. He's carrying college year-books to share memories. Tom was captain of the Blue Streaks basketball team at John Carroll, a Jesuit college in Cleveland. They didn't know each other in college, but years later Barragate read a column Tom had written questioning the value of long prison sentences for nonviolent first offenders. That was 1997, and Barragate, who had been a high-flying personal injury lawyer, was into the fifth year of a fifteen- to forty-five-year sentence for felony theft after siphoning money from his law clients to cover millions of dollars he had lost in risky stock ventures. There was no question about Barragate's guilt, but the sentence was un-usually tough for white-collar crime. He wrote Tom about his situation, launching a correspondence that prompted Tom to write several columns supporting Barragate's bid for parole so he could work and pay restitution to his victims. Tom testified on Barragate's behalf, ultimately helping to win his freedom. When I invited him to speak at Tom's me-morial service, he wanted to know if it was okay if he talked about his past. He didn't want to embarrass me. That's why I asked you, I replied. I want you to tell the story.

As I write this in 2007, a longtime friend and colleague from *Newsweek* calls to tell me his wife passed away after a long siege with breast cancer that had metastasized into her liver. She died in a hospital bed in their dining room. Three weeks earlier, when they decided as a couple to give up the fight, they asked the doctor the question they never had dared to before: How much time do we have left? Days, weeks, not months, he replied. Then they went home and went about their lives as best they could. It was the matter-of-factness of it that stands out in my friend's account of his wife's last days. She had e-mailed me after Tom's death, saying, "I don't know what we should wish for each other when the time comes to face our own death, but the comfort of looking back on a happy life and knowing that you did a pretty damn good job of appreciating it, well, that's a start."

EASTER SUNDAY, MARCH 27, 2005

Science vs. Religion

The uncertainty we all live with is not that we will die—that is a given—but when and how.
—Tom Brazaitis in a column, January 2001

TODAY IS EASTER SUNDAY, and the religious fervor around Terri's impending death is intensifying. I sit by Tom's bedside reading aloud to him from David Brooks's column in the *New York Times* about the Schiavo case, and how one side lacks rationality and science, and the other lacks compassion and morality. Tom looks wide-eyed and less than comprehending, but he likes the sound of the human voice. The Ray Charles CD I gave him for Christmas is playing on the boom box in the living room. It (the boom box, that is) goes back to when our kids were teenagers. Listening to the soulful music, the tears come. Maybe someday they will come in a flood, but for now I feel that crying would be surrendering to the despair I feel about life without Tom, and I want to keep a sense of possibility about the future alive. I don't want to give in to thinking I've been cheated somehow, that this is about me and not about Tom.

Scott Bojan, a fitness instructor we'd been lifting weights with since before cancer invaded our lives, comes by in the afternoon to visit, and Tom gives him a big smile. He clearly recognizes him. Signing up with a personal trainer was Tom's idea, one of his enthusiasms that seemed to come from nowhere, but probably had something to do with improving his golf swing. For me it was the recognition after years of running had given me legs like trees that I needed to pay attention to my upper body. Between sets, Tom and Scott would talk sports and joke around. It's like the old days as Scott gives a rundown on the weekend's West Virginia basketball game, except Tom can't respond. Scott stays as I feed Tom his lunch—Stouffer's Swedish meatballs—which he eats with gusto. I have no way of knowing it at the time, but it will be his last meal. I will later tell Scott he got the last smile and saw the last meatball go down.

PAT MAHONEY, the Presbyterian minister, is heading back to Washington. He's been fasting for nearly two weeks and getting only three or four hours of sleep a night. As the plane pulls out of the gate, he feels nothing but massive relief. He'd been under a lot of pressure as the chief organizer of the protests, and he knows Terri cannot survive. It has been nine days since the feeding tube was withdrawn. From what he understands of human physiology, it has reached the point where it would be cruel and inhumane to put the feeding tube back into this dying woman.

The last weeks have been an emotional roller coaster, with moments of high expectation that help was on the way to the crashing realization that the politicians were not going to deliver on all the promises that had been made, if indeed they ever intended to. He was completely exhausted, wrung out by the experience. He had failed to rally the area's religious community to Terri's cause. The big mainstream churches wouldn't even let the protesters use their facilities to hold rallies. One parishioner was quoted saying, "All those people bleating in Schiavo's front yard give Jesus a bad name." The Catholic diocese in particular took an aggressive hands-off stance toward the whole hullabaloo, as though it had nothing to do with the pro-life position the church champions. The Catholic high school where Bobby Schindler taught math was supportive, and the students discussed the family's struggle in their theology classes. But Bishop Lynch, who runs the diocese and whom Bobby regarded for lack of a better word as his boss, said this was a private family matter and that local priests should not get involved. Bobby thought it was scandalous the way the bishop treated his sister's situation. "For all intents and purposes, they turned their back on Terri," he says. He was told by a good source that the bishop had ordered the priests in the diocese not to speak about Terri from the pulpit. Bobby respected the authority of the church too much to make a big stink about it, but he wondered how the debate might have changed if the church had intervened. There are more than a hundred thousand parishioners in the St. Petersburg area that could have been mobilized if the church had put out the word.

It puzzled Mahoney too how the church made the distinction between what was worth fighting for and what just got lip service. For him, championing the worth of a severely disabled person like Terri is a continuation of his commitment to the dignity of life. "I'm opposed to the death penalty like I'm opposed to racial injustice like I'm opposed to abortion," he says. "It's all connected." But he has no illusions that opposition to hastening the end of life will get the same traction as the pro-life movement. "Hell no," he says. "Not even close." The difference, Mahoney explains, is that with abortion, there's a cute little baby you can invoke. With a severely brain-damaged person like Terri, people look at her and think to themselves, "I would not want to be in that position." On the plane, a fellow passenger recognizes Mahoney, who's been all over the news for weeks, and says, "You know what, Reverend Mahoney, I agree with what you're doing, but after all, isn't she going to be in a better place?"

Mahoney hears that a lot, and his stock answer is that it's true, that according to his faith tradition, what follows will be better. But this time, worn out with what has become a losing cause, he replies with sarcasm as he eyes his healthy seatmate. "You know what? You'd be in a better place right now too if you jumped out of this plane. Are you going to jump?" The metaphor hit its mark, silencing the man, who was clearly taken aback. After an awkward silence, Mahoney apologized and said he was wrong.

Wrong to be so combative with a well-meaning person, but not wrong in the sentiment he expressed when it comes to judging the worth of another human life. Mahoney didn't distinguish between saving unborn life and the life of a severely compromised individual like Terri. He welcomed the participation of the disabilities community as a way to broaden the debate beyond the pro-life base. Disability rights advocates generally lean liberal and progressive politically. They're not natural allies of the religious Right, but on this issue of hastening the end of life, they find common cause.

The Friday night before Easter, Bruce Darling, executive director of a disability rights center in Rochester, New York, was coming out of the grocery store with all the fixings to make dessert for his family's Easter dinner when his cell phone rang. It was someone from the national disability rights group Not Dead Yet asking if he would join the protest in Florida. Like most Americans, he had been following the Schiavo story, and he thought the controversy had been wrongly framed as part of the culture wars. It was far more complicated than right-wing pro-lifers battling secular liberals. Joining the protest in Florida offered an opportunity to get out a broader message about disability rights with all the world watching. He called his mother to say this big issue had come up and he wanted to make sure he and his people lent their presence. "And she was cool with it," he says.

The small contingent, five in all, arrive at the Florida hospice on Easter morning. The weather is hot and sticky and the grounds are crowded and chaotic. There is so much going on that Darling doesn't know what to process first. All the images he has seen on television, they are all happening at once—people reading the Bible either silently or more often aloud, people lined up and staring with red tape across their mouths (signifying what, he didn't know), people marching up and down saying their rosaries, and lots of crosses, with one really large cross being carried around by the protesters. It was a cacophony of noise with people chanting and singing and passing cars honking. This is quite a political machine, Darling thinks. He watches a man videotaping a woman off to the side. She talks for a while; the man videotapes her; then he stops and says, "Try it like this," giving her tips on how to improve her story and stay on message.

Darling is uncomfortable. It is brutally hot, and what shade there is, is taken. Even the women with cerebral palsy in his group who are always cold are hot. Everybody slathers on sunscreen, to little avail. They all get sunburned. Darling keeps saying he feels warm, and the others say, "You're in Florida, Bruce. Of course you're warm." He later discovers he is running a 103-degree fever. But his discomfort is less physical than personal. Bruce Darling is a gay man, and his politics don't generally align with the people he is suddenly in close proximity with. Once he and his group get their bearings and find people who seem to be in charge, they negotiate an arrangement to hold a press conference in the early afternoon.

With that settled, they head for lunch at a McDonald's about a block away. While they are eating, some of the religious protesters, seeing the wheelchairs, try to convince them to go out and do something to get arrested. "That would be front-page news everywhere if you got arrested," they urge. But that is not the group's intention.

At the appointed hour, the press conference gets under way. The small but hardy disability rights contingent has barely launched into their message about what implications Terri's situation might have for them when suddenly there is a commotion and someone yells, "They're going up the driveway!" Violating what Darling understood was a mutual nonaggression pact to let the press conference proceed undisturbed, the religious protesters charge up the driveway ostensibly to take water to Terri, prompting an arrest action that draws all the media attention and effectively shuts down the press conference. Darling is stunned and frustrated. Why would they do that? Why would they choose his group's moment to stage the disruption?

The reporters take off chasing the story, cameras in tow, leaving Darling and the others with a story to tell and nobody to tell it to, with one exception. A weekly magazine fellow who's had enough of the staged, camera-ready demonstrations stays behind. "If you've seen a bunch of people arrested down a driveway once, you've seen it," he says. "Yours is a story I haven't heard anyone talk about—would you guys mind talking to me?" The lone reporter lingers, and as they talk, the religious protesters start marching back and forth saying the rosary. Darling thinks, Okay, I'm Catholic, I know how this works. You don't just start the rosary and stop. They're going to be tied up for a while here.

Annoyed that the religious types have messed up the press conference, Darling and the others decide to counter with something equally dramatic. They will get out of their wheelchairs and flop down on the driveway. The point of leaving the chairs is to demonstrate they are not defined by the equipment that is tied to them, just as Terri should not be defined by the feeding tube that sustains her. The small band of disability activists moves to this level of civil disobedience because they know rational conversation cannot get through all the chaos. They will go with the emotion.

Darling has done direct action before, and as the others maneuver toward the driveway, he engages the officer in charge. "Look, here's the deal," he says. "We just want to talk, to share our perspective, and when it's over, it's over. We're not going to dirt you." By "dirt you," he means they aren't going to say one thing and do another. He doesn't know where he picked up the expression, but the officer gets it. He won't hustle them away. And after they have their say, they will get back in their chairs and leave. "Getting back in is always a little more difficult than getting out," Darling says with a laugh. And getting out isn't so easy, either. This is not an orderly transfer. It is rough. It is "throw yourself out of the chair and take your lumps," Darling says. A couple people get bruised up. Sitting in the driveway, they chant,"Don't devalue our lives" and "Let Terri live." Their props are tubes, which they hold up to show that for people with disabilities, tubes are part of their daily lives and not something scary. Once they are out of the wheelchairs and on the ground, cameras are plentiful and the media people who had fled the press conference suddenly wanted to talk to them again. Darling's cell phone rings. It is a friend from Texas. "You're in the driveway!" he exclaimed.

"Yes, but how do you know?" Darling replied.

"You're on CNN. I'm watching you right now."

To look at Darling, one would not suspect he has a disability in the classic sense of how it's generally defined. He's not physically disabled. He is what's called "face blind," a neurological impairment in the recognition of faces. He can recognize his mother and people he has continual contact with, but lacking a strong emotional connection, everybody else is a stranger. The medical term is *prosopagnosia*. Darling is also diabetic; his grandfather was a double amputee as a result of the disease. Within the disability community he is accepted as one of them, but he readily concedes he's not what others think of as disabled. He jokes that he's the kind of person everyone tries to get cut out of the benefits legislated by the Americans with Disabilities Act.

The religious fervor at the site frightens Darling. It feels as though it could spin out of control at any moment. Throughout the day, well-meaning people come up to the wheelchair users, touching their heads to pray for healing. They press a hot, sweaty palm on the person's forehead and then with their other hand apply pressure on the back of the head. Sometimes people place their hands over the eyes as well. By day's end, the accumulation of sweat, sunscreen and grime from the hands of nearly a hundred different people makes the recipients feel filthy. "It was like being a human doorknob for a public restroom," Darling says with disgust.

In the evening, as the crowd thins, he lays down on the grass, using his backpack to rest his head. Children play near him, tossing a ball. Once the ball lands by his head. It unnerves him. He worries about what could happen to him if he closes his eyes. He is sure that if these people knew he was gay, they would be just as quick to disrespect him as they were to defend Terri's life. He lays there wondering what punishment the Bible prescribes for homosexuality.

One of the odder alliances to emerge from the Schiavo saga is the bond between disability rights activists and the pro-life movement. One tends to be liberal and secular, the other conservative and religious. Yet they've been able to put aside those differences on discrete issues like Terri Schiavo, assisted suicide and medical futility cases. "Nothing about us without us," says Darling, whose mission is to gain a wider audience for the perspective of the disabled. He wasn't eager at first to embrace the Schiavo case but felt compelled to join the debate because of all the oversimplifying and overgeneralizing. Even the word *terminal* bothers him. Everybody's terminal in the sense we all will die. He has a disease that's likely to shorten his life. When does he start counting down toward the end? He thinks neither side in the culture war serves the cause of the disabled." The conservatives would recognize the sanctity of our lives while killing us by taking away services and medications through budget cuts. The liberals restrict our lives through medicalization and promote killing us as a form of caring," he explained to me in an e-mail. "To me, it looks like we may end up being the collateral damage of the culture wars."

The disability community makes the slippery-slope argument. If Terri's life is judged worthless, who among them might be next? "We're all clumped in the same pile," says Darling. He illustrates how society evaluates the value of life with this analogy. If a person with a mental disability walks into a hospital and says he wants to die, he is wrestled to the ground, medicated and given treatment. "If a person with a significant physical disability says, 'I want to be dead,' the response is, oh, that makes sense." And that's the crux of it for him, how people evaluate other people's core value. People say they don't want to live like that, with tubes and caretakers, but then when tragedy strikes, they adjust and find meaning to continue living. Christopher Reeve, the late actor, paralyzed after being thrown from a horse, is a celebrity example of someone who recovered from despair to contribute a great deal and inspire others.

There are data that show quadriplegics rate their quality of life higher than the medical professionals who attend them.

Darling's work is designed to bolster community services for the disabled so they are not forced to live in nursing homes. He tells the story of a Rochester, New York, man who became a quadriplegic after breaking his neck in a high school gym in 1967. Bill White lived on a ventilator in the rehab unit at Strong Memorial Hospital where he was held up as an icon and featured in the local newspaper for his indomitable spirit. He was quoted saying he had everything he needed, which was defined then as a supportive mother and access to the world through a computer. But then his mother died, and his computer broke and wasn't replaced, and he turned fifty, and he said he wanted to die. He made several attempts to disconnect his ventilator, but would then feel anxious and want it back. So he asked the hospital to sedate him with morphine so he could comfortably die after removing the ventilator. The hospital ethics committee supported his right to end his treatment and the hospital's intervention medically with morphine to assist in his death. The disabled community saw that as crossing the line from passively letting someone die to actively causing death. Bill White was one of the longest-known surviving quadriplegics on a ventilator when he died in August 1999. The local medical examiner ruled the cause of death was a gymnastics accident.

Darling thinks White became suicidal because he was depressed over a series of events, the loss of his mother, who was his real connection to the world, the loss of his computer, which increased his isolation, and turning fifty, an age that invites a midlife crisis. Instead of trying to boost his quality of life and improve his living situation, everyone nods their head and agrees he's made a rational decision in deciding he can't stand living like this anymore. Darling believes if White had access to less institutionalized care, he might have had more will to live. Whether that's realistic depends on the resources that are available. White needed twenty-four-hour care and in thirty-two years rarely left his hospital bed.

Darling lobbied hard in New York for the creation of a "nursing facility transition and diversion waiver," which allows people who need assistance to use the money that would normally go to a nursing home for services in the community. The nursing home lobby is strong, and the disability community had an uphill fight. Darling and his forces succeeded in part because of a fluke prompted by Darling's face blindness. He was working the state capitol in Albany as he usually does, accompanied by a colleague whom he relies on to provide verbal clues so he knows whom he's talking to. She ducked into the ladies room and left him briefly alone in the lobby of the legislative office building. A tall bald man in a suit, wearing glasses, approached. Darling thought, mistakenly it turned out, that he was an AIDS activist. "What's up?" the fellow asked. Thinking he's talking to a soul mate, Darling says, "We're in a big fight with the assembly." Then he proceeds to outline plans to disrupt Disability Awareness Day by storming the doors of the legislative chamber and dropping forty-foot "Free Our People" banners from the marble balcony while the Speaker is talking. "We're going to shut down the whole thing," he declares with gusto.

Just then his colleague arrived, so he concluded the conversation. He didn't get much of a reaction to the bold plan he outlined and figured maybe the fellow was having a bad day. "Do you know who you were talking to?" his colleague asked. "That was the legal counsel for the assembly." He had just tipped off the lawmakers what the disability rights community was up to, losing the element of surprise and probably rendering the plans moot.

At first Darling thought all was lost, but the opposite happened. The fellow of the mistaken identity went back to the Speaker and told him the disability activists were going to destroy Disability Awareness Day. Willing to do almost anything to avoid that spectacle, the assembly reversed its position and passed the waiver. "Sometimes fate is what it is," Darling laughs.

Thinking of Terri Schiavo as disabled is a reach for most people. She was not a good case to advance the cause of disability rights because she had such limited capacity. There had been better cases out there, but they didn't catch on the way Terri did with her wan smile in the videotape that played in an endless loop on cable television. Diane Coleman, an activist with Not Dead Yet, traveled to Florida in 2003, when Terri's feeding tube was first withdrawn. Coleman participated in a vigil at the hospice and at a Tallahassee court hearing, and she debated George Felos, a right-to-die advocate who would become Michael Schiavo's attorney, before the Tiger Bay Club in Tampa. The only thing that got him hot under the collar was when she raised his affiliation with a group called Last Act and Partnership for Caring, a coalition dedicated to educating people about end-of-life palliative care. She's all for good end-of-life care, she told me, but opposes anything that expands the power of guardians and reduces the rights of people like Terri who are in guardianship.

When polls showed that the overwhelming majority of Americans think government should stay out of end-of-life personal and family decisions, Coleman knew her side had lost the debate. The disability rights movement wants more government; they want civil-rights protections against bad decisions by guardians.

Coleman, who is fifty-three, was born with a neuromuscular disorder. She gets around in a motorized wheelchair, and for the past few years has been using a ventilator to help her breathe at night. She is the executive director of a center for independent living in Chicago. The case that made her an activist occurred more than twenty years ago, in 1985, in Los Angeles, where Coleman was living at the time. Elizabeth Bouvia, a twenty-six-year-old woman with cerebral palsy, checked herself into a hospital wanting to starve to death while receiving a morphine drip. The hospital turned her down, so the Hemlock Society brought a court case on her behalf. After two years of litigation, Bouvia won the right to assisted suicide. It was one of the first prominent disability rights cases focused on the right to die.

Bouvia had suffered a series of personal crises—a miscarriage, separation from her husband, the death of a brother, severe financial stress—that contributed to her wish to die. The disability community argued that if she weren't disabled, if she were just a woman with personal problems, the state wouldn't help her commit suicide. "Why are you making a distinction in her case just because she has cerebral palsy?" asked Coleman. "It was very difficult to get the media, the courts or anybody else to recognize our point of view in the matter." After winning the right to assisted suicide, Bouvia decided to live, but the legal precedent was established.

The case that Coleman wishes had taken off the way Schiavo did reached the California Supreme Court in 2001. Robert Wendlen's pickup truck had rolled over seven years earlier and left him in a coma that deepened into a minimally conscious state. His wife wanted to withdraw life support; his mother and sister fought her in court. The controversy offered a hint of the family dynamics that would come into full view with Schiavo. Wendlen's mother claimed in a CNN interview that her son kissed her hand and could throw a ball, whereas the wife said the only response that her husband offered was reflexive, and that he would not want to be kept alive artificially. The wife's judgment was supported by a court-appointed guardian.

What was unique about the case compared to Schiavo is that all parties agreed the subject of the controversy was not in a persistent vegetative state, that there was some very minimal awareness. The lower court denied permission to remove the feeding tube; the appellate court reversed the decision, and the case went to the state supreme court. Wendlen died before the high court issued its ruling siding with the lower court. He had contracted pneumonia, and under the appellate court ruling antibiotics were withheld. The supreme court said there had to be clear and convincing evidence of the person's wishes even when a guardian is charged with making decisions. This was a victory for the disabled community even though Wendlen was denied treatment that could have kept him alive.

Wendlen got some national attention but nothing like

Schiavo, even though many of the same players appeared in both. It was the first case of this kind that Wesley Smith got deeply involved in. Smith had thought the Wendlen case would be big. They had tapes of him sticking pegs on a pegboard, and he could roll a wheelchair down a hospital corridor, suggesting a degree of consciousness that Terri never exhibited. But his face wasn't on the Internet. He was hidden behind a hospital door. Terri was a marketing triumph. "The Face That Moved a Nation," as one newspaper headline put it.

For Ralph Nader, the consumer activist who joined with Smith, his longtime friend, to speak out for Terri, the issue is who decides, and he thinks Michael Schiavo forfeited his spousal right because he was in effect remarried with two kids, so he had a conflict of interest. With the parents willing to care for her for the duration, Nader told me, "The whole idea of this man saying I'm going to pull the plug on her was just outrageous." But the way Congress behaved is what really got to him, as it did to most Americans. Two hundred thousand people die every year from occupational disease, medical malpractice and air pollution, he says, and Congress doesn't rush back to pass legislation. "There are certain ways that people die that drive cultures up the wall," he says.

WHILE THE PROTESTERS are filled with religious fervor on this Easter Sunday, Tom's journey into nothingness is uncomplicated and even reassuring. Morphine is available to ease pain. He is at peace with where he's been, and where he's going. When he could still talk, a friend asked, "How are you?" a routine pleasantry. "I am not afraid," he replied.

MONDAY, MARCH 28, 2005

Comfort Kit

If there's anything good to come out of this Schiavo thing, it's that the GOP has really shot itself in its big fat pandering foot. Not that the Dems covered themselves with glory, of course, but hardly anyone noticed their craven cowardice.

—Katy Burns, friend, in an e-mail

In a conciliatory gesture, Michael Schiavo allows a drop of Holy Communion wine on Terri's tongue. Monsignor Thaddeus Malanowski, spiritual adviser to the Schindlers, says he and the hospital chaplain also anointed Terri with oil and gave her absolution and a papal blessing, completing the four elements that make up the Catholic rite for the dying. With the end approaching, Michael orders an autopsy so the extent of Terri's brain damage will be known.

A notice arrives that Tom's subscription to the *Secular Humanist* is expiring, and I decide to renew it in his honor. People of all ideological and religious persuasions are having conversations about what they would want should they find themselves in Terri's situation.

Tom's breathing is shallow and rapid today. He clamps his mouth shut when I fix him his usual cream of rice cereal. It is the first time he has refused to eat. I am sufficiently alarmed that I call Daphne, our hospice nurse. She's not scheduled to stop by today, but when I describe the changes in Tom's condition she says she's on her way.

When Daphne arrives, she suggests giving Tom morphine every two hours to ease the rapid breathing. She also pulls out the hospice "comfort kit," which is stored in my refrigerator. It was issued to us as part of the initiation process into hospice, and it contains an assortment of emergency medicines. Daphne adds Atavan to Tom's pharmaceutical banquet; it eases anxiety and also aids breathing. Tom is coughing and there is a gurgling sound in his lungs. I've had a cold and I think that he has caught my cold. But I'm also thinking something else—the death rattle. I ask Daphne about it, and she explains that in effect Tom is drowning in his own fluids. She prescribes a drug called Levsin, which is a drying agent, along with Robitussin DM for the cough. The Robitussin is delivered to our door, and it's the biggest bottle of cough syrup I've ever seen. It's enough to last a good long while. That must mean that this new phase Tom is in will last some time or surely they wouldn't stock me with this much Robitussin. Daphne writes out everything for me of what to give and when, along with instructions to call the hospice emergency number if Tom's breathing slows below a certain point.

I do not ask if this means the end is near, and Daphne does not volunteer any guesses about how much time Tom has left on this earth. I would later read Daphne's notation on Tom's "progress report" for this day that "patient appears potentially to have transitioned into 'active' dying process." She estimates Tom's physical pain as a six on a scale of one to ten. Under "Family perception" of the situation, she writes, "Aware of prognosis, accepting of prognosis."

My children have been taking turns staying in the house, and my brother and sister-in-law have been commuting back and forth from New Jersey, but as it turns out, we're down to the hard-core now—me. Brenda Stewart, the health aide who is here in the afternoons, is horrified that I am alone at this time, but it doesn't really bother me. Tom isn't going anywhere, I feel like medically things are under control, and I've convinced myself, thanks to that supersized Robitussin, that there's time enough for more family members to come and go. Brenda shakes her head. "I still think you should put out an SOS for someone," she says, giving me her cell phone number where I can reach her during the night. She cares for an elderly woman in the neighborhood and can come right over, she assures me. "I'll be fine," I say.

It's pouring rain today and Rev. Pat Mahoney is valiantly trying to hold a news conference in Lafayette Park across from the White House. He's attracted plenty of interest; there are twice as many photographers and reporters than demonstrators willing to brave the weather. The annual Easter egg roll is typically held on the Monday after Easter, and the downpour forces the White House to end the event early. Only about three dozen protesters are on hand when Mahoney begins his presentation.

"Dana Milbank mocked me," Mahoney later complains of the coverage he gets from a *Washington Post* reporter. The *Post* story leads with a Florida woman named Mary Porta who left the vigil outside Schiavo's hospice to fly to Washington with her giant five-foot-high Styrofoam spoon that says, "Jeb, Please Feed Terri." The spoon was still wrapped in United Airlines plastic and tagged with a security seal from the Department of Homeland Security when Porta carried it into the center square of Lafayette Park. Milbank has an eye for detail, and he notes that Porta used part of the airline's plastic wrapping as a makeshift poncho. Another protester, Brandon Fancher, came armed with a roll of red duct tape that he handed out in strips inscribed with the word *Life* for demonstrators to apply across their mouths as if they were being gagged. These are scenes any reporter would find irresistible, conveying the circuslike extremes that have overtaken the debate.

Mahoney knows that after eleven days without food or water, Terri is not going to survive. But he has come to Washington to press the Republican leadership to keep their promise to hold a hearing on her situation. He met this morning with the chief counsel to Republican Speaker Dennis Hastert, and he's gotten the message that the hearing is not going to happen. "They are lacking the political will," he says into a dozen microphones, blasting the congressional leadership for failing to follow through on the subpoena issued at the height of the controversy by the House Government Reform Committee to question Schiavo at a hearing in Florida. That was always grandstanding; it was never going to happen. "Is this a political stunt by the

Republican leadership?" Mahoney shouts, having concluded the answer is yes.

"I've been here since 1992, and this is the least-spiritual town I've ever been in," he tells me. Spirituality is personal; it's between a person and their god. In Washington, everything gets filtered through politics. He thinks Tom DeLay really believed in Terri's cause; he also knows DeLay used her to deflect political criticism in an ethics scandal that would eventually force him to resign his leadership post and then his congressional seat. "I felt completely betrayed by Congress and specifically the Republican leadership," Mahoney says. Even DeLay, a strong ally, became an albatross when he called for the impeachment of judges who did not rule on the side of sustaining Terri's life. "He really shouldn't have spoken. We were doing much better when it was a coalition with Harkin," says Mahoney. "I respect Senator Harkin. However we might disagree on other issues, Harkin for the disabled is really a champion." Referring to Harkin's support as a coalition is a bit of an exaggeration. Harkin was the only Democrat actively involved on the side of pressing Congress to intervene in the Schiavo case.

The cable networks are wall to wall with Schiavo. A report that Schiavo has been given small doses of morphine undercuts the argument that she is in a vegetative state and cannot feel pain. Dr. Cranford, the University of Minnesota neurologist who advised on the case, is on CNN's *Larry King Live* and MSNBC's *Scarborough Country*. He says it's not unusual to give patients in a vegetative state morphine "because sometimes it helps the family. ... It may reassure the family," and sometimes even the nurses, he adds. "Will this death be peaceful?" King asks. Cranford replies that it will be "absolutely horrible for the Schindler family who believes she's there." He says he doesn't know how it will be for Michael Schiavo. "I can't speak for him, but it will be peaceful beyond any doubt, Larry, to Terri Schindler. She's unconscious; she can't feel anything."

Appearing with Cranford is a woman, Kate Adamson, who was unconscious for seventy days as a result of a brain-stem hemorrhage. Her husband didn't give up on her; she doesn't think Michael should doom his wife. Cranford ex-plains that seventy days with a cerebral bleed is not the same as fifteen years in a vegetative state. "We have erred on the side of life," he says. "It's the longest right-to-die case in the history of American law."

Yet Bobby Schindler follows Cranford and with evident sincerity confirms that his sister Suzanne Vitadamo heard Terri crying out for help.

"Why not take in a tape recorder?" Larry King asks.

Bobby explains that they're not allowed, that it's against the court order to bring in cameras or recording equipment.

"Could you sneak it in?" asks King. "I mean, it would be very dramatic to see this. Might change things. … What's the reason for that?"

The reason is privacy and exploitation, and Michael Schiavo not wanting any more heartwrenching videotapes edited to suggest an awareness that Terri really doesn't pos-sess. Bobby says it's because Michael Schiavo and his attor-ney are hiding Terri's true condition so he can petition the courts "to have her killed."

Reading the transcript of this evening's *Scarborough Country*, I can imagine Dr. Cranford watching the show, waiting his turn to appear, and getting steamed as he listens to guests egged on by Joe Scarborough, a former Republican congressman from Florida, making wildly inaccurate statements about what is happening to Schiavo. Terri's sister, Suzanne, comes close to claiming a miracle, saying Terri is "very much alert," sitting in a chair and trying to talk. Terri was afraid of a bee sting, Suzanne declares; therefore, she would never want to be starved to death. Then, with a little prompting from Scarborough about "foul play," Suzanne goes on to allege unexplained broken bones and a neck injury suggestive of strangulation, implying Michael may have hurt Terri the night she collapsed and doesn't want Terri to speak again for fear of implicating him. It's tantalizing stuff, but Scarborough is skeptical, noting that he hasn't seen this picked up in the newspapers or on the cable news shows. Suzanne is undeterred. She says her family wants an investigation and she doesn't understand why they keep getting the brush-off.

There is a video clip of George Felos, Michael's attorney, saying Terri looks peaceful and calm, that there is music playing in her room, and that she has a stuffed tabby cat under her arm. He does acknowledge that her eyes look more sunken than when he saw her last, and that her breathing is a little on the rapid side, a sign that she is getting close to death, which he does not say.

The Schindlers' attorney, David Gibbs, is not as reticent. He let it slip on the Sunday show *Face the Nation* that Terri had passed the point of no return, medically and legally, a judgment the Schindlers vigorously refute for fear it will seal Terri's demise. Scarborough follows up with Gibbs, who says Terri's family is still hoping for a miracle. Pressed on the nature of that miracle, Gibbs says the Department of Children and Families in Florida had been on its way to take possession of Terri and put her on an IV until they were stopped by a court order. They're appealing that order with Gibbs's help. "If that could be reversed, that could be Terri's miracle," he says.

He's followed on the show by Mahoney venting about Congress and then Republican representative Chris Smith, an ardent pro-lifer, declaring it appalling they are using "water, which none of us can live without, as a weapon to kill her." He concludes that many Americans "don't realize that this woman is very likely feeling pain, and feeling it excruciatingly so." Scarborough concludes the segment with the hope that maybe Congress will also get involved "and come out from under the rocks from which they are hiding, because they are hiding tonight."

After the break, the camera turns to NBC correspondent Lisa Daniels in Florida for her interview with Dr. Cranford. She says she wants to be accurate and asks if it's true that Michael Schiavo asked him to examine his wife, and that he examined Terri Schiavo for about forty-five minutes. Cranford replies it was closer to forty-two, but forty-five is close enough. But there are lots of inaccuracies he wants to correct. "She's not starving to death," he says. "Do you understand that? She is dehydrating to death." When Daniels asks how he knows that, seeming to challenge his professional credentials, he snaps, "Because I've done it twenty-five to fifty times in similar situations. And they die within ten to fourteen days. ... And they are dying of dehydration, not starvation. ... And Joe doesn't have any idea what he is talking about. And you don't have any idea what you're talking about. I have been at the bedside of these patients. I know what they die from. I have seen them die. And this is all bogus. It's all just a bunch of crap that you are saying."

Daniels recovers nicely from the broadside, tossing it back to Cranford, "With all due respect, doctor, it sounds like you think that you know what you are talking about, so let's ask you about that. Are you 100 percent correct in your opinion that Terri Schiavo is in a persistent vegetative state?"

"I am 105 percent sure she is in a vegetative state," Cranford says. "And the autopsy will show severe irreversible brain damage to the higher centers, yes."

"Why are you so sure, doctor?"

"Because I examined her," Cranford says, along with four other neurologists at the hospice who examined her and found her in a vegetative state, a diagnosis she has carried for twelve years. The one neurologist who disagreed is Dr. William Hammesfahr, hired by the Schindlers and whom Cranford calls "a charlatan."

Daniels asks Cranford whether CT scans have been done on Terri. The Schindlers maintain that the tests that were done are outdated and Michael has blocked additional testing. Rapidly losing what little patience he has, Cranford says scans were done in 1996 and 2002, and they show severe atrophy of the brain. "The autopsy is going to show severe atrophy of the brain. And you are asking me if a CT scan was done? How could you possibly be so stupid?"

This is when Scarborough steps in to rescue Daniels, and to advance a pet theory pushed by the Schindlers, that the later scan, the one done in '02, actually shows improvement over the earlier scan, the implication being that a new scan might show additional gains.

A retired radiologist hired by the Schindlers, Dr. William Maxfield, was alone in asserting there was improvement. Judge Greer, the presiding judge throughout the case's long, tortuous legal history in Florida, "didn't buy it," says Cranford, "because the other doctors said it wasn't improved. It was probably worse than it was before."

"Is he a charlatan also?" Scarborough asks.

"Yes," Cranford says. From the perspective of mainstream medicine he's on safe ground with that description for Maxfield and Hammesfahr. Maxfield is into experimental therapies like hyperbaric oxygen and vasodilator to improve brain function, practices generally dismissed as quackery and that could not reverse the kind of brain damage Terri suffered. Hammesfahr, a neurologist, also offers therapies that are not widely accepted and has faced disciplinary action from the American Academy of Neurology.

"You tell me they are not charlatans," Cranford says, "just because you don't agree with me—I don't call everybody a charlatan." He cites Dr. William Cheshire, the neurologist brought in by the Schindlers, whose diagnosis of Terri as in a "minimally conscious state" shook up the media for a day or two but ultimately had no impact on the case. "I think he's a reputable neurologist. ... So, just because I disagree, I don't call them charlatans. But you have got your facts so far off that it's unbelievable, Joe. You don't have any idea what you're talking about. You've never been at the bedside of these patients."

"You were there forty-two minutes ... and somehow, in your forty-two minutes observing her, you have all the answers and everybody that disagrees is dead wrong, I guess," Scarborough says. That isn't what Cranford said, of course, but he doesn't control the microphone. And Scarborough smoothly segues out of the segment with a deft piece of character assassination, saying that he doesn't know this particular doctor's body of work, so he's not claiming Cranford is a charlatan or a hired gun, but as an attorney himself who has represented plaintiffs as well as defendants, he knows "too many doctors out there can be bought off by attorneys on either side. And then they come out, instead of telling you the facts, you get into a debate like you are talking to an attorney. It is very, very disappointing." He apologizes to Daniels for interrupting her interview, but she was getting attacked because of what he said. "I think that is unfair," he says.

Scarborough had resigned his congressional seat in 2001, saying he wanted to spend more time with his children. One had been diagnosed with juvenile diabetes, a particularly vicious disease for a child to cope with, and he expressed concern on air that a mild form of autism in one of his sons might be linked to vaccines he was given as an infant. A card-carrying conservative, Scarborough was pursued by Republicans to run for the Senate seat held by Florida Democrat Bill Nelson. Scarborough declined, apparently having too much fun as a broadcaster. Nelson went on to handily defeat Representative Katherine Harris, the former Florida secretary of state who had ended the presidential vote recount in 2000. By then, Scarborough had repositioned himself politically, becoming even more critical of President Bush and the Republican Congress than his liberal counterparts on cable television.

But as he hammered away at the Schiavo story night after night, his right-wing roots made him an aggressive advocate on the pro-life Schindler side, which he argued with the ferocity of a courtroom lawyer. Scarborough holds a law degree from the University of Florida, and was practicing in Pensacola when David Gunn, a local doctor who performed abortions, was gunned down in March 1993 as he entered his Pensacola clinic. The shooter was Michael F. Griffin, a self-described Christian terrorist and antiabortion activist whose family hired Scarborough to represent him, presumably based more on his opposition to abortion than on his expertise in criminal law. The judge refused to let Scarborough continue on the case because of his inexperience. Even so, the jury deliberated only three hours before sentencing Griffin to life in prison. The shooting led to the passage of the Freedom of Access to Clinic Entrances bill, passed in 1994, which prohibits intimidation by protesters like Griffin, who waited just outside the clinic for his prey to appear.

Given Scarborough's history, the substance of his "Real Deal" segment tonight, a knockoff of the rival Bill O'Reilly show, is not surprising. Both hosts love to take on the so-called elites while presenting themselves as warriors for the working class. "It's the elites that sniff and snort at any hayseed or redneck who dares to question their take—and you just saw one of them—on Jesus, Janet Jackson or Terri Schiavo," he says, alluding to Dr. Cranford, who had the temerity to question Scarborough's grasp of the facts but hadn't weighed in on religion or the wardrobe malfunction that exposed Jackson's breast for a split second on national television. When it comes to connecting the dots, Scarborough is just warming up. "You know," he says, "the *New York Times* told us in a headline last week that starving to death was the most gentle way to die. The AP cited a study that showed, on a sliding scale from one to nine, experts believe that dying from a lack of food and water was, all in all, a very good death. That's fascinating, isn't it? Why did we waste all that time in the mid-'80s with Live Aid? Why did we worry about famine in Ethiopia and across Africa? I mean, forget Live Aid. Next time, we will have Elton John sing 'Funeral for a Friend' or 'Better Off Dead.' Once again, they twist the facts to suit their agenda. It's dead wrong."

WE'VE LONG STRUGGLED with issues around the right to die. Dr. Jack Kevorkian, whose name is synonymous with euthanasia, was jailed in 1999 for practicing his illegal and unorthodox beliefs. "Dying is not a crime," he said. Suffering from hepatitis and diabetes, ill and gaunt, he was granted parole after eight years largely because of his health. Kevorkian's lawyer told ABC News shortly before the parole decision was made public that the controversial doctor was expected to die within a year. Kevorkian said in an interview before his release that he should have pushed for legalization of euthanasia as opposed to blurring the line to the point that he could be prosecuted for murder.

The case that proved his undoing involved a fifty-two-year-old man in the late stages of Lou Gehrig's disease who wanted to be euthanized but was unable to administer the injection himself. Up until then, with the more than 130 patients he had helped die, Kevorkian was careful to have a device that they controlled to bring about their death so that he could not be charged with the final act. He made the device, a "Thanatron," or death machine, which delivered drugs through an IV. Later, after he lost his medical license and couldn't get the drugs, he made a "Mercitron," or mercy machine, which pumped carbon monoxide into a gas mask. With the man suffering from ALS, or Lou Gehrig's disease, Kevorkian bypassed the intermediary niceties, administered the lethal injection himself, and allowed a videotape of the process to air on *60 Minutes*. He knew what he was doing, that the district attorney would have to charge him with homicide.

It wasn't the first time Kevorkian had faced the long arm of the law. He had been tried many times in his home county in Michigan, and had always been acquitted. There was even a growing network of support that said, sure, he's quirky, maybe even crazy, but he's got a point that should be reflected and debated. All those courtroom wins must have emboldened Kevorkian, who insisted on representing himself and, being a novice at the law, fully incriminated himself by declaring that, regardless of criminal prosecution, he would continue to defy the law and assist people in dying. The case was pretty cut-and-dried; he had killed somebody who could not kill himself. Guilty of second-degree homicide, Kevorkian was given a sentence of ten to twenty-five years.

Well before his conviction, though the religious Right had not yet reached its full ascendancy (that would come with George W. Bush's presidency), Kevorkian and the right-to-die issues he raised threatened and alarmed pro-life activists. "We were the ones who went through his garbage," boasts Rev. Pat Mahoney, clearly proud of the role he and others at the Christian Defense Fund and Operation Rescue played in early 1993 gathering evidence against Kevorkian. Knowing he kept detailed notes of all the suicides he assisted, and that the Supreme Court had ruled, as Mahoney puts it, "once it's on the street it's fair game," Mahoney and his fellow activists staked out the home of a longtime Kevorkian associate and saw him bringing out bags of garbage, putting them in the garbage can. "We got the bags," says Mahoney, and they proved a treasure trove.

Kevorkian had his own kind of language, sparing nothing in his graphic description of the final moments of a life. One document recounted the last minutes of a seventy-year-old man suffering from emphysema and heart disease who was breathing carbon monoxide through a mask from the device Kevorkian had designed. About forty-five seconds in the man became agitated and wanted the mask removed, which it was. After about twenty minutes, according to the seized document, he calmed down and turned on the flow of gas. Again he became agitated, crying, "Take it off." He immediately fell unconscious, signaling his demise. Prosecutors noted that on Kevorkian's final action sheet, the phrase "Take it off" appeared twice but had been whited out in the second instance. A lawyer for Kevorkian said his client had mistakenly typed in the phrase twice, and was only trying to correct an error.

The case did not prove decisive but contributed to the growing body of evidence against Kevorkian. "From an activist point of view, it was one of the most enjoyable moments I ever had," says Mahoney, "sitting in a van, hiding below the steering wheel and we see the state prosecutor and the police raid Kevorkian's home—and that's when he got arrested, and what we found led to some of the eventual charges."

A bent and frail Kevorkian emerged from prison on June 1, 2007, not exactly a free man. He still had to report to a parole officer, and a condition of his release was that he cannot assist in any further suicides. On *The McLaughlin Group* that weekend, John notes that an overwhelming majority of Americans, according to an informal poll taken by a fellow talk show host, Larry King, after Kevorkian appeared on his show, support some form of assisted suicide, or death with dignity. Question: Will Kevorkian's ideas take hold? Pat Buchanan says no, calling Kevorkian "a ghoul," an assessment seconded by Tony Blankley. John is looking for a different answer, and he gets it from me—and from Martin Walker, a British reporter who says he and his wife just filled out living wills to ensure they are not kept alive by extraordinary means.

Kevorkian is not the preferred face of the right-to-die movement, but the issues he raises cannot be dismissed in an aging society with the technological means to extend life beyond where it is meaningful. John is openly sympathetic to Kevorkian, as is legendary broadcaster Mike Wallace, now retired at age ninety, whose letter to the editor dated June 8, 2007, appears in the following day's *New York Times.* Wallace had interviewed the man they call "Doctor Death" for *60 Minutes,* and writes that he felt compelled to answer a *Times* editorial that called Kevorkian "deluded and unrepentant." He describes the Kevorkian he knew as a man who is "thoughtful and compassionate ... who speaks Japanese, plays the flute, reads voraciously and is of academic bent."

It's hard to see how language skills and musical ability have any bearing on the case, but Wallace goes on to describe an incarceration that sounds like cruel and unusual punishment. Kevorkian, age seventy-nine at his release, was kept in waist and leg shackles whenever he was moved around. His weight dropped to 113 pounds. Wallace quotes from a letter Kevorkian wrote to Chief Justice William H. Rehnquist in September 2000: "Today, more than half of all American physicians and an overwhelming majority of the public favor the decriminalization of euthanasia, and a significant number of physicians admit to performing it furtively."

The hospice movement goes to great lengths to separate itself from the movement for physician-assisted suicide. The purpose of hospice is to ease the passage to death, not to euthanize. Nevertheless, they are linked in the sense that an aging society is increasingly mindful of issues related to mortality. A case testing Oregon's assisted suicide law reached the Supreme Court in the fall of 2005, and in January 2006, the Court ruled by a vote of six to three that physicians who help terminally ill patients to end their lives under the Oregon law cannot be prosecuted.

The decision put a roadblock in the Bush administration's quest to extend its views on the culture of life into state legislation. Former attorney general John Ashcroft, an evangelical Christian, had challenged Oregon's Death with Dignity law, first passed by the voters in 1994, saying doctors were trafficking in controlled substances for purposes that were not legitimate medically. The state had survived two earlier attempts by Congress to override the law, which Ashcroft supported as a U.S. senator from Missouri, a state with a vocal and influential right-to-life population. Voters in Oregon reaffirmed their wish to have the law in place in a 1997 referendum.

Heated rhetoric about the potential for abuse and how the law would push the poor, the less educated and the uninsured into premature death proved unfounded. In the first eight years the law was in effect, fewer than three hundred people used it, and college-educated Oregonians with health insurance were eight times more likely to be part of that population. The law has safeguards in that two doctors must certify the patient is likely to die within six months, competent, fully informed and acting voluntarily before lethal drugs can be prescribed. A cancer patient in Oregon interviewed by Diane Rehm explained that he might never use the prescription to hasten his death, but he wanted the peace of mind from knowing it was there should the pain become too much for him to bear.

13.

Being There

While the law has spoken, law that is not tempered by mercy can be cruel. ... This is a moral issue and it transcends politics and family disputes.

—Reverend Jesse Jackson

THE PRESENCE OF Rev. Jackson, first at the Florida hospice and then in Tallahassee, the state capital, where he stands in solidarity with Governor Bush, adds to the surrealistic panorama blaring away 24/7 on the cable news networks. Jackson is drawn to controversy, but the Schiavo situation seems a stretch from his normal civil-rights activities. Rev. Mahoney had contacted Jackson along with Rev. Sharpton, an even more inflammatory figure in much of white America, to demonstrate that the country is more diverse on this issue of when to end a life than people realize. Mary Schindler and her son, Bobby, desperate for any opening, asked Jackson to come to Florida. "And I said yes, because I wanted to go to offer some comfort to them," Jackson told Joe Scarborough in a television interview.

Jackson's position is quite reasonable. After fifteen years of this, meaning Schiavo's vegetative state, he says we need not challenge Michael Schiavo's integrity. On the other hand, the parents' passion is understandable. This woman is not brain-dead. She is brain-impaired. All her vital signs are working. And to cut off food and water is heartless. Still, Jackson says Congress getting involved and imposing its will on the judiciary was wrong. The proper role for Congress, he says, is a renewed commitment to long-term health care for all Americans.

With the family still hoping for a last-minute miracle in the form of legislative intervention, Jackson meets with the Florida state senate's black caucus. Their opposition to reinserting Terri's feeding tube helped seal the legislation's defeat last week in a vote of twenty-one to eighteen. All Jackson gets is a promise that one senator would consider legislation requiring Schiavo get food and water, but only if she could receive it orally, which at this point, even if such a law were passed, would be a meaningless exercise in terms of extending her life. She is too far along in the cycle of dying even if she could swallow on her own, which she can't do or she wouldn't have been on a feeding tube to begin with. Reports that Terri's lips are dry and cracked and bleeding lead the news, but I'm skeptical of their accuracy. It sounds to me more like propaganda put out by the Schindler camp. The hospice workers I've dealt with would never allow that, and I am frustrated that my side—the hospice side—isn't doing a better job educating the public. The decision to stand aside from the public debate in order to respect Terri Schiavo's privacy has the unintended consequence of perpetuating urban myths about death and dying.

TOM IS NO LONGER EATING or drinking, and swabs to soothe his lips are on the nightstand next to his hospital bed. Hospice caregiver Annie Barnes, a gentle, middle-aged African American woman, feeds Tom juice and water with a tablespoon. She calls him Mr. Tom. The copious notes that Daphne the nurse takes record Tom's decline, initially gradual with a plateau for four to six weeks, and now a more steep descent is taking hold. It's been almost a month since she wrote, "Patient appears visibly more wasted; his face/eyes are sunken noticeably more in the last 1–2 weeks."

Tom has always had a Lincolnesque look, with his long, sharp nose, deep-set eyes and aura of melancholy, even when he was well. Whenever the Gridiron wanted to portray Lincoln or, more recently, the Democrats' 2004 presidential candidate, John Kerry, another Lincoln look-alike, the role fell to Tom.

The alertness in his deep-set hazel-colored eyes has dulled, which I interpret as unhappiness, but it may not be. People withdraw from the world at the end of life, and Tom is no longer with me in any active sense of the word. He made peace with his fate at the start of this process, but these past few weeks, he looks so sad that I feel haunted by his look. My son Eddie turned the hospital bed so Tom could look out the front picture window, thinking that might help. Brenda turns it back around. She feels it makes him too aware of what he's leaving behind, and heightens the melancholy.

I have often said throughout this process that if Tom were complaining or depressed, I couldn't stand it, that his accepting nature makes it easier for me. When the antidepressant prescribed by Dr. Hersh, the therapist he'd been seeing, ran out some weeks ago, the hospice nurse suggested we just drop it. Tom's taking so many pills, and she's dubious that, at this end stage of life, a baby-boomer designer drug can make a difference. But I believe otherwise, and I renew the prescription for Prozac, plus we add at the suggestion of Laura Wood, Tom's oncology nurse at the Cleveland Clinic, a prescription for Ritalin, which acts as a feel-good pill in adults. When it gets too hard for Tom to swallow the pills, I mash the antidepressants into his applesauce. I know it's what Tom would have wanted. "Yes, please, give me everything you've got" was his motto. He liked to quote the DuPont advertising slogan popularized during the sixties, "Better living through chemistry."

I vowed to myself early in the process that I wouldn't be a gatekeeper—refusing access to Tom because I was hiding his condition, or I was embarrassed for him. This is the human condition and there is nothing to be ashamed of. But I resent it when a friend asks pointedly whether he is still able to get to the bathroom. Somehow being able to care for one's own bodily functions is a demarcation in many people's minds between a life worth living and the retreat toward infancy that accompanies the end of life. Brenda the nurse is often there when friends stop by and reminisce about Tom's journalistic career, his basketball days and his intellectual and athletic prowess. She tells me she wouldn't let his professional colleagues see him like this. Daphne, a generation younger, brushes aside those concerns, saying that as long as people understand what to expect, that there won't be long meaning-of-life conversations like there are in the movies, then being there should be enough. Tom has been lying in that bed for more than two months, and the moments that stick in my mind have to do with friends and family, and how everybody rallied. When my older brother Ed arrived, the first of the reinforcements, he hadn't been to Washington to see me in years. He didn't know what kind of car I drive, and when I picked him up at Union Station, we were both astounded to discover we own the same low-end car, a Geo Prism. When he sees that I too have a stick shift, I go up greatly in my engineer brother's estimation. It must be in the genes.

There were calls from the Ohio politicians that Tom covered, John Glenn, the astronaut and former senator; Howard Metzenbaum, who for years had been the liberal backbone of the Senate; and Dennis Kucinich, once the boy mayor of Cleveland and now a member of Congress who ran for president in 2004 on a peace platform. When Dennis called and I handed Tom the phone and told him who it was, he said, "I know … the Almost President." Tom had followed the ups and downs of Kucinich's career and was both admiring and appropriately skeptical of the gadfly role he played on the political stage. Kucinich recalled that after he finally won election to the House after a couple of tries, Tom asked, "Now what?"

Kucinich is among other things a vegan, and he did inspire Tom to adopt for a period of time a macrobiotic diet in an attempt to stall the cancer. We spent a week at the Kushi Institute in western Massachusetts gaining a new appreciation of brown rice and Asian meditation while learning to prepare and eat a wide array of vegetables, some of which we'd never heard of before. We left armed with a new pressure cooker for rice and a host of recommended lifestyle changes. Eating right wouldn't hurt even if it didn't cure cancer, and the months Tom spent cooking and eating rice coincided with stability in his illness. But neither of us was under any illusion that we had found the answer, and the boredom of the diet made it hard to follow for any great length of time. I suppose every cancer patient has tried some side route away from traditional medicine.

Tom was never a believer in vitamins and health-food formulas, but cancer has a way of making people gullible. Around the time he was tiring of the macrobiotic diet, he heard from a fellow he'd gone to college with, Herb Scheidel, who had gotten an almost identical diagnosis of metastatic kidney cancer. They didn't know each other in college, but Herb had read Tom's columns about battling kidney cancer and wanted him to know how he had overhauled his entire lifestyle to adopt a holistic regimen of wellness that he credited with keeping his disease at bay for several years. He had discovered a doctor in Hawaii who practiced kinesiology, or muscle testing, to monitor cancer patients. Dr. John, or Dr. J as Herb referred to him, prescribed a diet heavy on vitamins and supplements along with fresh fruits designed to rid the body of food allergies and fungal infections and free the immune system to fight the cancer. Herb was such a believer that he and his wife had rented a beachfront home at an exorbitant sum on the island of Kauai to be near Dr. J. What did he have to lose? Tom said as we packed our bags for Hawaii to stay with Herb and his wife and visit Dr. J. Then came our Google moment: we found Dr. John on a Web site called GreedydoctorsofHawaii.com.

We went ahead with the visit, but our skepticism got the best of us when we met with Dr. John in what used to be a photo hut in a shopping center. He allowed us to sit in on his examination of Herb, which included asking him whether he needed more or less of a particular vitamin, and then relying on how high his arm raised for the answer. Tom had fun fantasizing about moving to Hawaii for six months to regain his health, but he was never serious about it and worried that the column he wrote denigrating Dr. J would ruin his friendship with Herb. A messy personal life caught up with Dr. J, but Herb remains a believer in the power of holistic healing. More important, eight years after getting a diagnosis of Stage 4 kidney cancer, he was still alive.

Tom's breathing is so labored that I remark to Brenda it's like he's running a race and trying to cross the finish line. As soon as I say it, I realize, of course, that's exactly what he is doing. He is actively dying, and it is not a passive exercise, a slipping away. He is working at it. Before I go upstairs to the bed we once shared, I give Tom morphine under the tongue to ease his breathing, as Daphne instructed. His face is turned toward me as he lies on his side working so hard to draw each breath. He looks anguished, his features contorted from the effort. His legs are scrunched up almost in the fetal position with white foam blocks placed between the limbs to keep them from chafing. When I place the dropper with the morphine between his lips, he takes it in as eagerly as he once did a gulp of water in the midst of a race.

When Tom learned that Marjorie Williams, a *Washington Post* columnist, had died of cancer at the age of forty-seven, he said, "People dying in our profession make me realize what a minor talent I was." Williams was a versatile and edgy writer and the tributes to her were deserved, but Tom too had earned his place in the Washington culture. I told him I saw Norm Ornstein in the greenroom at Fox and in the course of commiserating with me over Tom's illness, he said, "Tom is a beloved figure in the journalism community because he's such a decent fellow." Ornstein is one of the most quoted people in Washington. A resident scholar with the American Enterprise Institute, he's a recognized expert on Congress, the White House and just about anything anybody asks him about. "Did you write it down?" Tom asked. A journalist until the end, he was thinking about how he would be remembered, and didn't want to lose any of those special touches that make a piece of copy, or a life, come alive. I did write it down.

I would learn later that Williams was seeing the same therapist as Tom, Dr. Stephen Hersh, who specializes in treating people facing terminal illness. He told me that he showed her Tom's columns in an effort to inspire her to write about how awful she felt, and the emotional pain of leaving her two young children. "She was so diminished by her cancer and her pain that I'm not sure that without the inspiration that occurred in this office with Tom's help that she would have actually followed through on the writing," Hersh said. Tom had no idea that he was in any way responsible for the wrenching narrative Williams wrote about the course of her illness and how she came to terms with saying good-bye to her children.

When the social worker dispatched by hospice asked Tom what he was looking for in an occasional visitor, he replied, "Someone high on intellectual ability and low on egg-flipping skills." Hospice matches volunteers with the needs a patient expresses, and Tom wanted someone he could converse with. John Rehm, a friend given to examining existential questions with regularity and rigor, was now a hospice volunteer and a perfect match for Tom. The rapid decline toward the end of Tom's illness cut their time short, but early in the process John said he was struck by the smile on Tom's face. "It's the most peaceful sleep I've ever seen, a light sleep," he says. "I'm envious. He's made his peace with this." I tell John I couldn't stand it if Tom were depressed or self-pitying, or wondering, "Why me?" He says what I already know to be true: "I've never seen the slightest sense of self-pity."

A friend we've only recently come to know e-mails Tom: "I don't know your religious tradition nor your relation to it, and the older I get the more confused I am about the so-called 'big' questions of God, death and immortality. (It's not just that I don't know the answers—I'm not even sure I understand the questions!) But I am confident of this: in the case of a life lived so well as yours, a life of honesty and courage and compassion and love, death might be the last event of your life's trajectory, but it certainly won't be the last word on its meaning."

It still amazes me that I have been entrusted with the care of another human being at this transformational moment, but that is the core of hospice, that the end of life occurs in the context of the life that was lived. The hospice movement—and advocates do think of it as a movement—is struggling to overcome the perception that entering hospice means you have given up. Getting the medical profession to see hospice as a form of care that is appropriate for patients other than the terminally ill is the next horizon for the movement. There are already efforts under way to eliminate the six months or less life expectancy that is currently the admission ticket to hospice.

Art Buchwald, the Pulitzer Prize–winning humorist, did so well in hospice that he got better and they asked him to leave. He wrote a book, *Too Soon to Say Goodbye*, in the extra year of life he got. A study published in the March 2007 issue of the *Journal of Pain and Symptom Management* found that patients who chose hospice care at the end of life lived an average of one month longer than those who didn't, a statistic that helps combat another popular perception that hospice speeds death through the use or overuse of painkillers.

I visited Buchwald several times in the Washington Home hospice, where he had gone to die after he had surgery to amputate part of his leg and had decided to discontinue dialysis, a life-saving regimen, because of his failing kidneys. To his surprise, death didn't come. The first column he wrote from the hospice was titled "The Man Who Wouldn't Die." Further columns followed about "having a high time where you'd least expect it," "pulling the plug," in which he says a good surrogate is hard to find, and of course religion. In a column titled "The End. Or Maybe Not," Art ruminated on the hereafter. It comes up all the time, he says, people asking if he believes in God. "I believe in God, but not the one they're pushing—not any of the ones they're selling," he tells me. "All the problems in the world are caused by religion—underline *all*," he instructs me, as I write down his words, "all of them." I have him autograph his column about religion and his beliefs about an afterlife for me. It ends with the statement, "We don't know where we're going, and we don't know why we were here in the first place."

"Was it depressing?" a friend asks after one of my visits with Art.

"No, not at all," I say, telling her the mood was like a Paris salon with Art holding court each afternoon in a large sunny dayroom with a big-screen television and a stream of visitors out of *Who's Who in Washington*. Among them is the commandant of the Marine Corps. Art was in the Marines. "This is *big stuff*," he confides. "I didn't do anything fantastic, but as time goes by it looks better and better."

During one visit, Art chows down a roast beef sandwich on rye from Mel Krupin's brought by his son, Joel. There are all sorts of gifts and, with Easter approaching, three stuffed rabbits—the largest, from Ethel Kennedy, plays "Tara's Song." A smaller one sings a hippety-hop (not hip-hop) song. "Take that rabbit—I hate it," says Art. Joel stuffs it into a bag to take to his two young children.

Art is reclining in a lounge chair with his leg stump propped up on a pillow. Three women gather around him to pose for a picture. "I feel like Cary Grant," he says. They trade stories about Art, how he was the ringmaster for the annual pet show at the Kennedy home at Hickory Hill. It was raining cats and dogs on that day in 1978 but when he called that morning and announced, "D-day, Eisenhower speaking," they knew the show would go on. Looking around at the outpouring of support and pondering his own improved state of health, Art quips, "Dying is easy; parking is hard." It would become one of his signature lines.

On one of my Saturday visits, the hospice chaplain pulls me aside to say that she's worried that Mr. Buchwald isn't taking his situation seriously, that he jokes all the time, and isn't using his last days to reconcile whatever outstanding issues he might have with family members and with his own beliefs. She says he wonders why he hasn't died yet, and she suggests it's because he hasn't confronted the deeper issues, and he's not letting himself go.

She marvels at how upbeat he is. When I tell her he has a history of depression, and had been diagnosed with bipolar disorder, she is amazed. He's not at all depressed, she says. What's his secret? My observation is that he's dying the same way he lived, drawing comfort from the applause and appreciation of others, and expressing his hopes and fears in conversational humor. He did meet with a rabbi and consented to be buried and to have a religious service, which for him was a big move. He identifies with Jews culturally and was raised in a Hebrew orphanage during the Depression when his mother suffered mental illness and his father couldn't care for him and his two sisters, but he is nonpracticing when it comes to religion. He likes to joke that he's "covering all the bases," since he's met with the rabbi and talks to the hospice chaplain, a Protestant, whom he invites to bring a priest if she'd like, which she does. "Turns out he was a reader of mine," Art tells me. "He liked my Nixon stuff. He was *for* Nixon—and we had a nice conversation. I think she thought he would say, 'Let's pray,' or some bullshit."

Buchwald is doing it his way. Death is hard enough. Why does he have to make it more serious than it is?

After an aneurysm in his leg forced amputation of the leg below the knee, Buchwald also found himself facing dialysis. His kidneys had been failing for the past year, but coping with two major medical problems was more than he wanted to do at age eighty. His son, Joel, persuaded him to at least begin the dialysis and wait until he was done with the surgery and in rehab, and in better spirits, before making a definitive decision. He did four or five sessions and was more convinced than ever that it wasn't for him. His doctor was treating him with an experimental drug.

"We're going to make history with this," the doctor told him.

"I didn't want to make history that way," Art told me, recounting the story of an uncle who did an experimental cancer therapy and "died a horrible death."

When he moved from the rehab facility to hospice, he rebounded to such an extent that Medicare declared him "better" and stopped paying the bills. He paid the freight himself, the equivalent he says of a suite at the Four Seasons. Ironically, if he chose to resume dialysis, Medicare would pick up the charges, and that would be considerably more expensive than hospice. But dialysis three times a week for five hours at a stretch struck Art like a prison sentence. "And you either take the prison sentence or you take the other way out. And here's the funny thing about it all. If I'd taken the dialysis, nobody would care, nobody would know. This way everybody tells you how wonderful you are. There's a lot of payback from people who ordinarily wouldn't even get into your life. Depending on how you feel about things, and I feel pretty good, say all the nice things you want about me—say it all."

Fittingly, the hospice movement started in the 1940s as a love story when Cicely Saunders, a medical social worker at a hospital in London, fell in love with a young Polish man who had escaped from the Warsaw ghetto and was dying of cancer. He spoke little English but they managed to communicate, and with death looming, that's what they talked about, death and dying. When he died, he left her what money he had, which was five hundred pounds. He had told her, "I'll be a window in your home." Inspired by the experience and feeling that she was called by God to serve the dying, Saunders became a physician and two decades later, in 1967, founded St. Christopher's Hospice, named after the patron saint of travelers, in a leafy neighborhood in south London. It was a dramatic departure for its time in end-of-life care. The facility featured a hair salon and activities like creative writing, indoor gardening and various discussion groups, reflecting Saunders's belief that people should keep living instead of just waiting to die.

Hospice is derived from the Latin word *hospes*, which means a receiver of guests. In medieval times, hospices were way stations for travelers on their way to the holy lands. Saunders's strong Christian beliefs infused her hospice work, but she welcomed patients of other persuasions or those with no faith. She saw how a strong faith helped people at the end of life, but she also noticed that atheists often died as peacefully as Christians. The people with the most fitful exits were those who hadn't reconciled what they believed. Clergymen, surprisingly, fell into this category, along with the affluent. Perhaps the former spent too much time questioning, and the latter too little. In any event, it was Saunders's role to observe, not to judge. Relief of pain was of course central to her philosophy, and she was instrumental in getting the Church of England to recognize in a 1976 report on dying that everyone should have the right to "die well," without pain and with dignity. This was quite a breakthrough considering the resistance and even outright hostility that Saunders encountered from the medical establishment.

Saunders had been writing articles in medical journals about her radical ideas since the late 1950s. In 1963 she was invited to give a talk on hospice care at Yale Medical School. Since so much of hospice care falls to nurses, Yale's dean of nursing, Florence Wald, asked Saunders to repeat her talk for the nursing students and faculty. Listening to this British woman articulate what to Wald was the epitome of nursing—relieving pain, tending to a patient's emotional and spiritual needs, offering support to the family as well as the patient—so inspired Wald that she eventually stepped down as dean and devoted herself to helping found the first hospice in America. Connecticut Hospice treated its first patients in 1974. In an interview broadcast on public radio, she said, "What I have found is that people can die in good health," meaning with a sense of fulfillment, of a life that's come to terms with where it's been, and where it ends.

Another key figure in the evolution of hospice in America was Elisabeth Kubler-Ross, a diminutive woman in Birkenstocks and horned-rim glasses who launched the death-with-dignity movement in the 1970s. Born in Switzerland and trained in medical school there, she came to the United States in 1958 and worked as a psychiatrist in a New York hospital. She saw dying patients shunned when doctors could do no more, and she saw these same doctors conceal the truth from the terminally ill about their true condition. It was common practice then for doctors and families to withhold information, leaving too much unsaid and unresolved at the end of life. Kubler-Ross conceptualized the five stages of grief that people experience upon learning they have a terminal illness: denial, anger, bargaining, depression, and acceptance. Her book, published in 1969, *On Death and Dying*, offered the first practical guide on what to expect. The Hospice of the Florida Suncoast, which cared for Terri Schiavo, was originally the Elisabeth Kubler-Ross Hospice, founded in 1977 with fifty volunteers. Mary Labyak, president and CEO, spent a week when she was in graduate school training with Kubler-Ross, and says what she remembers most is the admonition to listen, that "dying people are our teachers, not vice versa."

When Kubler-Ross died in 2004, she was a New Age spiritualist looking forward to dancing among the galaxies. Saunders, who died in 2005, was a devout Christian. Wald, who is in her eighties, is an agnostic Jew. Despite their varied religious orientations, they shared the belief that addressing spiritual needs should be part of end-of-life care. Their vision became law when for the first time spiritual care was written into U.S. health policy as part of the Medicare hospice benefit passed by Congress in 1982. Acknowledging and treating emotional, psychological and spiritual pain along with physical pain is what sets hospice care apart in a medical world increasingly reliant on technology.

Establishing hospice care as a service covered by Medicare was a boon to older Americans and provided a stream of income to let the movement grow. Yet hospice is still misunderstood and underused. Doctors are reluctant to refer patients because it's seen as giving up, with the result that two-thirds of Americans die in a hospital, which is not what most people say they want.

Oregon senator Ron Wyden is sponsoring legislation to broaden the hospice benefit so people who enter hospice won't have to stop all curative care. Some hospice programs and health insurers have begun what they call "open access," where patients can continue potentially life-prolonging treatment like chemotherapy and dialysis while getting the benefit of the additional care at home that hospice provides. With the baby boomers poised to enter the Medicare years, the rules are bound to become more consumer friendly. "You think old people are a pain in the neck now, wait 'til the Baby Boomers come along," says Leon Panetta, President Clinton's former chief of staff and a former member of Congress from California. He was one of four lawmakers honored by the National Hospice and Palliative Care Organization for their leadership in passing the 1982 Medicare hospice benefit.

TOM WASN'T OLD ENOUGH to qualify for Medicare reimbursement, and we had to do some juggling with our private insurance, switching from his employer plan, which had an extremely limited hospice benefit, to my employer plan, which was more generous. If "open access" had been available and Tom could have continued those twice-weekly chemo infusions at the doctor's office, he probably would have. To be honest, it was a relief to be told there was no more chemotherapy, and to use these months to be at home and accept the inevitable.

14.

Saying Good-bye

If there's nothing more doctors can offer, you'll have to ask your-self, "How do I live as well as I can for as long as I can?"
—Tom Brazaitis quoting Dr. Stephen Hersh,
a Washington psychiatrist who specializes
in patients with terminal disease

THE SUN COMES IN my bedroom window well before six in the morning. We'll soon move the clocks forward an hour, but until then I'm getting up with the first rays of light. I come downstairs this morning and notice that Tom is very still. The bag that collects urine has not changed much since the night before. I push the thought away that he could have died. I don't want to face it, at least not yet. I am reassured when I see the sheet move slowly up and down. He must be breathing.

I partially shut the French doors leading into the living room like I have so many mornings, not wanting to disturb Tom and selfishly wanting to get my day started before I turn it over to his care. I go to the basement and ride ten miles on the stationary bike Tom had gotten me for my birthday, eat cereal for breakfast, feed the cats, feed the birds and the squirrels, and buzz up to Starbucks for an iced decaffeinated coffee, my normal morning routine. (In my telling and retelling of this momentous morning, a friend will gently advise, "Eleanor, leave out the part about Starbucks.") It has been my habit these last months to fortify myself with life's little pleasures before Tom is awake and the hospice caregiver arrives. I leave the door unlocked and a note on the stairs saying I'll be back in fifteen minutes, together with my cell phone number. I don't want anybody thinking I am slacking off. It's funny that I worry how others will judge me when I'm my harshest critic.

I am at the computer when the phone rings with a new health aide, Jordan Hammond, who is assigned to us that morning. He's waiting outside and wondering if he should come in. I race down the stairs and greet him at the door and, to my surprise, blurt out, "He's not doing too well. I think he might be dead." The words tumble out, words I didn't intend to say, words that give voice to a thought that I have pushed from my mind all morning. How could he be dead? Hospice just delivered a new supply of drugs, including the giant bottle of Robitussin that in my mind had come to represent weeks more of life.

With me hovering a few feet away, Jordan takes but a moment to render his verdict. "Yes, indeed he is. He's already cold."

The climactic event I have been preparing for these many months, if not years, has happened. How do I feel? Like somebody punched me in the gut. It's hard to breathe. I'm shivering but it's not from the cold—it isn't cold. It's from the shock. I'm aware that I'm crying, but at the same time my mind is racing. I should have sat with him the night before. I didn't realize he was that close to death. In retrospect, I should have known, but it's pointless to beat myself up over what I didn't do. Tom was no longer aware of his surroundings; he was in another place within himself. And we had said our good-byes. What had kept me sane was getting my rest and going to bed at a decent hour so that whatever I found the next morning I could deal with. To be honest, I'd come down the stairs every morning half expecting to find him dead.

Jordan says he'll clean him up, that Tom has had a bowel movement, which is normal at the moment of death. He gently straightens Tom's legs and closes his eyes and tells me, "He didn't have any stress on his face." Maybe they say that to everybody, but I'll take it. Then he calls the hospice to report, "Mr. Brazaitis has expired."

Daphne calls and says she'll be right over. She pro-nounces Tom dead at 10:40 A.M. I tell her that I knew he was dead much earlier and ask if she can estimate the time of death. "Eleanor, it doesn't matter," she says. Still, it is a weight on me that I feel a need to justify. I tell her how that morning I could see the sheet moving, and as I look down on my dead husband, I can still see the sheet moving. It is the air mattress generating the movement. Daphne asks if I want her to double-check that he has indeed passed away. No, I say. He is gone. He needed to die. She calls the fu-neral home.

Now comes the time I am grateful that Tom had already made arrangements to dispose of his body. Daphne asks if I want an immediate pickup or if I want some additional time with Tom. I choose the extra time, and the white van doesn't arrive until four o'clock in the afternoon. It is a scene straight out of *Six Feet Under.*

As I field phone calls and deal with letting people know, Tom lies peacefully in the living room. A friend, Bob Baggstrom, who had helped care for Tom these last months, arrives. He stands respectfully by the bedside for several minutes. A military man and a practicing Catholic, he tells me that he had performed last rites on Tom some time ago.

The medical supply house that delivered the hospital bed calls about picking up the bed while Tom is still in it. Comedy accompanies tragedy in death as in life.

I start to talk to him as I move around the house. "Tom, where did I put my Diet Coke?" It is a question I often posed and it had become a running joke between us. He looks so much like he has these last weeks that I keep expecting him to move, but he's frozen still. I don't want him covered with the sheet yet, consigned to anonymity. I am not the least bit bothered that I have a dead body in my living room. This is Tom, and it doesn't feel all that different from the months of illness as he lay in that bed.

When the undertaker arrives, he brings a stretcher and a caramel-colored plastic body bag. He enlists our friend Bob to help lift Tom from the hospital bed onto the gurney and into the body bag. Tom is tall and his head cracks against the metal at one end of the gurney. The undertaker doesn't change expression, but I know that isn't something he wanted to happen. He begins to zip the bag closed and asks if I want to close the part over Tom's face. I say yes. I lean over and kiss Tom for the last time, and then pull the zipper shut. His lips don't feel all that different—a little cool, but not unlike the winter nights when we turned the heat down in the house and crawled under the blankets. Our long fight has come to an end.

A WASHINGTON POST STORY about "death returning home" features families opting to care for and keep a dead loved one in the house for a longer period of time to get accustomed to the fact that the person is no longer there. A psychiatrist is quoted saying that he has treated countless people who never get over a death, and he wonders if being closer to the process can help people. I could see that Tom wasn't there anymore. He looked stiff and frozen, like a death mask of his mother who had died a year earlier at age eighty-seven.

I stand with a neighbor as the two men carry the gurney out to the van. I say that I wish this could be done under the cover of night. I hate the idea of everybody watching. This is a private moment, a private death. But then I say immediately after, Why should I care? Death is natural. There is nothing to be ashamed of. What am I hiding? The undertaker smiles at my concern and says even when he makes a pickup in the middle of the night, there's always somebody who's watching.

Daphne goes through the house to retrieve all the unused medicine. She knows where I kept everything, and she is thorough in retrieving it all. She comes downstairs with an armload of stuff she found on a shelf in the linen closet and says sternly, "I'm going to have to hold you responsible for Mr. Brazaitis's constipation. Look at all this stuff that you didn't use. We could have a bowel-movement party." Laughter and tears, reality and absurdity, is how death touches us.

People are squeamish talking about bowel movements, and I debate with myself whether I should reveal these details. Monitoring bodily functions is a major preoccupation for people on pain medicine, and I conclude I wouldn't be honest if I leave out this aspect. Morphine is great but it's very constipating. Myra Christopher with the Center for Practical Bioethics in Kansas City developed a recipe to combat constipation while caring for her dying mother. Get a melon ball scoop, fill it with petroleum jelly, freeze the scoops and then roll them in sugar. It greases the digestive tract. For an added touch, she colored the sugar pink.

Daphne flushes all the morphine she finds down the toilet. She misses one small vial, which remains in a corner of my linen closet. If I were to get a diagnosis like Tom's, I don't know if I could muster his fortitude and determination. He taught me a great deal, and part of the peace as I go forward in my life is knowing what happens when life ends, and how to prepare for it, and to say all I want to say in the time I have. People who do this well, dying, that is, are not necessarily extraordinary individuals. They are ordinary individuals hit with extraordinary circumstances, and they meet the challenge.

In the tribute I will write for Tom, I say he was a man who had trouble handling a sinus infection, yet when faced with Stage 4 cancer, he exhibited such grace and courage, it was probably as amazing to him as it was to me. The fact that Tom had a platform and that he used it the way he did, to help himself and other people, improved his quality of life and may have extended the time he had.

When he was feeling crummy and I was trying to jolly him into eating or watching some television show, he would say to me, "I wish you could feel how I feel for one day." He had his down times. There were days when he didn't get out of bed, and I would come home to a darkened house and a mood of heavy gloom that sometimes didn't lift until he faced a deadline for his column. I thanked the Gods of Journalism, but I can't sugarcoat this.

He had one of the more awful treatments for a person who uses his mind a lot—so in that context he really did brilliantly, and who knows whether it was his spirit, his energy, his intensity, or what it was that kept him going.

THIS IS TERRI SCHIAVO's thirteenth day without a feeding tube. David Gibbs, the Schindler family lawyer, is on *Larry King Live* holding out one last hope that the U.S. Supreme Court will step in and order a complete review of the case. His hope is misplaced. The Court refuses the case. There are no constitutional issues involved. Ever since the landmark *Cruzan* decision more than a decade ago, the courts have come down on the side of carrying out the wishes of the patient. Michael Schiavo had prevailed in repeated court challenges. Given the unshakable legal terrain, there is an air of unreality to the Schindler family's insistence that Terri be kept alive. Protesters at the hospice tell reporters that God will intervene somehow, and if Terri dies she will be a symbol for others to rally around. Gibbs will later say to me in an interview, "Let's just pretend—I'm not saying this will happen—but what if they come up with a drug that you can shoot into the brain that can dramatically enhance memory. Terri will never get the benefit of that."

King turned to the Schiavo story after a long opening segment honoring Johnnie Cochran, the flamboyant lead lawyer in the O. J. Simpson trial, who died yesterday from a brain tumor. A friend would send me a condolence card noting what fascinating company Tom would have in the hereafter with Cochran there to join him.

As media spectaculars go, the Schiavo case and the Simpson trial grandly and even grotesquely exposed the divisions in society. It was race and class in the Simpson trial; religion, abortion and the judiciary in the Schiavo case. Musing on the Schindlers and what the protest he helped lead had become, the Reverend Pat Mahoney reminds critics, "You know there are no classes for being a national celebrity. They're retired, they're living in Clearwater, he's a blue-collar guy from Philadelphia—and suddenly you're supposed to be an expert when people stick a microphone in your face. If they had said, don't come down, it's too exploitative, no one would have come down. Why did we turn it into this carnival-like atmosphere? I suppose it depends which side of the fence you're on. We were doing all that we could reasonably do to intervene peacefully to save her life. I have no control over satellite trucks and all that."

Another man of the cloth, the Reverend Hugh Westbrook, a United Methodist minister who is the retired chairman and chief executive officer of a chain of hospices he cofounded, says he cannot remember another time when a religious group pushed a government and its politicians over the edge this far with the exception of burning witches in Salem. "I'm still astounded they had the ability to pull off such an intervention," he tells me two years after the fact.

Westbrook talks about how dismayed he was at the beating the image of hospice took. Administrators stayed silent rather than risk overstepping their role as facilitators to carry out a family's wishes. "They got more advice on what *not* to say from lawyers. They were scared to death."

Westbrook traces his interest in caring for terminally ill people to the cancer wards he worked in as a divinity student in the late 1960s. Nothing more medically could be done for these patients and they had been left to die. Westbrook was active in the civil-rights and antiwar movements, and the pastoral counseling he was able to do with people at the end of their lives tapped into the deep emotional roots he had in the social activism of the era. When the bishop assigned him to Miami in 1973, he served a church but he also worked as a pastor in a hospital and nursing home. His career took an unintended turn a few years later when Anita Bryant came to Miami. She would plant the seeds for what would later become known as the religious Right.

A popular singer at the time, she was also the spokeswoman for the Florida Citrus Commission. A national advertising campaign featured her singing, "Come to the Florida sunshine tree," and she popularized the tagline "Breakfast without orange juice is like a day without sunshine." She came to Miami to lead a campaign against gay rights after Florida's Dade County passed an ordinance in 1977 prohibiting discrimination based on sexual orientation. Bryant was a Southern Baptist and had grown up in a strict religious household. Although her talent was obvious at an early age, her father had to be persuaded it would be a sin if he didn't allow his daughter to share the musical gifts she'd gotten from God. Bryant had three major hits: "Till

There Was You," "Paper Roses," and "In My Little Corner of the World." When President Lyndon Johnson died, she sang "The Battle Hymn of the Republic" at his graveside service.

Anita Bryant was a cultural icon, and when she stepped forward to lead what she called a crusade to overturn the Miami ordinance, the nation took notice. She called it Save Our Children, and it was the first organized opposition to gay rights. Jerry Falwell, who would soon found the Moral Majority to oppose abortion and gay rights, came to Florida to help Bryant. But she was the lead activist, and her inflammatory rhetoric, most of it wildly without foundation, guaranteed headlines. Among her assertions: "As a mother, I know that homosexuals cannot biologically reproduce children; therefore, they must recruit our children. ... If gays are granted rights, next we'll have to give rights to prostitutes and to people who sleep with St. Bernards and to nail biters." Bryant's hysteria caught on and the voters repealed the antidiscrimination ordinance by a margin of 69 to 31 percent. More than twenty years passed before it was put back into place, a legacy that Bryant can claim along with legislation she championed banning adoption by gays and lesbians that is still the law in Florida.

Observing Bryant's crusade from his religious perspective, Westbrook was offended. He didn't agree with her about gay people, and his Methodist church had a more tolerant view, more tolerant in some ways than today. He took action, organizing clergy and laity groups to oppose Bryant. It was not a popular move within the religious community, and he discovered that as one of the few straight ministers willing to take a public stand against Bryant, he got a lot of publicity. The result was that his bishop tried to move him out of his ministry on the grounds that he was a trouble-maker. He refused to go; his position at the church he was serving was really only a part-time job because the congregation had diminished in size. He managed to put together three other part-time jobs, an urban ministry, a campus ministry and a teaching gig at the local community college. The bishop backed off. "He thought I'd slink away anyway," says Westbrook.

Instead, Westbrook had found his calling. He and an oncology nurse at the college, Esther Colliflower, devised a curriculum on death and dying for nontraditional students called "Life Lab." They taught together for a year or so and decided to start a program to take care of terminally ill people by keeping them at home. This was 1975–1976. Their first patient was the wife of a professor at the University of Miami. Her oncologist regarded her as a "noncompliant patient" because she refused to go to the hospital for her cancer treatment. She'd had several rounds of chemotherapy and radiation and didn't want to become a perpetual hospital patient. Her doctor didn't do house calls, so he recommended his recalcitrant patient to Westbrook and Colliflower, who'd been agitating for the chance to test their theories and care for a dying patient at home. "He thought we deserved each other," laughs Westbrook. The woman turned out to be as much of a teacher as she was a patient. "She told us, 'I know you don't know what you're doing, but if you help me stay home, I'll teach you how to do it.' She was very clear how she wanted to die. She wanted to control her care and die at home in her own bed."

From six volunteers in the mid-1970s, Westbrook and Colliflower built one of the largest hospices in the country. The Miami facility they founded treats ten thousand patients a day and is the flagship for one of the fastest-growing hospice chains in the country, VITAS Healthcare Corporation. The National Hospice and Palliative Care Organization honored the duo at a Washington dinner in the spring of 2007 for their role in lobbying Congress twenty-five years earlier to cover hospice care under Medicare.

Westbrook took some heat for transforming his nonprofit hospice into a profit-making operation, and the business of hospice has made him a rich man. In 2004, in a highly lucrative merger, VITAS became part of Roto-Rooter, better known for plumbing and drain cleaning than end-of-life care. Hospice started out as a messianic endeavor to take death back from the sterile hospital wards and profit-making institutions, and the idea of making money from people dying made many hospice pioneers uneasy. But that bridge has been long crossed. Hospice is not cheap; it's cheap only in comparison to intensive care. And it's built on a trajectory of life where a person is pretty healthy up until a few months before death. It's ideal for cancer patients like Tom, but for people suffering through a longer decline, once hospice gets them stable, they can be kicked out. People like Art Buchwald are referred to as hospice failures, says Westbrook, chuckling at the irony. The health care system has yet to grapple with the looming prospect of millions of frail, elderly baby boomers who are not sick enough to die so they can enter hospice but need the kind of holistic support hospice provides.

Westbrook has thrived in the decades since his outspo-
kenness on gay rights shifted him into a new career path.
The same can't be said of the once popular singer whose
career and income declined because of the controversy. A
boycott of orange juice organized by gay activists and supported by a host of Hollywood celebrities took its toll, and
the Florida Citrus Commission didn't renew Bryant's con-
tract. Her marriage ended, and along with it the invitations
to sing at religious events that had been her mainstay. Still,
she was at the forefront of a movement that would config-
ure America's politics in ways that the founding fathers
would find unimaginable in a country where religion and
politics are supposed to be separate.

From his vantage point as an industry leader, Westbrook
cringed when he saw the news coverage of Jesse Jackson's
visit to Terri's hospice. He worried about the ramifications
for hospice in the African American community, where
there is a great deal of distrust. He determined that once
the controversy subsided, he would seek an audience with
Jackson. The two met some months later, and Westbrook
says that Jackson, without directly admitting it, indicated he
wasn't fully aware of what he was stepping into and the potential negative fallout for hospice in underserved black
communities.

When Westbrook met with Jackson, there were nineteen
hospice programs in the Chicago area, all ringing the city.
There were none in the South Side of Chicago, home to
much of the city's minority population. Westbrook was accustomed to promoting hospice as a move away from aggressive care at the end of life, an argument that resonates
among affluent white Americans. It falls flat in poor black

communities where the problem is not too much care, but not enough medical intervention at any stage of life. "It was one of those disconnects," says Westbrook.

The mistrust among African Americans is tied to this historical lack of care and to the medical experiments done at the Tuskegee Institute between 1932 and 1972 on poor, mostly illiterate black men suffering from syphilis. Without their knowledge, the men were denied treatment so researchers could track how the disease developed. Early remedies were extremely toxic, which was how they justified the study. But by 1947, penicillin was the standard treatment for syphilis, and withholding it could not be justified ethically or morally. A leak to the press ended the experiments and led to today's concept of informed consent. The Tuskegee men were told only that they had "bad blood" and were eligible for free medical care and burial insurance. Westbrook believes he has an ally in Rev. Jackson in wanting to see hospice and palliative care more available in black communities. Yet the legacy of suspicion left by Tuskegee has yet to be overcome.

People have been dying ever since we've been a species. You'd think it would be, if not routine, at least more openly discussed. But how we die and the cultural imperatives that accompany dying are new to most of us. Just a hundred years ago, by the time a person faced their own dying they'd had plenty of experience with brothers, sisters, parents, even their own children. My father was born in 1895, and his mother died as a result of complications from the birth. He was given the same name as a previous baby boy she had delivered stillborn. The first few months of life were hard, and people were just as likely to die in their teens as their forties. The average age at death was forty-six. People to-day are unfamiliar with dying because dying at the end of a long life is a relatively new phenomenon, and we're making it up as we go along.

15.

THURSDAY, MARCH 31, 2005

Learning from Terri

The essence of civilization is that the strong have a duty to protect the weak.

—President Bush, defending the government's right
to intervene in the Schiavo case

THE REVEREND MAHONEY has known for some time that Terri will not survive, but like the others who have taken up her cause, he keeps up a public facade of hope. He is back in Washington and this morning, as he did on so many mornings, he calls the protesters' command post in Florida for an update. Randall Terry comes on the line, and the hardbitten antiabortion activist is crying. "She doesn't have long," he says.

Shortly after nine in the morning, Father Pavone, the national director of Priests for Life and a Schindler family confidant, calls Mahoney to report that Terri has passed away. Mahoney is surprised at how hard the news hits him. "I definitely crashed," he says.

After all the seminars he had led about activism, he had violated the first rule, which is never get involved. He had bonded emotionally with Terri, and, at various points along the circuitous legal and political route, he had been sure they'd be victorious. At a rally in Tallahassee on the Sunday before Terri's feeding tube was removed, Mahoney was assured that a new version of Terri's Law would pass the legislature. Everything was wired, he was told. "In fact, they looked at me and said, 'Rev. Mahoney, please get out of town'—direct quote—'please get your supporters out of town. The outside presence will hurt this. The law is going to go through.'" It didn't happen. Republican lawmakers stood with Democrats to reject the measure despite what some had told Mahoney, perhaps to get him off their case.

Mahoney by his own description is "a little bit off the wall." He likes to mix it up, and he's drawn to what he calls "these national projects." He organized the demonstrations in Montgomery, Alabama, when a federal judge refused to remove a two-ton granite tablet display of the Ten Commandments from the rotunda of the judicial building. Mahoney is the man to see on the Right if you've got a beef against the government, but he regrets that his presence, along with Randall Terry, made it too easy for the media to pigeonhole the protesters as antiabortion zealots from the religious Right. He was the one who reached out to Al Sharpton, Jesse Jackson and Ralph Nader in an effort to broaden the face of the protest movement. He is so convinced that America is more diverse on this end-of-life issue that he went out and raised the money to commission a poll. Perhaps not surprisingly, the results of the poll reflect and reinforce his views: 80 percent of those polled said non-terminal patients should not be denied food and water. By three-to-one, the poll's respondents said a feeding tube should stay in place when a person's wishes are unknown, and a majority agreed that Schiavo's husband should have turned the guardianship of his wife over to her parents. The questions are worded in such a way by the polling organization, Zogby International, on behalf of the Christian Defense Coalition, they were certain to elicit the responses Mahoney is looking for. Even so, the data proved cold comfort, a coda to a narrative he had imagined would have a very different ending. He had gone seventeen days without eating and subsisting only on fluids, and now the drama had come to a crashing end. He would say later that this was the first event in twenty-nine years of ministry where he would not look back and draw one fun story from the experience. It was all dark.

Theresa Marie Schiavo dies at 9:03 A.M. with a teddy bear tucked under her arm. It has been thirteen days since the feeding tube supplying her with food and water had been withdrawn. Her husband is with her. Her brother, Bobby, along with Father Pavone, are with her until five minutes before her death. Pavone's eyewitness account, posted on his Web site, describes how he laid his hand on Terri's head and led the family in praying with her. "Okay, Terri, now here comes the tickle," her father says as he leans over to kiss her, brushing her face with his mustache. When her mother talks to her, Pavone writes, Terri makes sounds in response, though she could not articulate words. "Her mouth was open the whole time. It looked like it was frozen open. She was panting as if she had just run a hundred miles." As I have just learned with Tom, this is the sign of somebody working hard to reach death.

The previous night, Pavone had sat with Terri for more

than three hours. With Bobby on one side of the bed and her sister, Suzanne, sitting to his left, they held her hand and stroked her head. Pavone chanted in Latin, "Victimae Paschali Laudis," an ancient proclamation on the resurrection of Christ and the victory of life, even as, he writes, "I saw before my eyes the deadly work of the culture of death."

At least one police guard and at times as many as three armed officers stood guard in the room with Terri. Pavone noticed that when Bobby occasionally stood up and shifted position, the officer watching him would move to the foot of the bed to make sure he had a clear line of sight.

This morning, Pavone arrives early to be with Terri and her family, but he needs to leave for an interview scheduled in front of the hospice. To keep track of the time, he's brought with him a small timepiece, which he puts in his left hand as he leans over Terri and extends his right hand to bless her. He immediately feels a tap on his left hand. It is the police officer, wanting to know what he is concealing. Pavone says it is a timepiece, which the officer politely says he will have to hold as long as Pavone is there. "We couldn't have anything in our hands," Pavone later writes. "Maybe I was going to try to give her communion. Maybe I was going to try to moisten her lips. Who knows what *terrible* thing I was about to do?"

Pavone writes how ironic it seemed to him that on the night table in Terri's room there was a vase of flowers filled with water, roses among them, with another beautiful bouquet at the foot of the bed. He thought: *This is absurd.* The flowers get watered; the human being hasn't had a drop for almost two weeks. As he notes later, had he dipped his hand in the water and put it on her tongue, he would have been led out of the room and probably put under arrest.

The night before, in a widely broadcast interview, he'd called Michael Schiavo, his attorney, George Felos, and the Florida judge who ordered the removal of Terri's feeding tube "murderers." Some news outlets said he was "fanning the flames" because his outburst had triggered an angry response from the other side. He says all he did was rip away what he calls "the veil of euphemism," which allows the other side to present Terri's death as a merciful and gentle act. He notes in the account he writes of Terri's final hours that Felos "needs to manipulate the language to sell death in an attractive package. But a priest, seeing their work close-up and then telling the world about it, just didn't fit into their plans."

Pavone isn't just any priest with life issues as part of his portfolio. He comes out of the pro-life movement, where he spent a decade as an organizer and advocate before being ordained in 1988. He has dedicated his life and priesthood to opposing abortion rights, first in New York, where he was born and ordained, and more recently in Amarillo, Texas, where Priests for Life is headquartered. Working out of this dusty Texas outpost, Pavone hopes to attract like-minded priests to become a force within the church that is solely devoted to advancing the pro-life cause, including the questions around end of life that surfaced with Terri Schiavo. Dark hair frames his slender face and oversized glasses encircle his eyes, giving him an owlish look of intensity. A sought-after spokesman on pro-life causes, he is plugged into a web of organizations outside the Catholic Church, from Dr. James Dobson's Focus on the Family

Institute to Rachel's Vineyard, a retreat program for women who have had abortions. Norma McCorvey, the "Jane Roe" whose plight led to the 1973 Supreme Court decision *Roe v. Wade* legalizing abortion rights, and who twenty years later became an antiabortion activist, calls Pavone "the catalyst that brought me into the Catholic Church." (McCorvey claimed her pregnancy was the result of rape, a story she later recanted. She never did get an abortion. Her case took too long to unfold, and she gave up the child, a daughter, for adoption.)

In the intermittently sober reflection that follows Terri's death, just about everyone agrees that it's a good idea to draw up a living will so your wishes are known. But not Pavone, who believes a person who leaves clear instructions that he or she doesn't want to be fed, that is, doesn't want to be hooked up to a feeding tube, "is breaking the moral law by requesting suicide." Bobby Schindler, Terri's younger brother, her biggest advocate and a devout Catholic, feels the same way about living wills. "I don't agree with anybody giving permission in essence to kill yourself," he tells me. Pavone argues that the danger in our culture is not that we will be overtreated, but rather that we will be undertreated. Terri is Exhibit A, according to his thinking, because she was not dying, was not on life support by his definition, and did not have a terminal illness. He looks at a feeding tube not as a medical device but as a delivery vehicle for food and water, much like a spoon or a straw. Pavone does find common ground with ethicists who increasingly advise people to name a health care proxy, someone who knows you and your values and can speak for you in the event of a medical crisis that leaves you unable to speak for yourself.

Tom DeLay, the pugilistic House majority leader who more than anyone is responsible for propelling the Schiavo case through Congress, uses the occasion of her death to once again rally the faithful with a threatened assault on so-called activist judges and the independent judiciary that is at the heart of our democracy. In full swagger in an interview on the Fox News Network, DeLay throws down the gauntlet. "We promised the Schindler family that we will not let Terri die in vain. We will look at an arrogant, out-of-control, unaccountable judiciary that thumbed their nose at Congress and the president. When given the jurisdiction to hear this case anew and look at all the facts and make a determination, they chose not to participate, contrary to what Congress and the president asked them to do. We will look into it." Although under investigation for numerous ethics violations, he is still the number-two leader in the House at the time of her death. "The time will come for the men responsible for this to answer for their behavior," he declares. Perhaps it's an empty threat, but given the frenzy of the last weeks, who can be sure? DeLay describes a judiciary loaded with godless liberals when many of the judges who turned down the legal pleadings filed by Terri's parents were Republican appointees and pro-life adherents. They were following the law as opposed to a higher standard, which DeLay calls a "constitutional right to live."

News accounts point out that DeLay felt differently when his father lay grievously ill after suffering catastrophic brain damage in an accident. Told by doctors the then sixty-five-year-old DeLay would "basically be a vegetable," the family agreed to withhold dialysis, knowing the decision would lead to his death, and knowing that he would not want to continue in such a compromised state. DeLay did not question the decision, but it is at odds with his insistence that quality of life should have no bearing on whether to withdraw Terri Schiavo's feeding tube. "It's not for any one of us to decide whether she should live or die," he says at a press conference.

DeLay's tone and threatening words bring out the crazies, igniting a wave of anger against so-called activist judges, judges who follow the law as opposed to the dictates of an ideological minority. The nasty tenor of the public discourse coupled with a spike of death threats to Supreme Court justices over their refusal to take the Schiavo case prompt Justice Sandra Day O'Connor to invite congressional leaders, including DeLay, to the Court for an informal conversation over lunch about the state of disrepair between the two branches. At the lunch, O'Connor asks DeLay point-blank whether there is anything judges could do that would help alleviate the apparent unhappiness expressed by lawmakers. "And Representative DeLay indicated that he didn't think there was anything that could be done," O'Connor told me as she related the exchange. Was DeLay solicitous in her presence? "No," she replied. Supreme Court justices are accustomed to being fawned over; after all, there are only nine justices at a time, and O'Connor had a particular notoriety as the first woman named to the Court, and the justice most often the deciding vote in close decisions. The Republican House leader evidently made no effort to engage with her or her concerns; he was barely civil.

O'Connor retired from the Court soon after, and I met with her in early 2007. We chatted easily except when I mentioned *Roe v. Wade*, the Supreme Court decision that was one vote closer to being overturned since President Bush replaced O'Connor with the more conservative Justice Samuel Alito.

"Your gift was always that you seemed to find where the consensus was in the country," I offered, not realizing the trap I'd just walked into.

"That's no way to decide a legal issue," she said curtly. "That's not what governs the resolution of a legal issue."

Judges like to think of themselves as insulated from public opinion. "And so you would defend, I assume, *Roe v. Wade* on legal grounds," I ventured.

"I've never been totally approving of *Roe v. Wade*," she said. "I didn't say that, and I don't want you to say that I said that. I've written extensively on that, and I'll let that speak for itself; read *Planned Parenthood v. Casey*," she said, with a look that sent me scurrying to change the subject. (The 1992 decision affirmed *Roe* but upheld the right of states to impose restrictions on abortion as long as they did not place an "undue burden" on women. The phrase was crafted by O'Connor.)

I had been nervous about how to approach the subject of her husband's illness. I needn't have been. O'Connor is a straightforward westerner, and at the mention of the words *challenge* and *husband* in one sentence, she didn't duck the subject. Indeed, the words came tumbling out.

"Oh, gosh, he's got Alzheimer's," she said. "I think he's had it close to twenty years. But he could always function. It's only more recently that he really requires full care. He can't dress himself or bathe himself or shave himself—or handle the bathroom too well—and these things have become such that he requires full care, which I was no longer able to provide if I'm going to do anything. And we had this issue of where to live with him. We have two of our three sons who have families in Arizona, so it made more sense for him to be there, but that's a tug for me because I'm here. I talked to him on the phone yesterday. He thinks I've been gone a year and I've been gone four days. So it's very hard."

John O'Connor had known for some time that he had a problem with his short-term memory. An attorney, he compensated for years by writing himself notes. "There would be hundreds of little notes everywhere—on his dresser, in the bathroom, everywhere, for a long time," and that seemed to stave off the worst of the disease, "but now he can't read, and so now there's no conscious recognition of anything," she said, her words trailing off. The two met while law students at Stanford and married the year she graduated, 1952 (he graduated the following year). They'd been together for more than a half century, and as John's condition deteriorated, he had become anxious and agitated whenever his wife left even for a few hours. So in the months before she retired, she would bring him with her to the Court. "He would sit where you are on the couch," she said, her voice growing quieter, almost inaudible. "I couldn't take care of him anymore. I had to make a change."

In Washington, we're accustomed to hearing various professionals say they're leaving their chosen field to spend more time with their family, and it's almost always a cover story, but in O'Connor's case, it was all too true. She also may have gotten a nudge from Chief Justice Rehnquist, eighty years old and sick with cancer, who thought he could hang on for another year. O'Connor told Supreme Court reporter Jan Crawford Greenberg that Rehnquist told her, "I don't think we need two vacancies." O'Connor dutifully moved up her timetable, only to watch cancer claim Rehnquist, leaving the Court with two seats to fill. The tragedy is that once she announced her decision to step down, John's illness advanced more rapidly than she expected. If she had realized how close she was to placing him in an institution, she might not have given up her lifetime seat on the Court. Adding to the poignancy, O'Connor's oldest son, Scott, made public the news in late 2007 that his father had fallen in love with a woman named "Kay," whom he met at the Phoenix facility where they are both Alzheimer's patients. John O'Connor, seventy-eight, is like a teenager in love, the son said. Justice O'Connor made no public comment, but her son said she was "thrilled" with her husband's new outlook on life, which rang true to me, having seen her anguish over his mental state. He had been suicidal before finding this new relationship. Apparently, Alzheimer's patients forgetting their spouses or forming new romantic attachments is not uncommon, and O'Connor's willingness to share such information about her private life sets her apart in a positive way as a public figure.

On the day I met with O'Connor, *USA Today* had a front-page story on Justice Ruth Bader Ginsberg, now the Court's only woman, and how she misses O'Connor. "Oh, yes, and that's true," says O'Connor, echoing Ginsberg's lament that who would have thought in the modern world there again would be only one woman among eight men on the Court, the position that O'Connor, the first woman ever on the Court, filled for twelve years before Ginsberg arrived in 1993.

Ginsberg is a member of the Court's liberal bloc, whereas O'Connor was much less predictable, siding with the conservatives much of the time while providing the swing vote for a liberal majority on critical social issues such as affirmative action and reproductive rights. In 1990, when the Court heard the Cruzan right-to-die case, O'Connor had joined the majority in rejecting the Cruzans' plea to withdraw their daughter's feeding tube. But O'Connor had written in her opinion that artificial feeding was medical treatment, and Chief Justice Rehnquist had recognized a constitutional right to liberty that allowed competent people to refuse medical treatment. These assertions coupled with language saying the case could be reopened on the state level if new evidence surfaced about the patient's intent were enough to trigger a new trial that the Cruzans won.

Reminded of *Cruzan*, the first right-to-die case the Court took, O'Connor says, "The Court, we hope, doesn't have to get involved in these cases very often. It's painful when it does because these issues touch on problems of the heart as well of the mind, and that isn't where judges do their best work. We have had to look a time or two at whether there are constitutional limits that require state action one way or another in this area. One would like to think that courts should never be involved in these issues. They're not equipped to deal too well with them. In the Schiavo case, the issues had been raised and resolved in the Florida state courts, and here came a congressional requirement that the federal court—trial court and then the appellate court—review the action taken by the state courts. And that was a most unusual step when it was directed at one particular case. This was not a generic statute saying that in every case involving such and such, there shall be a federal court review. It wasn't that at all. It was a very strange thing. And once the federal district court reviewed what the state courts had done, they found no basis under federal law to overturn this decision. That went to the court of appeals, the same result. A petition for certiorari was filed here, which this court didn't take. There was no basis for taking it."

Asked if there was any debate or dissent about taking the Schiavo case, O'Connor said she wouldn't talk about any "unrecorded matters." But there were no dissents filed, and presumably the Court's decision to turn down "cert," short for *certiorari*, which is Latin for "to ascertain, to make certain," was unanimous. There was no constitutional basis to second-guess the lower courts.

O'Connor returned to the theme that the courts are not very well equipped to resolve end-of-life issues. "I'm not going to be able to enlighten you too much," she says. "And you have new members of the Court since *Cruzan*, and we don't know how new members will address some of the issues that they haven't addressed before." The Court is reluctant to get into these issues in part because they are better left to families, and in part because judges are like the rest of us. They prefer not to face these issues unless they have to.

O'Connor recalled her own bout with breast cancer, and how disbelieving she was at the diagnosis. She wanted to delay treatment until after she finished a couple more rounds of oral arguments. She was totally lacking in appreciation for the fact that everything had to stop; she had to focus, educate herself about the disease and make decisions about her treatment. Making decisions is her career and her calling, but she found herself quite unprepared to make so many choices: surgery and if so, how radical? What kind of follow-up treatment: chemotherapy or radiation or both? She applied the lessons she learned on the Court when faced with a difficult case—do the research, make the decision, and then don't look back.

O'Connor had a mastectomy followed by several rounds of chemotherapy. She is candid about the postoperative depression she suffered, and the debilitating fatigue that sapped her strength and her spirit. A person accustomed to having lots of energy, she could hardly get up in the morning and she needed a nap in the afternoon. It was frightening for O'Connor, who loves the outdoors and is an accomplished tennis player, golfer and skier. She slowly built back, crediting physical exercise with rejuvenating her mind and body.

The recovery was hard enough, but the worst, she recalled in a speech at Sibley Memorial Hospital years after her surgery, was the public visibility and the media scrutiny, which took on the aspect of a death watch. How does she look? When is she going to step down and give the president another vacancy on the Court? She looks pale to me; I don't give her six months. "There were people in the press box with telescopes looking at me in the courtroom to see just what my condition was," she said. "Press would call my office and say they'd heard all these dire rumors and I better tell them exactly what was what or they were going to publish them all. It was really difficult."

I COULD RELATE to that feeling of being under a microscope. I hated it when people would ask how I was doing and wouldn't settle for the perfunctory, Fine, thank you. They would press for more: How are you really? I was afraid if I let down my guard, I might reveal more than I intended or simply dissolve into tears.

The outpouring to Tom's death is overwhelming. I've got more than a dozen floral arrangements and fruit baskets in the living room plus two huge deli platters, enough to fortify a stream of mourners should I decide to hold a three-day wake. The truth is I don't know what to do. I don't have much experience with the rituals of dying. All I know is the living room looks terribly empty without the hospital bed, and the reality of what I've lost is beginning to sink in.

It's the week after Easter, and Congress along with much of official Washington is on recess. We had taped an "evergreen" (a show that didn't play off the week's events and in theory could run anytime) to air on this weekend's *McLaughlin Group*. But the passing of Terri Schiavo plus the approaching death of Pope John Paul make it too big a news week to go with the pretaped show. John calls me at home to see if I feel up to doing a show at our regular time on Friday afternoon. I don't see much point in staying home with the flowers and the cold cuts, much as I appreciate the expressions of sympathy. I welcome the chance to do what for me is normal—bat around the issues of the day in a highly charged political environment.

Admittedly, it's not standard fare for the grieving widow, and a friend who calls to see how I'm doing counsels me against popping up on television so soon after Tom's death. "It will further the impression of you as somebody with ice water in your veins," she says, a comment that chills me on several levels. Is that what people think of me? Because I get in there with the big boys and express my opinion, that I'm heartless? Maybe she's right; maybe I shouldn't do the show, I think. My son Woody, wanting to bolster me, goes to the Internet and plugs in two words—*bereavement* and *widows*—and downloads an article that tells me I'm okay, that grieving is individual, there are no rules. Some people sit in a darkened room with the shades drawn, whereas others find solace or at least distraction in activity. My friend's remark is searing, and it throws me off, but I see my son's reaction, which is basically, Go for it, Mom. If it's okay with him, how bad could it be? The incident reinforces my own instinct that for me, continuing my work life, my normal routine, is my salvation.

As for my friend, I learned throughout Tom's illness that people project their own feelings. She had apologized earlier for not visiting while Tom was bedridden. She said she couldn't handle it, that she had issues around her mother's death and not getting to her bedside that made seeing Tom too difficult. I don't hold that against her, and wish her well in resolving her own anxiety. People do in these circumstances what they can, and it's best not to pass judgment.

Terri's saga is issue 2 on that Friday's show. "Perhaps everything that can be said about Terri Schiavo's pilgrimage to death has been said," says John. "But more can be said about the impact of the Schiavo saga on public policy and politics. Question: What will be the impact on public policy and politics?"

Lawrence O'Donnell, who often takes a contrarian view, says, "There will be none. The story will disappear in the coverage of the pope and we won't get anything out of it," with one caveat. He would like to see an adjustment in marriage law. He says it's "utterly preposterous" that a spouse in name only like Michael Schiavo gets to decide whether Terri lives or dies.

"Who should do it?" McLaughlin asks.

"If you have a division between parents and spouses ... I am with the parents," O'Donnell says. He has one child, a daughter who is not yet a teenager, and he promises with great gusto her "prenup will specify that the husband not only does not get to decide about her feeding tube, he doesn't even get a vote."

Tony Blankley, too, is with the parents in the Schiavo case, but he's not with O'Donnell on shifting away from spousal rights. "For some of us who trust our wives more than anyone on the planet, I would want to have it there," he says. He predicts a policy debate waged primarily in state capitols, resulting in the modification of state laws.

I point out that the debate is already under way in state capitols, and that President Bush when he was governor of Texas signed a law that allows hospital officials to remove a feeding tube over the wishes of a family if they conclude the treatment is futile. The debate is not new, but it gains momentum both to advance such remedies and to resist them, as we saw in the Schiavo debate. "Technology ensures that about 85 percent of us will face a decision something like this. And I think there is a continuum between life, when you want to prolong life, and when you want to begin to end it. And it's a very personal, individual decision."

They listen to me perhaps more respectfully, knowing what I've just been through. Pat Buchanan, upon seeing me in the greenroom before the taping, offers his sympathy, saying quite memorably, "You took a big hit, kid." It was heartfelt and kind and rakish all at once, like Humphrey Bogart in the movie classic *Casablanca*, underscoring why Pat is so popular among both his ideological foes and friends.

Pat predicts a war on judges led by politicians and people who believe Terri was sentenced to death by the judge in Florida, and that she didn't die a "natural death," but succumbed to starvation and a lack of water. "There's going to be a war over these judges, Supreme Court judges and appellate court judges, and it's going to be a bloodbath," he says.

John wants to know who was the political winner, the Democrats or Republicans? O'Donnell says there was no winner, an answer that displeases John, who jumps in to declare the Republicans "the political losers, no question about it. The Democrats were the political winners."

Buchanan hoots at that. "The Democrats didn't even stand up," he exclaims. "They're hiding in the weeds." He's right that the Democrats went along with the stampede to save Terri, fearful that the GOP had found a winning issue. Still, the Democrats win by default because they didn't lead the charge.

McLaughlin says the White House and Congress are political losers. "Right, Eleanor?"

"Right," I say, grateful for the softball. I predict that congressional popularity levels are going to go down, and that Tom DeLay is a big loser because a lot of his Republican colleagues blame him for leading them into this fight, which has backfired on them. "He's one indictment or ethics charge away from getting out of there," I say, a prediction that will soon become true.

"We're going to do that next week," John says, rushing through his winners and losers to Florida governor Jeb Bush. "Does he look like a rigorist in this or does he look like he's got a tender conscience?" John asks in the Jesuitical language that has made him such a force on television for so long.

Blankley gives a qualified answer, saying Bush "probably nets out a winner." He believes the majority of conservatives know that Bush acted as vigorously as the law permitted him to. But he did run afoul of a hard-core base that wanted him to break the law and be in contempt of court and send in the highway patrol to grab Terri.

What about Michael Schiavo?

"He's not a winner to me," O'Donnell interjects.

I counter to say, "He's been demonized, but we're not going to change the marriage laws in this country."

Hearing that is like red meat for O'Donnell, who's really on a rampage about the legal prejudice in favor of a spouse, "which in this country is a frequently temporary relationship, and certainly was in that case," he says.

Buchanan cites the ACLU as a loser because they backed the husband and fought to "put this woman to death" when they otherwise "go to the penitentiary gates to defend a serial killer against execution if there's one small factor in there" to win a stay.

My turn to counter Buchanan: "A winner will be science when the results of her autopsy come back and reveal that she had no brain activity. And I don't think we count that as a meaningful life that should be sustained."

The ultimate winner or loser—Terri Schiavo—which is it? John thunders.

Buchanan: "I think she's a heroine of a movement and of a cause, and I think Terri Schiavo to a lot of Americans is a saint who was put to death. And even the folks on the other side—nobody's against Terri Schiavo, so she's a complete winner."

"I don't think we can improve on that," John says.

I agree.

John ends the segment with a "political repercussion scale," with zero meaning zero political repercussion from the Terri Schiavo saga and ten meaning "nuclear-scale repercussion politically." Buchanan says it's an eight or nine in terms of poisoning and polarizing American politics. I give it a six, with the advantage going to the Democrats. Blankley gives it a three. O'Donnell agrees with me, that it's a six. "I'll go with a six," McLaughlin booms, and the sixes win.

The show closes with a tribute to Tom that John prepared earlier. The producer tells me that he had planned to deliver it live but couldn't get through the read without his voice breaking up. Tom's picture appears on the screen as John announces "In memoriam: Another death occurred this week much closer to home, Tom Brazaitis, a member of this television family, Eleanor's husband. Tom was a gifted journalist, a generous man, a loving father and husband, a witty, talented athlete, singer and dancer, without a mean bone in his body. He was sick for a long time and died at home with his beloved Eleanor, who I asked to be with us today, which is what Tom would have wanted."

It was a beautiful farewell and Tom would have loved it.

Epilogue

A WEEK TO THE DAY after Terri Schiavo's death, armed guards escorted Dr. James Bernat, a neurologist who heads the medical ethics committee at Dartmouth Medical Center, through a special entrance reserved for senators and into a hearing room to testify before the Senate Health and Education Committee. Bernat's task was to define "vegetative state" and to help the senators understand and clarify the muddy moral debate that had gripped the nation. The American Academy of Neurology had asked Bernat to testify, and he had readily agreed, eager to do his part to educate the public about this little-understood neurological state. In the days preceding the hearing, there were death threats, and the head of public affairs at Dartmouth called Bernat and suggested he consider not going.

As he was led into the hearing room, the first thing Bernat noticed was the number of people from the disability community, some in wheelchairs, so many that an overflow room had been set up for the testimony to be broadcast into. The atmosphere was charged with tension, which Wyoming Republican John Enzi, chair of the committee, did his best to defuse. Enzi made a reasonable and measured statement about the importance of the decisions that drove the Schiavo controversy. Senator Ted Kennedy, ranking Democrat on the committee, spoke next. According to Bernat's account, Kennedy excoriated the entire Congress for a totally inappropriate invasion of privacy—for butting into a family controversy where it didn't belong. He said it was unconstitutional and wrong. He concluded by rhetorically asking, "What will we do with the next case? The American people don't want this."

Preceding Bernat was a speaker brought in by the Republicans, Rud Turnbull, a lawyer whose perspective is shaped by his experience as the father of a mentally disabled son. A soft-spoken, scholarly man, Turnbull talked about the importance of government in protecting the disabled and spoke movingly of his son, a thirty-seven year old with a mental age of about six, and the struggle to establish his rights as a full human being. Bernat listened respectfully but thought it was off the point to portray Schiavo as disabled.

Senate rules say only the chair and ranking member can make statements; the other members of the committee can only ask questions. But that didn't deter Republican Richard Burr, a freshman from North Carolina, from launching into a speech about how Congress had acted to protect this innocent person. He was very proud of this, and his grandchildren would be proud. As Bernat relates Burr's self-serving remarks, he can't resist an editorial comment—"It was a little disgusting actually." Then Burr posed a hypothetical question that Bernat recognized as a setup. If someone came into the emergency room and a full battery of testing was not done, would the doctor be liable? Bernat said it depends on what the problem is and what the standard of care is. "What I'm getting at," Burr persisted, "is she didn't have a PET scan and an MRI." He asked the question and left without waiting for an answer. Burr had won the seat vacated by Democrat John Edwards in 2004, and as a newcomer to the Senate was eager to get into the *Congressional Record* his justification for voting the way he did. He wasn't challenged for his violation of protocol because there was nobody there to challenge. Kennedy had left earlier to attend an event with a visiting foreign leader. "It was an interesting lesson in how they do things," Bernat said later. Political positioning is what politicians do best.

THE AUTOPSY REPORT on Terri Schiavo was made public two and a half months after her death, on June 15, 2005, and for most people put to rest what was left of the controversy. Her brain was "grossly abnormal," atrophied to half the normal size for a woman her age. "Damage and neuronal loss in her occipital lobes" had left her blind, forcing those who bought into the highly edited video of Schiavo to reexamine what they saw if she saw nothing. "The vision centers of her brain were dead," Dr. Jon R. Thogmartin, the medical examiner, said. "No amount of treatment or rehabilitation would have reversed" the damage she suffered. The autopsy found no evidence of any long-ago trauma, noting that numerous examinations of Mrs. Schiavo in the hours, days and months after her collapse never detected any signs of strangulation or blunt injury, indirectly addressing some of the more virulent rumors spread about Michael Schiavo and what he did or didn't do the night his wife collapsed.

In a curious mix of medical and legal language, the report concludes the "mechanism" that killed Schiavo was "marked dehydration." She did not starve to death, a myth that the media should have done more to dispel. The "cause and manner" of death was severe anoxic brain injury, meaning her brain had been denied oxygen, but exactly why that happened on that winter morning fifteen years earlier, the report says, "cannot be determined with reasonable medical certainty." Both sides generally agreed her collapse was triggered by low potassium levels. But nobody could say for sure whether the underlying cause was an eating disorder, a question that is beyond the scope of an autopsy. "The manner of death will therefore be certified as undetermined," the report said, a sentence that the Schindler family and their allies grabbed ahold of as evidence that Schiavo had suffered an untimely death.

No examination of a brain on autopsy can prove or disprove that the deceased person was in a vegetative state. "PVS is a clinical diagnosis arrived at through physical examination of living patients," the report says. However, the condition of Schiavo's brain—shriveled, discolored and scarred—was consistent with persistent vegetative state, according to the neuropathologist brought in by the medical examiner. In his press conference, Thogmartin compared the state of Schiavo's brain to that of Karen Ann Quinlan, the young woman at the center of the first nationally recognized right-to-die case. He said Quinlan, whose parents sued the state to let her die, had more brain tissue, 835 grams as opposed to Schiavo's 610 grams, which is half the 1,200 to 1,300 grams considered normal for a forty-one-year-old woman.

Most people would accept these facts as evidence of a life long over, but many months later, when I met with Bobby

Schindler, he had a different reading. He thought it was misleading to compare his sister to Quinlan because Quinlan was not "starved to death." She died with a feeding tube in place. Her parents won the right to remove her from a ventilator. Schindler says the medical examiner did not take into account the ravages of the severe dehydration Terri suffered. He says, without any medical expertise to back him up, that Terri could have gone blind because of the dehydration. He is unshaken in believing that his sister could have benefited from therapy and rehabilitation. He faults the medical examiner for handing out the autopsy report at a press conference, giving reporters little time to absorb the technical information and ask probing questions.

Two days after the report was released, Governor Jeb Bush announced an investigation into the circumstances surrounding Schiavo's collapse. Most people accepted the medical examiner's conclusions and wanted to close the whole sorry debate. Even many Republicans thought Bush was mistaken in pressing for more legal action once it had been established there was no evidence of foul play or indication that Schiavo could have benefited from further treatment. Bush said he sought the probe because the autopsy report revealed a possible gap between the time Schiavo fell to the floor unconscious and when her husband called paramedics. The report says a 911 call was placed at about 5:40 A.M. on February 25, 1990. Michael Schiavo in a 2003 interview with Larry King on CNN said he had discovered his stricken wife on the floor outside their bedroom at about 4:30 A.M. and immediately called 911. The hour's difference had been raised before but had never been a serious point of contention in the long and acrimonious legal battle between Michael Schiavo and the Schindlers. Bush asked the state attorney in Pinellas County, where the Schiavos were living when Terri collapsed, to conduct the inquiry. It didn't take the state attorney long to echo the medical examiner's findings, and in a report dated June 30, he said Michael Schiavo's statements had been consistent over the years. Schiavo said he "ran" to call 911 that fateful morning, but he wasn't wearing a watch or looking at a clock. The state attorney said the discrepancies he'd been asked to investigate did not suggest criminal behavior.

With that, Bush finally brought down the curtain on a remarkable legal drama. In truth, Terry Schiavo died like some two million people do every year in the United States after a decision has been made to withhold life-sustaining treatment. Despite the best efforts on the part of her parents and fiercest advocates to portray a forty-one-year-old woman as a child, the weight of legal opinion was with her husband and his view of what his wife would have wanted. Michael Schiavo infuriated the Schindlers when he had "I kept my promise" engraved on Terri's burial marker in a Florida cemetery, along with the day in 1990 she "Departed the Earth" and the 2005 date she was "At Peace."

BACK HOME IN IDAHO, Brandi Swindell keeps Terri's picture in her nightstand drawer along with her Bible and the books she reads at night. It is part of her commitment to never let Terri's memory die. Swindell had fasted for fourteen days to demonstrate her solidarity, and after Schiavo died, she knew she had to eat, but it was some time before her appetite returned. "It was a hard transition," she says, tears welling up as she recounts the time spent healing from the experience. Swindell is an activist, and the period for mourning soon gave way to the need to advance the greater cause. In May 2006, a little more than a year after Schiavo's death, Swindell bought a hundred-dollar ticket to a bioethics conference at the University of Pennsylvania. Among the featured speakers was Michael Schiavo, who appeared on a panel moderated by a conservative radio host who, unlike most of his counterparts in right-wing radio land, had supported withdrawing Terri's feeding tube. Swindell sat quietly through the panel discussion and when the moderator invited questions, she submitted one. It was about the Zogby poll commissioned by Pat Mahoney that asked, as Swindell recounted the question, "If somebody is severely brain damaged and has no written directive, should the feeding tube be removed?" The response was overwhelming, with something like 80 percent of those polled saying the feeding tube should stay in place. Swindell went up to the moderator and asked him why he didn't read her question, which she thought was compelling. He explained there were too many questions, and besides, she knew it was a one-sided event. "And that's fine," she said. But she wasn't about to leave without confronting Michael Schiavo, whom she blamed for Terri's death. She stood in line patiently for her turn to talk to him. "Hi Michael, I'm Brandi. I want you to know it's never too late to admit that what you allowed to happen to Terri was wrong." She was initially calm and polite, but her presence rattled Schiavo. His face reddened with anger, and the encounter rapidly escalated into angry volleys. Swindell says she left on her own, but one of the blogs said she had to be escorted out. The conference organizers refunded her money, and she didn't go back. She wasn't there as a protester, she says; she was there as a voice for Terri, and she'd said her piece.

WHEN POPE JOHN PAUL II became gravely ill the same time that Terri Schiavo's life was slipping away, Carlos Gomez, the Cuban-born physician and hospice administrator, told me someone should write an article called "The Death of Two Catholics." We were having lunch in a small French restaurant in Georgetown, and I thought the conceit could easily be expanded to three Catholics. Tom's drift from the church and his unwavering embrace of atheism even as he faced his own mortality rounded out the imagery. Gomez had his own issues with the church, its dogmatic position on abortion and even birth control and the shameful cover-up of information about priests practicing pedophilia, and no longer considered himself a practicing Catholic. But he was steeped in church tradition, and he thought the story line that emerged after the pope's death wasn't the whole truth.

The story went like this: The vicar of Christ reached his time and experienced a "natural death," whereas Terri, a lowly layperson, decades younger, had a medically assisted death. John Paul died the day after Terri (and two days after Tom) in his quarters at the Vatican after a protracted battle with Parkinson's disease. He refused heroic measures and chose to die at home rather than the hospital. But the chain of events that led to his death was hardly "natural," says Gomez. The eighty-four-year-old pontiff first entered the hospital for a urinary tract infection, where he was put on a catheter and treated with antibiotics. After he was sent home and the antibiotics stopped, he spiked a fever, "*gravissimo*, to use the Latin, very grave," says Gomez. Then he suffered a heart attack that sent him back to the hospital, where the hardiest bugs await, resulting in an infection that strained his metabolic processes. This in turn led to congestive heart failure, which made his kidneys shut down.

"Now, could he have lived longer?" asks Gomez. Probably, but that's not the point, given the pope's age and multitude of ailments. "The point is that medical intervention in and of itself isn't always the best thing." Asked what he would have done if he were the attending physician, Gomez says, "I would have asked him what it is you want—and I'll tell you how I can get you there. And if he'd said, 'Cure me,' I would have said that's not in the cards." The tradition in medicine is first, do no harm. Cure when possible, and when you can't cure, palliate. When the holy father is suffering, Catholics would say this is the way of the cross. "I have a very different sense of Jesus," says Gomez. "He was a healer; he helped the lepers. I don't think this is a vale of tears. I think suffering is a crock." When I told Gomez that Tom had often cried out in pain, he grimaced at the notion that morphine for a dying man had been rationed for any reason. He believes there should be no limit to the amount of pain medication. "You give it until the patient is out of pain, and if you can't control the pain for one reason or another, then you sedate. You do not want someone to be conscious when they're dying." It's extremely rare for a person near death to be conscious and aware, says Gomez. That only happens in Hollywood.

Anger at the judges who ordered Terri's death took shape at a nationally televised gathering of evangelical Christians called Justice Sunday. Convened on April 24 at a Baptist church in Louisville, Kentucky, the event took aim at Senate Democrats who were blocking President Bush's judicial nominees and was subtitled "Stopping the Filibuster Against People of Faith." It featured such right-wing evangelical figures as Focus on the Family's James Dobson, former Watergate felon Chuck Colson, and, by videotape, the biggest catch of all, the majority leader of the U.S. Senate, Bill Frist, lending the prestige of his office to an unprecedented partnership of church and state to wage war on federal judges. An acclaimed pediatric heart surgeon before he entered politics, Frist was once considered a natural for higher office. But he had embarrassed himself with his rosy assessment of Schiavo's condition based on watching her on videotape, and the disconnect between his long-distance diagnosis and the actual state of her brain function put the final stake through Frist's presidential ambitions. Pandering to the conservative wing of his party had been part of his strategy, and it had backfired, destroying his credibility in the process. Frist had become a laughingstock. He didn't run for reelection, and nobody was surprised when he said he wouldn't enter the '08 presidential race. As Senate leader, he had floated the "nuclear option," threatening to eliminate the minority's right to filibuster judicial nominees in order to win confirmation with a simple Republican majority. Cooler heads prevailed, fortuitously as it turned out, since the GOP would be thrust back into the minority after the '06 election and rely on the filibuster to block Democratic initiatives.

Two more Justice Sundays followed, one in August '05 and another in January '06, but they didn't attract nearly the attention as the one held in the immediate aftermath of Schiavo's death, when the outrage over the judicial rulings was still raw. Frist became a conspicuous no-show, having delivered a soulful speech on the Senate floor in support of embryonic stem cell research, breaking with the White House and with the conservative movement he had so assiduously courted, and returning to his roots as a doctor and a scientist.

The zeal was still there on the Right to remake the judiciary, but with the resignation of Supreme Court justice Sandra Day O'Connor, a prochoice centrist, and the appointment of two young, intellectually rigorous justices drawn from conservative ranks, John Roberts and Samuel Alito, the politics shifted. President Bush had delivered. With a reliable and often decisive conservative bloc on the Court, the Justice Sunday movement lost steam. The religious Right resigned itself to protecting the gains it had won, which were considerable given the youth and commitment of Bush's Court appointees.

ON THE ONE-YEAR ANNIVERSARY of their daughter's death, the Schindlers came to Washington for a press conference to announce their foundation to "save" others in Terri's situation. Of all the politicians who had so vocally championed their cause, only one showed up for the event, Kansas senator Sam Brownback, who would run for president on a "culture of life" platform. Tom DeLay, who had resigned his leadership post in the midst of an ethics scandal, was the only other politician who hadn't backed away from his support for the Schindlers and their cause.

DeLay didn't attend the press conference, but he welcomed the Schindlers in his Capitol Hill office. It was the first time they had met, and Bob Schindler says the former House whip was practically crying as they talked. A picture of Terri hung on the wall right next to the photo of a fallen police officer, placed there, an aide told Schindler, as a constant reminder of how life's heroes could become victims. Schindler was so touched by the apparent sincerity of the man who had done more than anybody to elevate the issues surrounding his daughter's death that he told DeLay he would fly to Texas and vote for him if he could. A week later, DeLay announced he would not run for Congress again, formalizing his fall from grace.

I caught up with the Schindlers in the lobby of their hotel as they prepared to fly back to Florida. Their list of politicians who've disappointed them is long, but they are most bitter about Senator Frist. "He turned on us," says Mary Schindler, grimacing as she recalls Frist's answer on *Meet the Press* when asked if he had any regrets about his role in the Schiavo case. Frist said the lesson he took from the experience is, "The American people don't want you involved in these decisions."

Mary Schindler is a short woman with dark hair and a sour expression. She sits with her arms folded across her chest, body language that reinforces her defiance—at the politicians who abandoned them, the medical professionals who couldn't see Terri's potential, the judges who sided with Michael Schiavo, and the son-in-law she believes mistreated her daughter for his personal gain. Bob Schindler is more curious than angry about what motivates the people who aren't on his side. A working-class guy, he didn't suit up in Washington attire for the press conference. He was dressed like he was going to brown-bag it at an assembly plant. I instantly liked him, whereas I found his wife unapproachable. She fretted about getting to the airport, while her husband patiently took my questions and didn't seem to mind recounting the whole sorry tale—including fisticuffs with Michael. This is a family that knows how to hate, and Michael Schiavo more than reciprocated.

Son Bobby is the keeper of the flame. Slightly built, with dark, keen eyes and a lithe intensity, he told me I could ask him anything. "Don't feel like you're going to upset me with any questions you might ask." More than a year after Terri's death, he was still steaming at the politicians who backpedaled. When he heard Democratic senator Joe Lieberman say unequivocally on *Meet the Press* that he had no regrets over his support for congressional intervention in the Schiavo case, he wrote a letter to Lieberman thanking him. Whereas most Democrats who went along with the Republican majority on Schiavo did so because they feared a backlash if they didn't, Lieberman's support was different. He really meant it. Lieberman often staked out positions at odds with Democratic orthodoxy, and he would ultimately break with his party over his backing for President Bush's war policies in Iraq. He won reelection in '06 as an independent. Another politician who didn't run and hide, in Bobby's view, is DeLay. Bobby met with him and came away thinking that unless DeLay is a great actor, he was sincere. "He was the only one who called my mom after Terri died," Bobby said, adding that he might be forgetting somebody else but he didn't think so.

ON SATURDAY, MAY 14, 2005, more than three hundred people assembled in the National Press Club ballroom to pay tribute to Tom. Diane Rehm graciously agreed to moderate the event, and our friend Bob Trask, a motivational speaker and the closest thing Tom had to a spiritual adviser, flew in from Seattle to fill the role of a chaplain. They had met standing in line in Red Square waiting to see Lenin's tomb. It was the height of the cold war, Ronald Reagan was president, and few Americans were touring the Evil Empire. Tom was on a reporting trip for the *Plain Dealer*, and when he heard Bob and his wife, Mary, speaking English, he approached them and in a conspiratorial tone, they thought, offered to move them ahead in the line on the strength of his connections. Bob and Mary thought this bearded stranger was probably KGB, but they took him up on his offer. The chance encounter produced a lasting friendship. The beard didn't fare as well. Tom shaved it off after Senate hearings into Reagan's Supreme Court nomination of Robert Bork, a conservative jurist who was voted down by the Senate. Demonized as an extremist by his liberal critics, Bork's beard added to his satanic caricature. That wasn't what bothered Tom; it was that facial hair had been co-opted by the Right.

Tom had left me as a guide the program from a memorial service at the Press Club that he had attended, where I learned later he was seen sitting quietly in the back and taking notes. I had packed in more speakers, wanting to acknowledge the Ohio politicians Tom had covered in addition to his professional colleagues, his personal friends and his family. In the interests of time and to keep things moving, everybody was instructed to keep their remarks between three and five minutes, which everybody pretty much ignored. Tom was a stickler for keeping time, and as I sat in the front row, I imagined him with his stopwatch, timing everybody and whispering to me how he would have edited down their remarks.

When Phil Barragate took the podium, he announced right off that he wouldn't abide by the time constraints. Then he told the story of vying with other convicts in a prison library for recent copies of the *Plain Dealer*, where he'd come across a column Tom had written about some kids who had removed a stop sign as a prank and were facing prison because an accident occurred, which resulted in a death. Tom proposed a more constructive punishment, such as community service or lecturing other potential youth offenders. Barragate had served almost five years, exhausting every legal avenue he could think of as a once successful trial attorney to win his release. He wasn't in some Club Med for white-collar criminals but in one of Ohio's toughest state prisons. When he read the column, he saw a parallel between what Tom was advocating and the restitution he was proposing, a chance to repay the people he had defrauded in exchange for parole. He wrote Tom in July 1997 and soon they were corresponding regularly. Tom saw merit in Phil's argument that as a first-time nonviolent offender, his sentence was excessive (fifteen to forty-five years), he'd already been behind bars for a big chunk of time, and society along with his victims would be better served if he could become productive again. Tom was captivated by Phil's tales of prison life, the jockeying for favors, the absence of privacy, the racial tension, and encouraged him to keep notes for a possible book.

Drawn into the fight along with its policy implications, Tom convinced his editor to do a full-page story on Barragate's proposed restitution plan, and to invite public reaction, which was largely positive. There still would be more twists and turns before parole was granted in September 1998, but having Tom as his bulldog in the public arena proved decisive. Ironically, the parole board did not require restitution, though Phil made some attempt to earmark money he earned for his victims. When finding gainful employment as an ex-con proved harder than he imagined, the payments stopped. Phil worried that his fall from grace might somehow embarrass Tom. At the memorial celebration, he told of worrying about the reception he might receive at an event in Cleveland, and he sought Tom's advice. "What should I say if they ask me my name?" "Tell them your name, and that you're my friend," Tom replied.

The Gridiron chorus provided a musical interlude of songs Tom had either written or performed, and to my amazement, John Glenn sang the lyrics of a song he and Tom had performed together in the spring of '99, shortly after Glenn retired from the Senate. Glenn had made history in 1962 as the first American to orbit the earth, and then made a second trip into space in 1998, at age seventy-seven. The lyrics offered advice to other Senate oldsters seeking media attention. When I asked him if he would reprise the song, he demurred, saying Tom had gotten him to sing in public, but he wasn't going to do it again. So I was surprised when he took out his song sheet and began to warble. He'd always been a favorite of Tom's, along with his wife, Annie, whose battle to overcome a debilitating case of stuttering had been chronicled by Tom in the *Plain Dealer Sunday Magazine*.

Two other Ohio Democrats spoke, Rep. Dennis Kucinich, a faithful and long-standing friend whom Tom had dubbed "the Almost President," and former representative Louis Stokes, who told me how much it meant to him that Tom had flown to Cleveland to be there when he announced his retirement from Congress after thirty years. A courtly and savvy legislator, Stokes was the first African American to serve in Congress from Ohio. Senator George Voinovich couldn't be with us, but he credited Tom with launching his political career with an endorsement in a small weekly newspaper when he was running for local office. Voinovich, a moderate Republican, would go on to become mayor of Cleveland, governor of Ohio and, finally, senator from Ohio, all the while ribbing Tom, whose liberal leanings were well known, for what he started. They were friends.

Other strange bedfellows attending, as noted in *U.S. News*'s "Washington Whispers" column, were conservative columnist Bob Novak and retired ambassador Joseph Wilson, whose wife's identity as a CIA operative had been revealed in a Novak column. *U.S. News* quoted Wilson saying when he spotted Novak, he felt like he needed a drink, and me saying Tom was a ham and would have loved everything about the occasion.

Lots of wonderful things were said about Tom, and though the celebration (a word I still stumble over using) ran longer than intended, when we concluded just short of two hours, it looked like that's what we planned all along. Tom's two adult children, Mark and Sarah, shared their childhood memories, evoking knowing laughter about Tom's obsession with golf and conveying the strong bond they had with their father. Robert, my youngest son, spoke for the Clift boys. He was thirteen when Tom and I married, and it wasn't always smooth sailing. He said he came to understand Tom a lot better *after* he was diagnosed with cancer. "Here was a man who I saw throw his golf clubs for having his shot disturbed, make choosing the Christmas tree into an Olympic event, and institute rules like 'no eating' in his gold Toyota Tercel," Robert said. "Yet when Tom was diagnosed with cancer, he never complained once—there was absolutely no self-pity—and at a time when those around him wanted to throw up their hands at the prospect of living without him. Tom was at peace with himself, his life, and the fact of his death—all the while copiously researching his condition and fighting to continue his life. I learned a lot about Tom during this time. What I had incorrectly assessed as a preoccupation with rules was really the reflection of a fighting, competitive spirit. Tom understood life's game and accepted its rules—its ups and downs, its beauty and its ugliness. And as long as you talked to him straight, fairly, and by the rules, you could always count on him. And in the many years he was in my life, he never failed to come through. He was a true leader and role model, and I can only hope to play my life as honorably as he played his." Robert's words were simple and to the point, and Tom would have appreciated the sports metaphor—he and Robert shared a love of sports. But if he were there stage-managing, I suspect he would reserve his highest praise for the fact that Robert kept his remarks within the allotted time. And he'd point out that "no eating in the car" was a losing battle.

Tom was interred in the columbarium at Arlington National Cemetery in a service with full military honors. The niche with his name and date of birth and death is engraved with the atheist symbol of an atom. Later that same year, 2005, my oldest brother, Robert Roeloffs, was also laid to rest in the columbarium. Sixteen years older than me, Bob was like my father, teaching me to drive and serving as my political mentor. A New Deal liberal, he shaped my liberal beliefs, and like Tom, he had long ago lost faith in organized religion. His niche also bears the symbol of an atom.

The summer after Tom died, I traveled with my son Robert to the tiny island of Föhr in the North Sea for a family reunion. Both my parents had emigrated from there, and we have many relatives on the island. Föhr's cobblestone streets and thatched-roof houses remain untouched by time. Standing in a church cemetery by the gravestone of my father's mother, who had died soon after giving birth to him, I felt immersed in the seamlessness of life and death. Tom was gone, but what did that mean?

A few days later, visiting friends in Berlin, I tripped over a piece of luggage and broke my left wrist. The first thing the nurse told me in the Berlin emergency room was to remove my wedding ring because of the swelling. I had been wondering what the protocol was for the recently widowed, and discovered after consulting the Internet that there was no set rule. A freak accident three months after Tom's death made the decision for me, and I moved the ring to the pinkie of my right hand, where it remained until Valentine's Day the following year. That's when it slipped off my finger unnoticed, I think on a crowded flight to the West Coast. A sympathetic seatmate helped me scrounge around on the floor of the plane to search for it, but to no avail. I'm not superstitious, if that's the right word, but if I were, I could imagine Tom sending me signals that he wants me to continue my life as fully as I can.

On what would have been our sixteenth wedding anniversary, I hear a review of Joan Didion's book *The Year of Magical Thinking*, about the aftermath of her husband's sudden death, and how others marveled at her strength while she struggled with the craziness her overwhelming grief roused in her. I am out jogging and listening to this on NPR. It is a beautiful fall day, Tom's favorite time of the year, and the thought crosses my mind that I should take his ashes for a walk. Didion talks about setting out her husband's shoes in case he comes back. I find myself fantasizing about breaking into the columbarium at Arlington, where the individual niches are sealed, and liberating Tom. It's totally irrational, but imagining is my way of remembering.

Acknowledgments

THIS BOOK IS DEDICATED TO the A-Team, a trio of Tom's former colleagues whose visits lifted the spirits of the man they called "Chief." It had been years since they worked for him in the *Cleveland Plain Dealer* Washington Bureau, but their war stories brought laughter and they came together to care for the Chief when he could not care for himself. Thank you Tom Diemer, Judy Grande and Keith Epstein, and a special thanks to Bob Baggstrom, who had a sixth sense about when he was needed, which was often.

I know Tom would want me to express his appreciation to the Cleveland Clinic and especially to Laura Wood, his oncology nurse, and Dr. Ronald Bukowski, the physician who oversaw the clinical trials that may have extended Tom's life, but then again, maybe not. Researching this book, I became even more aware of Tom's phenomenal will. I am grateful to Dr. Stephen Hersh for sharing his notes to help me document Tom's thinking as he faced his impending mortality.

Of the many interviews I did, I want to particularly thank Dr. Ronald Cranford, the neurologist most associated with declaring Terri Schiavo in a persistent vegetative state. I spoke with him in March '06, not realizing he was ill, and his views about the power of the video images of Terri are reflected in the book. He died two months after we spoke of kidney cancer, the same disease that struck down Tom.

I also want to single out Dr. Carlos Gomez, a hospice administrator when we met who shared with me his views as a Catholic on the intersection of science and religion at life's end. He is now the medical director for the District of Columbia's first citywide program to deliver pediatric palliative care. Caring for someone at the end of life is a transforming experience that has made me an advocate of hospice and led me to accept an invitation to serve on the board of the National Hospice and Palliative Care Organization.

In bringing this book to fruition, I owe much to my research assistant, Marcia McMullen, who can find anything anywhere and who tracked down interview subjects with skill and grace. Her belief in the project kept me going during those inevitable times when I felt bogged down.

I want to thank my agent, Deborah Grosvenor, for introducing me to Bill Frucht, the editor at Basic Books whose vision made this book possible. He said I had a personal story to tell, and I should tell it in the context of the debate over Terri Schiavo. The concept took me on a journey that confirmed much of what I believed, but also challenged some of my easy assumptions about the debate that shook the nation. Without Bill's guidance and encouragement, this book wouldn't have happened. Thanks also to his able assistant, Courtney Miller, for shepherding the manuscript.

Finally, my family deserves a special commendation. My three grown sons, Eddie, Woody and Robert, all in the midst of busy lives, stepped in to help provide the care that was needed, as did my brother, Ed Roeloffs, and sister-in-law, Eileen Cox. I want to end with a general statement of thanks to all the people who reached out to Tom, and to me, during this time. Many are acknowledged in the book. Those that aren't should have their names enshrined somewhere, so here goes: Maryalyce Greicius, Frank and Maureen Greicius, Anne Renshaw, Maxine Champion, David Crossland, Susan King, Page Crosland, Tara Sonenshine, Katy and Don Burns, Carol Iantuono, Karen O'Connor, Sally Baker, and Frank Uhlmann, together with all the unheralded hospice workers who make a positive difference every day.

Appendix

Minus One Kidney, but Still Flossing

JULY 4, 1999

WASHINGTON—The first clue that something was wrong came in a phone call from Ginger, my urologist's secretary.

"The doctor wants to schedule another test," she said. "I'm sure he told you about the large mass in your kidney." Since the doctor had told me no such thing, I figured Ginger must have called the wrong patient. Some other poor guy had to cope with a "large mass" in his kidney. The doctor had not called me. I wasn't scheduled to see him until the next day to get the results of my tests.

"Oh, I'm sorry, I thought the doctor had spoken to you," Ginger said. "He still wants to see you tomorrow, and he definitely does want to schedule another test—a bone scan."

The next morning, my urologist greeted me, "How are you?"

"That's what I'm here to find out," I said.

Back in April, I had reported seeing blood in my urine to my primary-care physician, the third under a new "managed choice" health plan. The first two doctors had dropped out of the plan, which they felt was overmanaged.

This was my first visit to Doctor No. 3. He tested a urine sample and found no trace of blood. He gave me a container to take home to capture a sample if and when the blood returned. He told me not to worry.

More than a month later, at a regularly scheduled prostate check-up with the urologist, I offhandedly mentioned the blood in the urine. Without hesitating, he said, "We'll have some tests run."

"But my doctor said the urine sample was clean," I protested.

"That often happens, but it's not conclusive," said the urologist.

Several weeks later, sitting opposite me in an austere examining room, the urologist's voice turned grave as he answered his own question about my well-being. I took notes, as if gathering information for a story about someone else.

This was not—could not be—me he was talking about. I was the picture of health for my age (58) or any age. The only night I've ever spent in a hospital was when I was born. Did I mention that I ran four miles that morning before seeing the doctor?

"You need another test—a bone scan," the urologist said. "You've got something pretty big in your left kidney. I don't like the looks of it. In my experience, there is an extremely high likelihood that this is cancer. The kidney needs to come out as soon as possible. The cancer may have spread to the lymph nodes around the kidney."

"But I feel fine," I protested.

"Kidney cancer can grow without causing any trouble," he said.

By the time you read this, I should be in my third day of recovery from a radical nephrectomy, the medical term for removing a kidney.

MY WIFE HAD SUSPECTED the worst. I called her to confirm her suspicions. "To paraphrase Ronald Reagan," I said, "I don't have cancer—my kidney does."

That's what Reagan said to counter his doctor's solemn announcement to the press corps: "The president has cancer." Reagan figured that cancer was his prostate's problem, not his.

The doctor told me not to bother looking up the survival projections because we don't know yet the kind and extent of cancer we're dealing with. Naturally, I went straight to the Yahoo search engine on the Internet and plugged in "kidney cancer" and "survival."

(For the record, the five-year survival rate ranges from 87.5 percent for localized kidney cancer to 9.2 percent for cancer that has spread to other organs or bones.)

Doctors like patients to think that surgery isn't so bad. "The anticipation's the worst part," they say. Yeah, sure.

The anticipation so far has been a breeze. I'm in denial. There is an aura of unreality about it, as if I'm watching *E.R.* and this is happening to somebody else—the guy Ginger was supposed to call when she called me by mistake.

Once in a while, reality intrudes. I played golf over the weekend to get my mind off things. It was a sunny, blue-sky morning, and it felt good to be alive. But as I stood on the fifth green waiting for my playing partners to putt, I felt a chill—the dreads, I call it—a reminder that I've got an appointment with fate.

The one thing that keeps the dreads at bay is humor. One of my wife's friends, herself a cancer survivor, conquered the dreads by working on a book about her battle with the disease, titled, *You May Be Hitler, But I'm Not Poland.*

The late Howard Simons, managing editor of the *Washington Post* when the newspaper broke the Watergate story, set a standard for journalists coping with cancer. He kept his sense of humor to the end.

Gene Weingarten (author of *The Hypochondriac's Guide to Life. And Death.*) recalled his interview with Simons when his death from pancreatic cancer was imminent:

> I asked Howard if he was angry, and he said, "You mean like this?" And he looked to the heavens and cried, "Why me, and not Pol Pot?" Then he smiled and said he was not angry.
>
> ... I asked him to tell me how the impendence of death had altered his perspective on the meaning of life. This is what he said: "Mostly, you no longer worry about flossing."

Well, I'm still flossing. And one of the last things I did before heading off to the hospital was to order two new pairs of running shoes to get back in shape once I'm on my feet again.

Life after Surgery Begins
AUGUST 1, 1999

WASHINGTON—Let me set the scene for you.

The time is 3:30 in the morning. The place is a private room on the third floor of George Washington University Hospital.

Hours earlier, doctors had operated to remove a cancerous left kidney. I am hooked to an array of tubes. One drips sugar water into my veins. Another injects painkiller into the epidural space of my spine. A third lets me administer an extra jolt of anti-pain juice as needed, but no more than once every 20 minutes. And then there is a catheter to drain the processed fluids out of my system.

The morphine that had produced a giddy high in the recovery room has begun wearing off and I am conscious of a throbbing ache where my kidney used to be.

In spite of it all, I am laughing at the antics of my nurse, Marita, a 4-foot-10 dynamo from the Philippines. She is standing on tiptoe on the nightstand reaching up with forceps to turn off the light above my head because the pull-cord has snapped off.

This was the highlight of my hectic first night in the hospital. Sleep was interrupted constantly by the beep-beep-beep signal that an IV had run dry, or by a nurse's aide popping in to monitor my temperature and blood pressure.

At daybreak, the team of doctors that had operated on me came to check their work. One of them peeled off the bandage over the 12-inch incision and announced, "It looks very good." Looking down, I could see the tops of the two-dozen staples holding flesh in place across an angry red scar.

Less than 24 hours after the surgery, I was on my feet—well, sort of. Attempting to navigate the space between my bed and a chair, my knees gave way and I collapsed into the arms of Darlene, a tall, solidly built nurse's aide.

"Shall we dance?" I asked through teeth clenched in pain.

On hearing about this, the anesthesiologist concluded that I was getting too much pain medicine. She cut back the dosage and advised me, "You may experience some discomfort." This, a resident doctor later told me, was medical jargon. "Roughly translated, it means I am about to slice you open with a rusty butter knife," he said.

I laughed. It hurt to laugh.

It's been a month since the operation. The staples are out and the pain has diminished to the point where two Extra-Strength Tylenol capsules every six hours do the trick. I'm taking long walks, morning and night, and only occasional naps. I'll be fit for full-time work in another couple of weeks.

Kidney Cancer and a Sequel

OCTOBER 8, 2000

WASHINGTON—Nearly 20 years ago, I met an extraordinary woman named Laurel Lee. Divorced with three children and suffering from cancer, Lee lived by the dictum, "When life gives you lemons, make lemonade."

She turned a hospital journal written for her children and illustrated with her own quirky drawings into a best-selling inspirational book, "Walking Through the Fire."

The glow of her unexpected publishing success vanished when a follow-up examination showed the Hodgkin's disease had returned. When she told her agent, he was appropriately sympathetic. Then, brightening, he asked, "Laurel, have you thought about a sequel?"

Lee laughed when she told the story. She could afford to because by then she had once again beaten back the cancer and produced a second bestseller, "Signs of Spring."

Well, dear readers, I've got a sequel of my own to write. A month and a half ago, I learned that the kidney cancer I thought I had conquered with the surgical removal of my left kidney in July 1999 had returned, this time in a lung.

After the surgery, I was told I had a 70 percent chance of living out my life cancer-free. The odds were in my favor, but I lost. With metastatic kidney cancer (when microscopic cells develop into tumors in other parts of the body), the odds are reversed. The statistics now suggest I have a 20 percent chance of living to 2005. The median life span for metastatic kidney cancer is 18 months.

Although President Nixon declared war on cancer in 1971, the weapons at the disposal of medical science 30 years later still are primitive—rocks and clubs against a stealthy and nearly impervious enemy. In the case of kidney cancer, the two most effective weapons, chemotherapy and radiation, are powerless, even when the cancer is detected early, as mine was.

Kidney cancer conquers when the body's immune system is weakened. The FDA-approved treatments—Interleuken-2 and Interferon-alpha, separately or in combination—attempt to arm the immune system to fight back. The possible side effects (nausea/vomiting, anxiety and confusion, constant flu-like symptoms, to name a few) can be brutal.

(You may have read recently about a new "cure" for kidney cancer, based on stem-cell transplant. Most of the stories left out the vital information that the patient must have a perfect-match sibling, which I don't, and that the treatment can be very toxic and, like the other treatments, can cause death.)

One kidney cancer patient said he feels like a soldier hitting the beach in *Saving Private Ryan*, seeing buddies on all sides falling one by one and wondering, "Am I next?"

In the face of all this, doctors, family and friends urge me to keep a positive attitude. So, I spend a part of each day visualizing my newly emboldened T cells attacking and defeating the enemy.

Tomorrow morning, I report to the Taussig Cancer Center of the Cleveland Clinic Foundation to begin a month of outpatient treatment, followed by two weeks of rest, then a CAT Scan to see if I'm making progress.

I chose the Cleveland Clinic because I'll be under the care of Dr. Ronald Bukowski, one of the world's leading authorities on kidney cancer, and research nurse Laura Wood, herself a specialist in treating this disease.

Like many kidney cancer patients undergoing treatment, I'm part of a clinical trial exploring cutting-edge drugs. Along with the FDA-approved drugs, I will receive a third immune booster with the unromantic name of GM-CSF.

As for the odds, I'm told mine are better than most because the cancer so far is without symptoms and confined to a lung. If enough of the smaller tumors can be zapped by the treatment, surgery may be an option to remove the rest.

Stephen Jay Gould, the paleontologist, evolutionary biologist, and science writer, exposed the fallacy of statistics after suffering from abdominal mesothelioma, a rare cancer with a median mortality of only eight months.

Gould's scientific mind immediately concluded that a median is not a hard reality, but an imperfect measure, an abstraction subject to countless variables. True, half the deaths would be scrunched in the narrow range between zero and eight months. But the other half could extend out for years and years.

"I possessed every one of the characteristics conferring a probability of longer life," Gould wrote. "I was young; my disease had been recognized in a relatively early state; I would receive the nation's best medical treatment; I had the world to live for; I knew how to read the data properly and not despair."

Eighteen years after his diagnosis, Gould is alive and well. He's my role model.

Steve Dunn, a metastatic kidney cancer survivor who launched an Internet site to help other patients, sums up Gould's experience with an addendum to his on-line signature: "The possibilities are infinitely greater than the averages."

My sentiments exactly. Lemonade, anyone?

Gladiator in the Ring

JANUARY 2001

We all live with uncertainty—it is part of the human condition—but I've had an extra dose of it ever since I was diagnosed with metastatic kidney cancer five months ago.

Many of you have sent letters and e-mail or left phone messages asking about my condition, so today's column is a progress report.

I spent one morning last week undergoing tests to see

whether the treatment I've been enduring has done any good. In the afternoon, research nurse Laura Wood spread out a dozen large slides from my CT scans on a wall-mounted light box and Dr. Ronald Bukowski, my oncologist, interpreted them.

My wife and I had spent a restless night anticipating this moment. The possible results ranged from the most negative (the disease had spread to other organs) to the most positive (the cancerous nodules in my left lung had miraculously disappeared).

The highest probability was for a result somewhere in the middle, which is what I got.

Pointing to a slide showing the largest nodule in my lung—a blob about the size of a pencil eraser—Dr. Bukowski observed that it had shrunk in the last month and was now less than half the size it had measured before I started the treatment three months earlier. The other nodules in the lung were too small to measure accurately, but Dr. Bukowski said they hadn't grown since the last CT scans.

"How am I doing?" I asked.

"You're doing great," Dr. Bukowski said.

He didn't add "so far," but he might have. Outcomes for the immunotherapy I am undergoing are varied and unpredictable. Early progress is a good sign, but no guarantee that the final result will be positive—thus, the constant uncertainty.

At best (and this is only in three to five percent of the cases) the treatment results in complete remission of the disease. For some patients, the treatment is effective for several cycles, and then stops working. Others have had to drop out of the treatment because they cannot tolerate the side effects of chills and shakes followed by fevers as high as 105 degrees.

My prize for showing continued improvement is that I qualify for another round of toxic treatment, starting tomorrow. For a month, I'll be injecting myself with three FDA-approved drugs, Interleuken-2, Interferon-alpha and GM-CSF. Adding GM-CSF to the other two drugs makes this a clinical trial.

Food tastes awful while the treatment is underway, so I lose weight. I restore the lost pounds during the two-week break between cycles by loading up on previously forbidden foods like peanut butter, ice cream, hamburgers and potato chips. My already thinning hair is falling out at a faster clip thanks to the drugs and spotty nutrition.

If I make it through a fourth cycle, Dr. Bukowski said I would revisit a surgeon to see if the remaining cancer can be removed surgically, my best hope for a recovery. If not, I'll continue the immunotherapy. A couple of Dr. Bukowski's patients have been on it for two years.

Kidney cancer is relatively rare in this country. In a population of 281 million, only 30,000 cases are diagnosed each year. I had a better chance of being gunned down in the streets [than] I did contracting this disease. But I have learned to stop asking, "Why me?" There is no sure answer to that.

My cancer is classified as Stage 4 (the designation for terminal cases) but I am better off than many others in this category. My metastasis was discovered early and is limited in scope, at least so far. Although the treatment causes chronic fatigue, I've had no symptoms from the cancer itself. This increases my odds for durable remission or at least several years' extension of my life beyond the 18-month median lifespan for Stage 4 patients.

Years ago I came across the "Eschatological Laundry List—A Partial Register of the 927 (or was it 928?) Eternal Truths" by psychologist Sheldon Kopp, the author of *Guru*. Item 4 on the list reads, "We are all already dying and we will be dead for a long time." I find some comfort in the reminder that we're all on the same boat—the *Titanic*.

The uncertainty we all live with is not that we will die—that is a given—but when and how. My illness has focused this uncertainty on my periodic CT scans, when, like a gladiator in a Roman arena, I am given a thumbs up or thumbs down.

Because my column has been appearing most Sundays during the treatment, some readers have assumed that I'm back to good health. Most of my writing actually takes place at 2 or 3 a.m. after the side effects have come and gone and I am jolted into hyper alertness by the process.

In the weeks ahead, I'll be writing as frequently as I can. (You wouldn't want George W. Bush to get a free ride in these pages, would you?) If my column is missing on any given Sunday, you'll know that the previous week was especially hard.

To all who have written, e-mailed or sent phone messages, thank you. It is comforting to know that I'm not in this alone.

The Long, Tortured Road to a Cure

JULY 29, 2001

I spent last weekend at an airport hotel in San Francisco with 150 others who were searching desperately for clues to the biggest mystery in our lives.

Officially, we were participants in the annual conference of the Kidney Cancer Association. My wife said it reminded her of one of those weekend dinner-theater gatherings where a crime is staged and the guests compete to solve it.

In our case the crime was not a fake murder, but a real disease that pits those who get it in a life-or-death race against the calendar and the odds. The median life expectancy for patients with stage IV metastatic cancer that has spread from the kidney to other organs or bones is 18 months.

There is no known cure for kidney cancer. Interleukin-2 (IL-2) is the only FDA-approved drug to treat the disease. It produces a response in about 15 to 20 percent of patients. Five percent get a complete response, meaning the cancerous tumors disappear. But there is no guarantee the disease will not recur months or even years later. The longest disease-free survival so far has been a dozen years.

We were told repeatedly during the session to "ignore the statistics."

I was diagnosed with renal cell carcinoma (RCC), the medical term for kidney cancer, in the summer of 1999. My left kidney was removed surgically. Thirteen months later, a CT scan showed the disease had reappeared in my left lung. Since last October, I have been undergoing IL-2-based immunotherapy. My disease has not gotten worse, but neither has it gotten measurably better.

"Stable is good," is the mantra for patients like me. Stability buys time. If you can keep the disease in check, you might still be alive when a cure is discovered.

The Kidney Cancer Association conference opened with a tour of Chiron Therapeutics Laboratories, where Interleukin-2 is made. Although we were in the home of the most potent drug against kidney cancer, a Chiron official confided, "If I were diagnosed with kidney cancer, I wouldn't be satisfied with my options." A company oncologist told us, "The drug discovery process is long and frustrating, and yields are low."

Many drugs have shown great potential in tests on mice, only to fail when tested in humans. One scientist joked, "We know two things: how to give mice cancer and how to cure cancer in mice."

Later, there was a great deal of discussion about the relative merits of taking high-dose IL-2 in the hospital versus low-dose IL-2 at home, which is the treatment I am on. The debate glosses over the fact that neither method is particularly successful.

My oncologist, Dr. Ronald Bukowski of the Cleveland Clinic, addressed the conference and made an appeal for patients to cooperate with researchers to find a new way of treating kidney cancer.

Citing the low percentage of positive responses under the current regime, Bukowski said, "We need a new drug as first-line therapy." Finding it will require some patients to participate in studies where they may be part of a control group getting only sugar pills.

"We don't like placebo studies, but it's something we have to do," Bukowski told the patients who worry that being in the placebo group would cost them precious time in the battle against the disease.

Dr. Robert J. Amato, another kidney cancer expert from Texas, reinforced Bukowski's call for trials of new drugs, saying, "Ten to 15 percent success is not good enough. We need to evolve into new treatments."

We discussed the pluses and minuses of "compassionate use" programs that allow patients in desperate straits to try drugs that have not yet gone through randomized clinical trials under controlled conditions. Patients see compassionate use as a right for those who can't wait for the tedious process of scientific evaluation. Drug companies see it as a big expense with little payoff in the sense that results, good or bad, don't provide precise data for FDA approval. Doctors worry that widespread distribution of drugs before they are tested would limit the pool of patients for trials where they might get a placebo.

With no cure in sight, much of the emphasis in cancer treatment these days is on living with the disease. We learned, for instance, about the role of nutrition in combating the effects of cancer and the benefits of visual imaging. It is hard to believe that merely imagining T-cells ganging up on cancer cells will improve our chances, but anything is worth a try.

After three days, we were no closer to finding a solution to this deadly mystery—but then we didn't really expect to be.

Jim Hunter, a 10-year survivor, summed up the feelings of a lot of us when he said, "I look at the treatment as a survival thing. I don't think about a cure. I worry about the next six months, the next year."

A Cancer Patient Looks at Terrorism

OCTOBER 14, 2001

New members signing on to the Internet site for cancer patients are greeted with this sardonic message: "Welcome to the club that nobody wants to belong to."

Now, in a way, we are all members of a club we'd rather not belong to. Call it the Club of Anxiety. It came into being on the morning of Sept. 11 and almost instantly recruited 281 million members in this country and millions more abroad.

As a kidney cancer patient myself, I am aware of the similarities between cancer and terrorism. In the days after the Sept. 11 attacks on the World Trade Center and the Pentagon, I told friends that being a Stage IV cancer patient (there is no Stage V) is like being on the 90th floor of one of the towers in New York: You don't know whether you can make it out, but you're sure going to try.

For Americans, even those far from the sites of the plane crashes on Sept. 11, the news hit like a cancer diagnosis. From that day forward, life would not be the same. I was reminded of an exchange between Daniel Patrick Moynihan, who was working in the White House at the time, and journalist Mary McGrory on the day President Kennedy was shot.

"We'll never laugh again," McGrory said.

"Oh, we'll laugh again," Moynihan said, "but we'll never be young again."

So it is with the onset of cancer or terrorism. From then on, there is an agonizing uncertainty to life's calendar. True enough, no one is ever given a guarantee of another dawn, but the real and present danger of an invader, whether it is cancer or terrorist, makes us more conscious of the ultimate odds against us.

Terrorists, like cancer, hide in the shadows, sometimes lurking for years before striking. We had our first visit from Osama bin Laden's strain of terrorism eight years ago with the attempted bombing of the World Trade Center. Six people were killed and hundreds injured.

We thought that was an isolated incident, a bizarre aberration, which was quickly forgotten. We were cured!

Then came Sept. 11 and an attack so devastating it left us wondering whether we would ever be whole again. Millions of people not directly affected by the attacks nevertheless feel the pain. One of every four of us reports feeling depressed a month after the horrific explosions.

Laura Wood, the research nurse who is monitoring my care at the Cleveland Clinic, said she imagines that many people now feel the same way that cancer patients feel, that they have lost control of their lives. More accurately, we have become aware that we've never had any real control over anything.

President Bush promises to "smoke out" the terrorists and rid the world of this scourge. But terrorist cells, like cancer cells, multiply rapidly, lie dormant for years before attacking, and defy attempts to blast, burn, suffocate or starve them.

Terrorism, like cancer, attacks the heartiest among us. A healthy diet and daily exercise cannot grant a person immunity any more than capacious oceans to the east and west and friendly neighbors to the north and south can guarantee a country invulnerability.

When the diagnosis is cancer, a man or woman has a choice to make: Learn as much as possible about the attacker and try to defeat it or pretend that life will go on as always if you ignore it. The same holds for terrorism.

Many who never gave much thought to global politics before now feel driven to learn who Osama bin Laden is, what he wants, and why a whole generation of militant young people in the Muslim world seem to hate us deeply. Becoming aware that we really do live in a global village is a good thing.

And we can take some comfort in the knowledge that the odds of our being killed by terrorists are very long. We face a much greater risk of death by motor vehicle accidents, firearms, poisoning, falls, even suffocation, not to mention heart disease or cancer.

One e-mail correspondent, Polly Morey, saw even the Sept. 11 attack as a glass more than half full. If all 50,000 people had been doomed in the World Trade Center and all 23,000 in the Pentagon and if the planes that crashed had been filled to capacity, 74,280 could have been killed. As it was, 93 percent survived or avoided the attacks.

"That's a higher survival rate than for heart attacks or breast cancer," Ms. Morey trumpeted. "Pass this information on to those in fear. Don't fear the terrorists."

Life will go on, as it did after the Civil War, after World War I, World War II and Vietnam, after the influenza epidemic of 1918 that killed 550,000 in the United States and after the Great Depression that crippled the nation economically and psychologically.

Now we have our own life-threatening peril to deal with, and, as the late Sheldon Kopp said in his "Partial Register of the 927 (or was it 928?) Eternal Truths," we have only ourselves and one another; that may not be much, but that's all we have.

Welcome to the club that nobody wants to belong to.

The Cancer Phase Called "Now What?"

MARCH 24, 2002

When a cancer patient sits down with his or her oncologist to discuss the findings of the latest CT scans and X-rays, a kind of Kabuki dance takes place, following a well-worn script. Any deviation from the script signals trouble. In my case, I had been undergoing immunotherapy treatment for metastatic kidney cancer for 17 months under the care of Dr. Ronald Bukowski, a kidney cancer expert, at the Cleveland Clinic Foundation.

Every six to eight weeks, I would report to the clinic for blood work, a CT scan and an X-ray, then meet with Dr. Bukowski and clinical research nurse Laura Wood to review the results and plan the next phase of treatment. Our script went like this:

BUKOWSKI: How are you?

PATIENT: That's what I'm here to find out.

BUKOWSKI: No change. Everything's stable.

Stable is good in the cancer game, where the goal is not necessarily a cure, but long-term survival.

When I was tested in January, however, Bukowski said one of the lung tumors appeared to have grown, but that it was hard to tell because of the "slice" the CT scan captured.

He said if you slice an egg at one of the ends, you get one diameter, if you slice it in the middle, the fat part, you get another, bigger diameter.

He pronounced me "stable with a question mark."

Ten days ago, after another set of scans, the Kabuki dance varied ominously.

BUKOWSKI: How are you?

PATIENT: That's what I'm here to find out.

BUKOWSKI: Let's go out to the hall. I want to show you the films.

Nobody had to tell me that the news was not going to be good. The films showed that one tumor, apparently the one that had raised a question previously, had grown from a few millimeters in diameter when treatment began in October 2000 to 1.5 centimeters by this March.

It was enough to knock me out of the clinical trial I had been on involving injections of Interleukin-2, Interferon-alpha and GM-CSF.

Bukowski suggested that I take a few weeks off and then pick another trial. He offered two possibilities at the Cleveland Clinic. One would require me to travel from Washington to Cleveland every week; the other, I learned later, would not accept patients with a particular kind of cataract, which I happen to have.

Many kidney cancer patients are faced with this predicament. Having failed Interleukin-2, the only FDA-approved treatment for kidney cancer, they must go shopping among other treatments offered in the United States or overseas.

(Who or what is on trial here, the patient or the drugs? Carl Dixon, president and executive director of the Kidney Cancer Association, says patients don't fail treatments. He says treatments fail patients.)

The leading experts are well known in the kidney cancer community. Besides Bukowski, there is Dr. Janice Dutcher in the Bronx, Dr. Robert Amato in Houston, Dr. Robert Figlin in Los Angeles and, of course, the National Cancer Institute right in my backyard in Bethesda, Md.

On the Internet, where patients exchange information, promising new drugs appear and disappear quickly. Somebody finds a new trial in Boston or Seattle or New Orleans and there is a buzz for a while as hopes rise. But there is no magic elixir for Stage IV kidney cancer.

One of the first things I came across in my search for clinical trials was a press release from one drug company blithely stating that "patients with renal cell carcinoma who fail IL-2 therapy have a median survival of approximately six months."

That's not me, I told myself. My overall health, the relatively small size of the tumors and the fact that they have not spread beyond the left lung suggest that I will be on the long end of that median. Still, it does suggest that time is of the essence in pursuing another path of treatment.

The fact that Interleukin-2 failed in my case eliminates me from many clinical trials that are based on some combination of IL-2 and other drugs. In picking a new course of treatment, it's also important not to close off too many other options if the second trial also fails.

Surgical methods that are less invasive than resecting or removing a lung might be used to lessen the tumor load, but that is only a delaying tactic for someone with multiple metastases.

So many possibilities, yet so few promising prospects. So far, this particular kind of cancer has defeated every challenge modern medicine has produced. And we who are stuck with the disease sigh and go about our lives.

In the movie *28 Days*, Sandra Bullock, who plays a recovering alcoholic undergoing treatment, says, "They tell us to live one day at a time—as if we had a choice. Two, three days at a time?"

Of course, all of us live one day at a time. Some of us are just more aware of it.

Cancer Patients Experiment, Try Alternatives

DECEMBER 22, 2002

Cancer patients are vulnerable. I speak from experience on this.

Writing about my own battle with kidney cancer has prompted plenty of feedback from readers offering curative advice ranging from coffee enemas to vitamins and visualization techniques.

Conventional medicine has little to offer kidney cancer patients. Interleukin-2, the so-called gold standard of treatment, cures only 6 to 8 percent of patients. Given that kind of success rate, the siren song of alternative treatments is hard to resist.

Conventional treatments often have nasty side effects. For 17 months on a combination of Interleukin-2, Interferon and GM-CSF, I endured chill-induced tremors, high fevers, loss of appetite and other unpleasantness. Many alternative treatments, by comparison, boast of being free of side effects.

After I was taken off conventional treatment, a friend and fellow kidney cancer patient persuaded me that macrobiotic diet was the way to go. He says it saved his life.

For the last four months, I have been following the diet—not because I think it will cure my cancer, as some believe, but because healthy eating can't hurt. Since August, I have eaten more organic brown rice and consumed more steamed vegetables than in all my prior years on the planet combined. And I've learned how to cook, a side benefit that my wife appreciates and that I enjoy.

In addition to the diet, Michio Kushi, a leading teacher of macrobiotics, recommends singing a happy song every day. Fortunately, I can carry a tune.

My friend's cancer had been more or less stable for several years. So it came as a surprise to me when he announced he was abandoning macrobiotics for another alternative treatment offered by a doctor on one of the Hawaiian Islands.

Macrobiotics had stopped the cancer in its tracks, my friend said, but he wanted to get rid of it completely. He was convinced that a doctor transplanted from Florida to an island paradise in the Pacific could cure his cancer—and mine, too. I did not have to be talked into taking a trip to Hawaii to see for myself. I sat in on one of my friend's three-times-a-week treatments.

The doctor, an osteopath, explained that his treatment

differed from most conventional treatments that attempt to rid the body of cancer. His treatment went deeper, he said, by attacking the fungal overgrowth, parasites and bacteria that cause most cancers.

The treatment consists of a healthy, organic diet (less rigid than the macrobiotic diet), prescribed medications, supplements and intravenous doses of vitamins and minerals.

What caught my attention was a technique the doctor called "forensic kinesiology." He demonstrated on my friend. Lying on his back on the examining table, my friend raised his right arm straight up. The doctor asked a series of questions. My friend didn't say a word, but his arm "answered."

After each question, the doctor attempted to pull down my friend's arm using two fingers. If the arm went down, the answer was "yes." If it stayed up, the answer was "no." Based on the arm's answers the doctor adjusts the kinds and dosages of medicines and supplements he prescribes.

"With this treatment, the underlying reason for my cancer will be gone and the tumors will melt away," my friend says. I hope he's right. I'm pulling for him.

I have nothing against supplements and high-dose Vitamin C and certainly have no objection to spending a few months in Hawaii (other than the cost, which runs into the tens of thousands of dollars for the full schedule of treatments, plus living expenses). But the divining arm diagnosis is not for me.

Another kidney cancer patient in California called me to say he was cured by a combination of intravenous vitamins and medicines administered at a clinic in Reno, Nev. He said he's been cancer-free for five years. He urged me to get on the next plane to Reno.

Anecdotal evidence like this is what makes complementary and alternative medicine a multi-billion-dollar business.

The American Cancer Society's Guide to Complementary and Alternative Cancer Methods lists more than 100 methods for which there is no scientific evidence that they can cure or influence the course of any cancer. The list includes the macrobiotic diet and applied kinesiology.

Recently on the Internet discussion group for those with kidney cancer, one patient wrote, "I have been on supplements including Cantron and Protocel for over four years and truly believe they have extended my life. ..."

A woman who lost her husband to kidney cancer answered that her husband went four and a half years with lung metastases "without any significant visible change." After a relapse, he took massive doses of shark cartilage for two years, only to watch the disease progress.

"I am not opposed to trying alternatives," she wrote. "I simply suggest looking at the evidence regarding them. Is it hard evidence, or evidence like yours? People with kidney cancer can go from rapid progression to a complete standstill for years without any treatment."

That's just it. Kidney cancer marches to its own quirky drummer.

I have been off treatment since March. My most recent CT scans and X-rays earlier this month showed that my disease is in an "indolent phase," as my oncologist put it. So, for now, we're taking a wait and watch approach. My next tests will be in April.

My best hope is that a promising trial will come along while I still have a chance to take advantage of it. Meanwhile, I'll keep eating healthy and singing a happy song.

Going after Cancer with a "Knife"

OCTOBER 5, 2003

As I lay on the operating table about to undergo brain surgery one day last week, I thought of Dan Quayle. It was Quayle, trying to quote "a mind is a terrible thing to waste," who declared, "What a waste it is to lose one's mind. Or not to have a mind is being very wasteful. How true that is."

I would have reminded the surgeons operating on me of this indisputable wisdom, but they had abandoned the room, leaving my brain and me at the mercy of a machine.

"Wait a minute," you're thinking. "Did he say brain surgery?" Let me explain.

A week earlier, I had reported to the Cleveland Clinic for diagnostic tests measuring the extent of cancer still in my body resulting from a cancerous kidney originally diagnosed and surgically removed in July 1999.

Because I had complained of headaches and dizziness recently, my oncologist, Dr. Ronald Bukowski, ordered a brain scan. Sure enough, the CT scan showed two tumors, one on each side of the brain. Double-checking with a more sensitive MRI scanner showed the larger of the tumors had a smaller tumor orbiting around it like one of Jupiter's moons—three in all. I was scheduled for consultations with a neurosurgical oncologist and a radiation oncologist, who explained that the best option for treating these "lesions," as they called them, was Gamma Knife surgery.

The Gamma Knife, I learned, is not really a knife at all, but a multimillion-dollar machine developed in the 1950s by a Swedish neurosurgeon that has been used since the 1980s to treat a broad range of brain disorders, including cancer. The surgery, I was happy to learn, did not involve cutting open my head. Rather, technicians would screw a frame to my skull (ouch!) and attach to it a mask that would focus radiation beams on the lesions to eradicate or at least shrink them.

Dr. Michael Vogelbaum, the neurosurgical oncologist, and Dr. John Suh, the radiation oncologist, told me I was eligible for a national clinical trial seeking to recruit 480 patients to help settle the question whether targeted Gamma Knife radiation could be made more beneficial by following up with broadly dispersed whole-brain radiation.

I wanted to do my part for science—I really did—but I was stopped by one almost certain side effect of whole-brain radiation, namely the loss of my already thinning hair with the odds against having it grow back fully. I decided to go for the Gamma Knife and keep the whole-brain option as a last resort.

I reported to the Gamma Knife Center at 7 A.M. Nurse Betty Jamison applied a topical pain duller and injected a muscle relaxant while she and Vogelbaum fitted the frame tightly to my head. The slightest movement, they explained, could misdirect a beam into healthy tissue. Radiation therapy technician Debbie Henry wheeled me off for a CT scan and an MRI that would determine the coordinates for firing the radiation beams.

For more than an hour, Vogelbaum and Suh analyzed the scan data and developed a surgical plan involving precise mathematical calculations, angles of attack and radiation intensity. I received five bursts of between five and 15 minutes each, with mask changes and position adjustments between doses.

Left alone in the lead-lined operating room, I listened to classical music on the radio, not seeing, hearing, feeling or smelling the radiation coursing through my skull. The only painful part was the screwing and unscrewing of the frame.

In an hour or two, I felt practically normal. My wife and I went out to dinner that night and I drove back to Washington the next day.

I'll go back in six weeks to find out whether the treatment is working and whether any more lesions have cropped up that might require treatment. One sour note is that even if the brain metastases are eradicated, the fact that I've had lesions on the brain makes me ineligible for some promising trials for the cancer elsewhere in my body.

Dr. Bukowski said he was pondering other options, but I know there is no magic elixir to treat renal cell carcinoma. Like many cancer patients, I'm hoping to live long enough to take advantage of a breakthrough treatment if one should come along.

Meanwhile, I'll be doing my best to fend off the inevitable. But then, isn't that what we all do?

Fighting Cancer with Every Tick of the Clock
NOVEMBER 16, 2003

I think I can empathize more than most with the plight of the Browns. My season, like theirs, is on the line. One more loss may be one too many. The difference is that whether they win or lose this year, there will be other seasons. For me, this could be the end game.

My three-year battle with metastatic kidney cancer now has me playing "prevent defense." In football, to prevent the opponent from scoring a winning touchdown in the final minute or two, the defense gives ground in the middle of the field, hoping the clock will run out before the opponent can score.

Any fan can tell you that prevent defense fails at least as frequently as it works. But in my case, the prevent defense is not simply the best option available, it's the only one.

The sole FDA-approved offensive weapon against kidney cancer—a drug called Interleukin-2—failed me more than a year ago.

My doctors at the Cleveland Clinic and I were "watching and waiting" for a promising drug trial to come along. What came along instead was cancer's equivalent of "the long bomb," a scoring strike to the brain.

The clinic's urologists, radiologists and neurosurgeons struck back with a high-tech weapon of their own—laser gamma knife surgery—which eliminates or shrinks brain metastases as much as 80 percent of the time.

Last Monday, six weeks after the gamma knife surgery, I was looking for good news as I sat in the office of neurosurgeon Michael Vogelbaum while he posted films of my follow-up MRI on a wall-mounted light box.

"I have good news and bad news," he said. "On balance, it's bad news."

The gamma knife surgery had significantly reduced one of the brain tumors, but the larger one had continued to grow. Worse, three new brain tumors had popped up.

After reviewing the options open to me—from doing nothing and letting the cancer take its course to putting up the equivalent of a goal line stand against the disease—I chose the most aggressive course available.

In less than 24 hours, I underwent a second round of gamma knife surgery, using focused laser beams to try to kill the three new tumors that had surfaced in a mere six weeks.

Since the gamma knife had not worked on the larger tumor (now almost an inch in diameter), Vogelbaum proposed conventional brain surgery to excise the large tumor and a much smaller one orbiting it like a moon around Jupiter. Vogelbaum was leaving town, so he put me in the hands of Dr. Gene Barnett, the chief neurological surgeon.

After a day off, I was back on the operating table, this time under anesthetic, for Barnett to drill a 1- to 1-1/2-inch hole through my skull like an ice fisherman, open the membrane that covers the brain and, following a computerized map of my head, fish out the tumor.

The risk of temporary or permanent damage, such as to vision or motor skills, is relatively small, Dr. Barnett said, but added ominously, "The bad news is, it's not zero, and if it's you, it's you. But you've got to compare that to the risk of doing nothing and letting the tumor do bad things to you."

Before giving my OK for surgery, I wanted to see the results of a CT scan on the rest of my body. If the cancer was
growing as rapidly in my lungs as in the brain, what would
be the use? But the CT scan showed the lung tumors and
one in a buttocks muscle had not grown appreciably.

"We're on the cusp," Vogelbaum said. "The danger is in
losing control."

Vogelbaum speculated that the new tumors in the brain
could be the result of a shower of metastases coming from
elsewhere in the body.

If such a shower were a one-time event, then the brain
surgeries followed by two weeks of whole brain radiation
could calm the storm, at least temporarily. And if one or
two new tumors appear, they could be controlled by the
gamma knife.

"The odds are now more against you than for you," Vogelbaum told me straight out. "But in terms of your prognosis, the odds don't tell us much. It's much more in the
hands of your cancer. We still have reason to be optimistic."

By the time you read this, I should be in my hospital bed
recuperating from the surgery and watching the Browns
take on Arizona. We'll know soon enough whether the
Browns have any hope of making the playoffs. And sometime in January, tests will show whether the prevent defense
devised by my medical team did its job.

Meanwhile, please join me in a chorus of "DEEE-
FENSE!"

CT and MRI Have Gloomy Tales to Tell

JANUARY 24, 2004

At a dinner over New Year's, I was the only one in the room who wore a hat—indoors.

It was my first night out in public after undergoing whole-brain radiation, which left my head Kojak-bald. As I face side effects ranging from extreme fatigue and nausea to cognitive impairment, baldness should be the least of my concerns. Still, I was embarrassed.

I sat next to an attractive investment banker from New York. Answering her quizzical look, I doffed my hat and asked, "Hat or no hat, what do you think?"

"With the hat on, you look like a dork," she said, kindly. "Without it, you're kind of handsome."

The "kind of" notwithstanding, the hat came off.

The goal of three weeks of whole-brain radiation was to kill microscopic metastases in my brain before they could sprout. Alas, when I underwent an MRI three weeks after the radiation treatments, it showed three new brain metastases.

As I write this, I am seated in the Gamma Knife Center at the Cleveland Clinic awaiting surgery to zap the three new tumors.

A CT scan of the rest of my body showed my systemic kidney cancer progressing like a smoldering forest fire.

More than at any time since my original cancer diagnosis in the summer of 1999, I am running out of options.

A Washington psychiatrist who specializes in patients with potentially terminal diseases told me it might be time to lower my expectations—to "redefine hope" from beating cancer to controlling it.

"If there's nothing more doctors can offer, you'll have to ask yourself, 'How do I live as well as I can for as long as I can?'" he advised.

My oncologist at the Cleveland Clinic, Dr. Ronald Bukowski, cautioned me not to give up on treatment—not yet.

Brain metastases make me ineligible for most clinical trials for metastasized renal cell carcinoma (kidney cancer). Bukowski said options remain, including Thalidomide, once the scourge of pregnant women. Three weeks after the brain metastases are treated, we can go back to work on the systemic disease, he said.

Dr. Michael Vogelbaum, the neurosurgeon in charge of my brain treatment, said that stabilizing the systemic disease (now lodged in my lungs, pancreas and left buttock, to name a few of the sites) is a prerequisite to a cancer-free brain.

The Catch-22 is this: Systemic treatment cannot begin for at least three weeks, time enough for new brain metastases to emerge. If the latest Gamma Knife treatment fails, I might require another open-brain surgery.

I told Vogelbaum I was beginning to feel uneasy about the amount of money (so far, most covered by insurance) it is costing to keep me alive, money that might be better spent on patients with brighter prospects.

Vogelbaum said his job is to treat patients, period. As long as a viable treatment exists and the patient is willing, he's prepared to try, he said.

Vogelbaum said that in some democratic systems, where government controls who gets certain treatments, I would not have gotten a third Gamma Knife surgery, or a second or possibly even a first.

"It doesn't work that way in our society, thank God," he said. "It's nice to live in a society where every life counts."

For now, that's good enough for me. It's a presidential election year, and I don't want to miss it.

References

BOOKS

Barragate, Phillip L. *Whatever Happened to God?* Waldoboro, Maine: Goose River Press, 2006.

Bartholome, William G. *Meditations.* Kansas City, Mo.: Midwest Bioethics Center, 2000.

Byock, Ira, M.D. *Dying Well: Peace and Possibilities at the End of Life.* New York: Riverhead Books, 1997.

Caplan, Arthur L., James J. McCartney, and Dominic A. Sisti, eds. *The Case of Terri Schiavo: Ethics at the End of Life.* Amherst, N.Y.: Prometheus Books, 2006.

Colby, William. *The Long Goodbye.* Carlsbad, Calif.: Hay House, 2002.

Gibbs, David. *Fighting for Dear Life: The Untold Story of Terri Schiavo and What It Means for Us All.* Minneapolis: Bethany House, 2007.

Schiavo, Michael, with Michael Hirsh. *Terri, the Truth.* New York: Dutton, Penguin Group, 2006.

Schindler, Mary, and Robert Schindler, with Suzanne Schindler Vitadamo and Bobby Schindler. *A Life That Matters: The Legacy of Terri Schiavo–a Lesson for Us All.* New York: Warner Books, 2006.

Notes

Chapter One

Frank, Mitch. "The Legal Struggle: A Timeline of Events." *Time*, April 4, 2005, 24.

Gostin, Lawrence O. "Ethics, the Constitution and the Dying Process: The Case of Theresa Marie Schiavo." *JAMA* 293, no. 19 (May 18, 2005): 2403–7.

Perl, Peter. "Delay's Next Mission from God." *Washington Post*, April 9, 2006.

Sellers, Jeff M. "When to Pull a Feeding Tube." *Christianity Today*, April 15, 2005.

Chapter Two

CBS News. "Schiavo Feeding Tube Removed." Pinellas Park, Fla. March 18, 2005.

Noonan, Peggy. "'Don't Kick It': If Terri Schiavo Is Killed, Republicans Will Pay a Political Price." *Wall Street Journal*, March 18, 2005.

Chapter Three

Allen, Mike, and Manuel Roig-Franzia. "Congress Steps in on Schiavo Case." *Washington Post*, March 20, 2005, A1.

CBS News. "[Attorney Andrew Cohen Analyzes] Trial by Legislation." March 19, 2005.

Goodnough, Abby (and Lynn Waddell, contributor). "Protestors Hold Vigil for Schiavo at Hospice." *New York Times*, March 20, 2005.

Hinderaker, John. "It Wasn't Fake: We Now Know the Truth about the Schiavo Memo." Washington, D.C., *Weekly Standard/Daily Standard*, April 8, 2005.

Chapter Four

Fagan, Amy. "Congress OKs Schiavo Bill." *Washington Times*, March 21, 2005.

Chapter Five

CBS News. "Bush Signs Bill into Law." March 21, 2005.

Goodnough, Abby. "US Judge Hears Tense Testimony in Schiavo's Case." *New York Times*, March 22, 2005.

Chapter Six

Goodnough, Abby, David Kirkpatrick, Christine Jordan Sexton, and Lynn Waddell. "US Judge Denies Feeding Tube Bid in Schiavo's Case." *New York Times*, March 23, 2005.

Chapter Seven

Goodnough, Abby, and Adam Liptak. "Court Blocks Bid: New Schiavo Tack by Governor Bush." *New York Times*, March 24, 2005.

Klien, Rick. "Parents Lose Appeal on Feeding Tube: Schiavo Fading Quickly, Lawyer Tells US Court." *Boston Globe*, March 23, 2005.

Larry King Live, CNN. "Guest Panel Discusses Terri Schiavo Case." Panelist: Arthur Caplan. March 23, 2005.

Richey, Warren, and Linda Feldman. "Who Speaks for Terri Schiavo?" *Christian Science Monitor*, March 23, 2005.

Chapter Eight

Countdown with Keith Olbermann. Jay Wolfson interviewed. "Some Truths in the Schiavo Case." March 24, 2005.

Goodnough, Abby, Dennis Blank, Shiaila Dewan, and Linda Greenhouse. "Supreme Court Refuses to Hear Schiavo Case." *New York Times*, March 25, 2005.

Chapter Nine

CNN. Daryn Kagen and Bob Franken. "Schiavo Legal Path: What's Left? Schiavo Backlash for Bush? Before Terri Schiavo." CQPolitics.com, March 25, 2005.

CNN News Night with Arron Brown. "Battle over Terri Schiavo." March 25, 2005.

Kaplan, Karen, and Rosie Mestal. "The Terri Schiavo Case: Medical Perspectives." *Los Angeles Times*, March 23, 2005, A21.

Lyman, Rick, Dennis Blank, and Lynn Waddell. "Schiavo in 'Her Last Hours,' Father Says Amid Appeals." *New York Times*, March 26, 2005.

The McLaughlin Group. Panel: Pat Buchanan, Eleanor Clift, Tony Blankley, and James Warren. Host: John McLaughlin. March 25, 2005.

Schwartz, John. "The Schiavo Case: The Medical Situation." *New York Times*, March 25, 2005, A14.

Chapter Ten

Lyman, Rick. "As Legal Moves Dwindle in the Schiavo Case, the Focus Returns to Governor Bush." *New York Times*, March 27, 2005.

Chapter Eleven

CBS News. "Schiavo's Protestors' Passions Rise." March 27, 2005.

Isbitts, Steven. "Police Ready for Unruly Hospice Protests." *Tampa Tribune*, March 27, 2005.

Roig-Franzia, Manuel. "Schiavo Family Urges Protestors to Stay Calm." *Washington Post*, March 23, 2005.

Chapter Twelve

Larry King Live, CNN. "The Long Debate over Terri Schiavo Nears Conclusion." Panel: Ronald Cranford and Jay Wolfson. March 28, 2005.

Lyman, Rick, and Abby Goodnough. "Husband Says Autopsy Will End Suspicions." *New York Times*, March 29, 2005.

Milbank, Dana. "With Giant Spoon Florida Woman Helps Stir Up Protest from White House." *Washington Post*, March 29, 2005, A3.

Chapter Thirteen

Rehmann, Marc. "Walberg Win Makes Michigan Rep. Schwarz First GOP Primary Loser." CQPolitics.com, August 9, 2006.

Scarborough Country. Guests: Paul O'Donnell, Jesse Jackson, Ronald Cranford, Chris Smith, Patrick Mahoney, David Gibbs, and Suzanne Vitadamo. Host: Joe Scarborough. March 29, 2005.

Sidlow, Edward. *Freshman Orientation: House Style and Home Style*. Washington, D.C.: CQ Press, 2007.

Chapter Fourteen

Larry King Live, CNN. "Remembering Johnnie Cochran; Analysis of Terri Schiavo." Panel: David Gibbs, Gregory Murphy, Fr. Frank Pavone, Randall Terry, Dr. Ken Druck, Dr. Henry Lee, and Dr. Carlos Gomez with CNN correspondent Susan Candiotti, March 30, 2005.

Roig-Franzia, Manuel. "Schiavo's Parents File Late Appeal." *Washington Post*, March 30, 2005.

Chapter Fifteen

"Faithless Politics: Priests for Life Defies Constitution and Conscience." *Catholics for Free Choice*, August 2006.

Greenburg, Jan Crawford. *Supreme Conflict: The Inside Story of the Struggle for Control of the United States Supreme Court*. New York: Penguin Press, 2007.

Pavone, Fr. Frank. "Terri Schiavo's Final Hours: An Eyewitness Account." Priests for Life, Staten Island, N.Y.

Interviews

Aberle, Daphne. March 13, 2006.

Bernat, Dr. James. June 19, 2006.

Buchwald, Art. March, April, May 2006.

Byock, Dr. Ira. June 20, 2006.

Caplan, Dr. Arthur. June 10, 2006.

Christopher, Myra. October 17, 2005.

Coleman, Diane. December 2006.

Collins, Dr. Frances. August 21, 2006.

Connor, Ken. May 15, 2006.

Cranford, Dr. Ronald. March 29, 2006.

Danforth, John. May 9, 2006.

Dobies, Pam. May 22, 2006.

Edmondson, Drew, attorney general, Oklahoma. September 29, 2006.

Felos, George. May 18, 2006.

Flanigan, Sr. Rosemary. February 13, 2006.

Gibbs, David. March 26, 2007.

Gomez, Dr. Carlos. March 28, 2006.

Harkin, Senator Tom. May 2, 2007.

Hentoff, Nat. January 2007.

Hersh, Dr. Stephen. June 5, 2006.

Klayman, Larry. February 28, 2006.

Labyak, Mary. August 28, 2006.

Lynn, Dr. Joanne. August 17, 2006.

Mahoney, Rev. Pat. September 29, 2006.

Nader, Ralph. January 9, 2007.

O'Connor, Justice Sandra Day. January 26, 2007.

Paris, Father John. September 7, 2006.

Schindler, Bobby. September 20, 2006.

Smith, Wesley. October 30, 2006.

Sulmasy, Dr. Daniel. October 25, 2006.

Swindell, Brandi. October 9, 2006.

Turnbull, Rud. May 22, 2006.

Veatch, Dr. Robert. August 28, 2006.

Westbrook, Hugh. May 1, 2006.

Wholberg, Rabbi Jeffrey. January 2007.

"The Legacy of the Terri Schiavo Case: Why Is It So Hard to Die in America?" University of Pennsylvania Center for Bioethics, Tenth Anniversary Symposium, April 30–May 1, 2006.

Tom Brazaitis memorial service, National Press Club, May 15, 2005.

Diane Rehm Show. "Tom and Eleanor Living with Cancer." February 7, 2001, and November 11, 2003.

Moyers, Bill. *On Our Own Terms: Moyers on Dying.* PBS, 2000.

Index